"This collection of 39 letters is as unique as its creator/editor, who conceived of a way for psychoanalysis to reach out and touch parents in order to enable them to comprehend what makes parenting so perplexing at times and how it may well become the most exciting adventure that life has in store, one that becomes rewarding in ways one might never have imagined. Upon reading her Introduction, I sensed Andy Cohen is one who understands from experience how psychoanalysis works, and is one who has a talent for communicating her understanding in plain English. Her conception has lead to the birth of this extraordinary collection of letters from parents around the globe. These authors are moms and dads who have themselves been analysed during their training to become psychoanalysts. Cohen urges each reader to 'dream their way through these letters' that speak to each writer's experiences of failure and success in navigating the fascinating minefield that is parenthood. I am convinced that this book should be on the shelf of every prospective or present-day parent and may well lead to their own emotional and mental development, as well as that of the children".

Judith L. Mitrani, PhD, FIPA, *Psychoanalyst, author and novelist*

"As a broadcaster and founder of 'Baby Brunch' a parenting support podcast, I engage in many enriching conversations. In nearly all these exchanges, I find that people either use their talents to help others or draw from personal experiences to do so. Andy Cohen is one such person, offering both. While countless books have been written on this subject – and I've had numerous interviews about it – never before have I felt such a deep sense of connection with stories that resonate so closely with my own. Andy's book captivated me for days. It encouraged me to approach my own parenting challenges with more care, thanks to the wisdom shared in these heartfelt letters. While I thought I knew a lot about parenting – as a stepmother of two and mother of four – this book reframed parenting for me: It reminded me that the feelings we go through are valid and surmountable, allowing us to better understand ourselves and evolve into the parents we are meant to be. The deeply personal stories from these leading international experts will engage, inspire, and ground you. It's a powerful journey that brings joy and enlightenment, and ultimately, a true rebirth for every parent".

Elana Afrika-Bredenkamp, *Radio personality and host of South Africa's leading parenting podcast*

Parenting Psychoanalysed: Letters to a Parent

The first book of its kind, *Parenting Psychoanalysed: Letters to a Parent* collates the musings of a thoughtful group of psychoanalysts with a series of candid letters, each addressing the aspect of parenthood they most want to share and what they wish they knew before becoming a parent.

Written in the simplest of terms, each contributor shares a letter that reflects both personally and professionally on parenthood, sharing their feelings, insights and psychoanalytic reflections with the parent-reader. Drawing on their deep understanding of the mind and the personal work done on themselves, each writer digests what it really means to be a parent, what they didn't expect when they were expecting, the pleasures and anxieties of parenting, the ordinary ambiguities and ambivalence evoked by their children at various life stages, as well as many other gems that no other parenting books are talking about. This international collection begins an important conversation with mothers, fathers and caregivers; encouraging them to consider how their inner worlds, worries and wishes matter deeply and hold important clues about how to parent in an open and authentic way. Each letter shows how understanding this dynamic is key to raising a healthy, balanced family and living more freely.

This thought-provoking book connects parents through personal stories and profound psychoanalytic insights, and is an essential read for every mother, father and caregiver.

Andy Cohen is a psychotherapist and candidate psychoanalyst with the South African Psychoanalytical Association (SAPA). Andy is passionate about making psychoanalytic thinking more accessible, seen in her TEDx Talk, "A Mom Can't Always Act Like a Grown-Up – Here's Why", which explores the unconscious forces between parent and child. She holds an MA in Fine Art and trained as a community art counsellor at Lefika La Phodiso, a non-governmental organisation providing art-based psychodynamic mental health services to at-risk communities. She currently lives and works in Johannesburg, South Africa.

ANDY COHEN, EDITOR

Edited by Andy Cohen

Parenting Psychoanalysed

Letters to a Parent

Routledge
Taylor & Francis Group

LONDON AND NEW YORK

Designed cover image: *Mail Art Collage* by Ruby Silvios, 14.5 cm x 11 cm, cut images on vintage envelope. Lined paper background courtesy of Getty Images.

First published 2025
by Routledge
4 Park Square, Milton Park, Abingdon, Oxon OX14 4RN

and by Routledge
605 Third Avenue, New York, NY 10158

Routledge is an imprint of the Taylor & Francis Group, an informa business

© 2025 selection and editorial matter, Andy Cohen; individual chapters, the contributors

British Library Cataloguing-in-Publication Data
A catalogue record for this book is available from the British Library

Library of Congress Cataloging-in-Publication Data
Names: Cohen, Andy (Psychotherapist), editor.
Title: Parenting psychoanalysed : letters to a parent / edited by Andy Cohen.
Description: Abingdon, Oxon ; New York, NY : Routledge, 2025. |
    Includes bibliographical references and index.
Identifiers: LCCN 2024056440 (print) | LCCN 2024056441 (ebook) |
    ISBN 9781032472010 (hardback) | ISBN 9781032471976 (paperback) |
    ISBN 9781003385042 (ebook)
Subjects: LCSH: Parenting—Psychological aspects. | Parent and child.
Classification: LCC BF723.P25 P38 2025 (print) | LCC BF723.P25
    (ebook) | DDC 155.9/24—dc23/eng/20250208
LC record available at https://lccn.loc.gov/2024056440
LC ebook record available at https://lccn.loc.gov/2024056441

ISBN: 978-1-032-47201-0 (hbk)
ISBN: 978-1-032-47197-6 (pbk)
ISBN: 978-1-003-38504-2 (ebk)

DOI: 10.4324/9781003385042

Typeset in Bembo
by Apex CoVantage, LLC

For R, my person.

Contents

Letters

Permissions

Introduction

Andy Cohen

Dear Parent,

I remember first encountering psychoanalysis as a new parent. Beyond seeing caricatures of Freud behind the couch and hearing those bad jokes about cigars, it was an unfamiliar field. At the time my daughter was only six months old, and I was really wrestling with motherhood. I began searching for answers that would dismantle my distress. I looked everywhere: into spirituality, coaching, academia, general psychology, art making, self-help, even religion . . . but nothing quite hit the spot. I read a lot too but found that every resource was either too abstract or was a "how to" offering quick-fix parenting hacks. There were so many resources dedicated to solving the "what" of parenting, but nothing addressing the "why". And certainly nothing providing guidance on all the unfamiliar feelings that were getting in the way of my mothering.

DOI: 10.4324/9781003385042-1

Then I stumbled upon this thing called "psychoanalysis": a theory of mind, first developed by Sigmund Freud, and then refined by generations of subsequent analysts. I also discovered it is a therapeutic treatment grounded in these theories. I came to understand that both the theory and the treatment aim to understand human suffering and relatedness, by exploring the interaction of conscious and unconscious forces in the mind – namely, the part of the mind that contains thoughts, memories, desires and feelings that are not accessible to conscious thought. The theory explains that all of this greatly influences a person's life – like the persistent back-seat driver that won't let up!

In truth, at the time, psychoanalysis was just *another* thing I was willing to try, but the moment I really engaged with it, it just hit differently. The theories I began to explore gave name to invisible experiences, and my own analysis delivered a satisfaction similar to playing that old 1980s Tetris game: remember how after some time of playing, your screen filled up furiously with increasing speed, putting you dangerously in the red? But then, at the last moment, by some chance, a single brick slid in, all the solids lined up, and you experienced that triumphant relief as multiple bricks broke in tandem. Clearing your screen and giving you another chance to play! This is what psychoanalysis has felt like for me. Albeit hard, it has brought me the reprieve I was searching for and, in time, I was able to create more mental space for myself, my kids, my husband *and* my new profession, when I eventually decided to train as an analyst myself.

Great story, but here's the problem: despite my very proactive search for clarity, I still only *just* stumbled upon psychoanalysis. I came very close to missing out on the learnings psychoanalysis provides because it remains tucked away from mainstream media. Years later, as if rescuing a past version of myself, I reached out to analysts worldwide and asked them to *write* this wrong. So, this book seeks to engage with parents who are curious about themselves and their children and who are eager to explore more, even if they have no prior knowledge or experience in psychoanalysis.

I strongly believe that our profession should be in dialogue more with parent-readers like you. While not everyone can, will or wishes to reach the inside of an analyst's consulting room, everyone can still benefit from our rich theoretical insights. This book attempts to de-mystify analytic theory and speak to parents in the same way that we might address these things with our patients in the room; simply (without compromising on nuance), respectfully and delivered with love.

So with this in mind, this book was born. Whether you are a mother, father, guardian, caretaker, caregiver, still expecting, parenting a toddler, tween, teen or preparing for an empty nest, my colleagues and I have written this book for you. Written in plain English, each of the letters in this compilation offers a rare glimpse into a psychoanalyst's parenting experience. The 39 contributors, from 30 countries, are of various ethnicities, and come from vastly different cultural contexts. Between them they have racked up around two centuries of professional experience! Not only are they analysts, but they are also mothers and fathers, new and long-standing parents, some are grandparents, and even great-grandparents.

It is also worth mentioning that every contributor in this book has also undergone their own personal analysis. Indeed, unlike other mental health professions, psychoanalytic training requires analysts-in-training to experience their own treatment, multiple times per week[1] on the couch, for several years,

---

1 Psychoanalytic societies differ in their training models and the required frequency of a training analysis.

to deeply explore their own unconscious minds. A cardiac surgeon need not operate on their own heart to qualify. An analyst, however, must know their own mind extensively, to engage the struggle in others.

So now that you have a better sense of the people who have written to you and why, you are probably curious *what* I asked them to write about. In this book I tasked each contributor with one challenging question: *What did you struggle with as a parent and how did psychoanalysis help you work it out?* I asked them to draw on personal experience and to couch their responses in psychoanalytic theory but to do so using jargon-free language. Essentially, my request was to candidly share their learnings and yearnings with you, dear Parent. To my knowledge, this has never been done for parents, in this format, before.

As you read you may notice that each letter is unique. Some letters are about mothers and others are written more specifically about fathers. There are letters about the newborn situation, adoption, separation, adolescence, adult children, racial and political tensions, and more. Try not to worry if a letter's specificity isn't directly in line with you and your current family constellation or situation. Freud discovered that in the unconscious mind, there is no sense of time. Revealed in dream life where *then* is *now* and *now* is *then*. Think of each letter as a dream, try and imagine yourself or your child at the age of those discussed or as the other partner in that given scenario. Feel free to dream your way through this book. It will be more fun that way!

Like a matryoshka doll, the letters in this book also stack and layer different parts of the parent/child mind and you can expect to see themes overlap, reinforce and interplay with each other. Though I prefer not to elaborate in too much detail. What I will say is this; in South Africa, where I live, we use a particular phrase to describe a woman who becomes pregnant: we say that she "falls" pregnant. It wasn't until an American colleague pointed out the strangeness of this phrase that I began to wonder about its meaning. It suggests that parenting is a *fall*, a *tripping up* and a *stumble* of sorts. "Falling" conveys a sense of something out of control, which contrasts starkly with how other cultures, like the United States, describe the same life stage with the phrase; a woman "gets" pregnant. This implies something that is far more *in* control, considered and aspirational. This is such an interesting geographical split to describe the same phenomenon! This interplay of falling and holding steady conveys the catch-22 of parenting. Just as this book brings analytic minds from either side of the globe together, it also marries some of the contradictory views and conflicts we all face as parents. Each letter examines this tussle that unfolds between parent and child, between partners, and very importantly inside the parent's mind.

Finally, I would like to point out that most mainstream parenting books tend to focus on delivering the *dos* and *don'ts*. They try to contain anxieties and manage external difficulties by suggesting concrete strategies. This book adopts a different approach. The letters spend a lot of time in the "grey area" where there are no clearcut answers. They explore difficult, often uncomfortable internal feelings about parenting like love, hate, competition, loss and mourning. There are also beautiful moments of optimism, playfulness, gratitude and adventure. For the writers of this book, there was a lot of grey too, as these letters have straddled a fine line between the professional and the personal and this required a lot of careful thinking. Despite the complexity of the task, I am really struck by how each contributor has really poured him and herself into the page, and I am so thankful for what this book has become: a meeting place to think about what it really means to be a parent. Because exploring and engaging with these elusive dynamics can ultimately make your parenting voyage that much more manageable and pleasurable. I sincerely hope we have succeeded.

So here is what I'd like to invite you to do; just start reading. As you engage with the ideas in each letter, notice your own thoughts. They are as important as the analysts' words that you are reading. For patients in analysis, there is usually only one rule we ask; "say whatever comes to mind". These fragments of thoughts, known as free associations, are seemingly random but do have an important underlying logic (Schwartz 2023). Each one is a little clue to your unconscious processes. As you read, notice your own thoughts and feelings – what grabs your attention, makes you uncomfortable, gets you excited, renders you sleepy or irritates you. Each response may be a valuable breadcrumb leading to a deeper understanding about yourself and your child. You may even want to jot your responses down as you go along. The themes you feel strongly against might be the very ones you need to explore further. These thoughts are like your own little footnotes that will enrich this reading experience, as the best learning is done with both heart and mind. Let us begin . . .

Warmly,

Andy Cohen

Your editor and mother of two | South African Psychoanalytical Association | Johannesburg, South Africa

Letters

1

~~~~

Sergio Eduardo Nick

Dear Parent,

I heard an interesting story from an analytic colleague, about a pregnant woman who she once worked with: she described her first meeting with this pregnant woman, where she asked the mother-to-be why she had chosen the name "Alice" for her daughter. The pregnant woman, without hesitation, explained that when she was a child, she had a doll that she would not part with for anything in the world. She explained "I took her with me when I went out, when I showered, when I slept and when I ate. Her name was Alice."

While this story may seem rather dull, dear Parent, the important thing is that it was here that I learned that what we call an "imaginary baby" has its roots in early childhood! The "imaginary baby" can be described as that child who inhabits the depths of the parent's mind, long before its birth. This can influence both the desire for what its physical characteristics

DOI: 10.4324/9781003385042-3

will be like, as well as aspects more linked with whom the baby will become, how it will relate to each of its parents and what shapes its future destiny as a person in the world.

The mother and the father hold different ideas about the child, as they were conceived long before the parental couple was formed. One of the challenges of parenthood is precisely allowing each partner to share their fantasies of what the unborn child will be like, as well as to tolerate that the other parent has a different idea of the child that will, in time, be born. Here in Brazil (as well as in many other countries) this can be seen when deciding what the child's name will be, or in more prosaic situations, in choosing which football team the child will support. It's as if each parent must accept that the child is not just theirs. That there is a partner with whom to share the desires, fantasies and expectations of what this child will be like.

A second challenge, not so easy for each parent to become aware of, is accepting that the baby who was actually born has a completely different nature to that of the "imaginary baby". Going through this transition is crucial for a good parent–baby relationship. This includes knowing how to distinguish what the baby demands from their parents from what they expect from it. Perceiving the baby as it is, and not through the way we imagine it to be, can be particularly challenging, and this is what I want to talk to you about today.

Did you imagine having a smart and communicative baby, but she is shy and not very outgoing? Or were you expecting a boy, only for a girl to be born? Or did you perhaps think that everything you gave your baby would be willingly received, that he would immediately calm down when picked up or accept the breast immediately? Has your child acted quite contrary to these expectations?

And so it is. Being a father and a mother demands a lot of tolerance, and a lot of willingness to abandon many of your own ideas of what your newborn would be like! Not surprisingly, the postpartum period is considered a very special phase of life, a delicate period where a good outcome greatly influences the mental health of that newborn child.

One of the richest experiences I've ever had as a father was being attended to, together with my wife, by a psychoanalyst willing to accept our dreams, conflicts and demands in relation to my daughter's birth. We went from being a very harmonious couple pre-pregnancy, to fighting over small and superfluous things. Each one feeling misunderstood by the other! In this couple's therapy, we started talking about the pregnancy, about what we expected as parents and about the love we already felt for a baby that was still far from being born. "Making room for the baby" was a rich and valuable experience for our little girl's arrival, now with a space in each of us and shared by both parents.

I now know from my clinical work with pregnant or postpartum couples how much these conflicts can disrupt the proper development of a child. Often, by helping parents put what's troubling them into a narrative, we see some of the baby's symptoms disappear as if by magic! But as we know, there is no magic in these mental processes, and I will try to explain this by sharing with you, dear Parent, a difficult experience I once had, while trying to calm my few month old daughter:

Imagine seeing a struggling baby crying loudly. Immediately, you pick her up, believing that she will stop crying and calm down. But the exact opposite happens. My daughter was still crying and still struggling! And now?! What do I do?! Well, let's walk around the house, sing a song, while rocking her on my lap. Nothing solves the issue! Anguish begins to invade me. I think to myself that I don't know how to take care of her. Worse: there's still over an hour until mom returns! My daughter continues crying, and I'm desperate because I don't know what else to do.

Suddenly, a childhood memory comes to mind: I was crying a lot and my nanny, who had stayed with me while my mother was travelling, promised me that she would stay by my side while I slept. I took a nap, like I did every afternoon, but when I woke up, I realised she wasn't by my side. I cried for I don't know how long! An immense anger filled me. A deep feeling of betrayal invaded me, and I found myself completely inconsolable! Can you imagine how much of my personal analysis was taken up by this childish scene?

Well, it was from this memory that I began to imagine that perhaps my daughter, still breastfeeding, could be feeling something similar. Remembering personal situations I had experienced, I decided to talk to her, as if she were capable of understanding what I was saying. "Calm down, my love! I know what you're feeling. Being without your mom by your side is horrible, right?! I know. I've been through this and suffered a lot too. Just the way you are feeling right now! Nothing calms us down because we want mom and no one else but her, right?"

And so, I spoke, mixing my memories with what I imagined she was going through. I walked around the house with her on my chest, whispering these things in the most sincere and loving way possible. Her crying slowly cooled down and I talked about how hard it was to feel anger when we had no way of expressing it properly. But I understood that she must be angry. Sooooo angry!

And with that, she calmed right down and with wide eyes open, she was astutely listening to me in a very tranquil way. How to explain such a phenomenon? Some might reason that she got tired of crying, or my embrace calmed her down. Well, you haven't met my daughter, capable of crying inconsolably for hours!

My explanation would rather be psychoanalytic, based both on recent theories about communications that occur without words, and on this (and other) experiences with babies.

My childhood trauma blocked my ability to deeply understand the anguish that gripped my little girl. Added to this was the fact that I, also without realising it, allowed her to be the one who expressed an anguish of separation that belonged to both of us. As she screamed nonstop, my baby grappled with the inconvenience of longing for her nurturing mother, but in those moments her angst was *also* an expression of my own pain, so old and yet still so present within me!

These phenomena are rare and difficult to capture. Catching that memory evoked in that moment helped me connect my daughter's inconsolable anguish to an understanding that I myself had already suffered something similar, albeit in another time. Then, once I realised that I had in fact survived that trauma, I was able to calm down and was *then* able to deal with the pain that my daughter was experiencing, in this present moment. I think that was how she calmed down, by believing that the pain was bearable. That it wasn't the end of the world!

Here it's worth mentioning that our unconscious knows no time. Just like in dreams, in our unconscious minds, the past and present are interchangeable and old ideas can invade new moments without warning. It depends, of course, on the level of communication we have between our conscious and unconscious mind. And, as it occurred to me, it also depends on whether we're able to capture old memories and relate them to present situations.

They say we have to stay calm when taking care of a baby. That's the truth! But this calm is not achieved by giving strict instructions to our brain or just taking several deep breaths. In my opinion, it depends on us making contact with our own memories, our own pain and our own anxieties. When we know them better, it becomes easier to understand and accept our children's suffering. They, in turn, will benefit from this good experience, and internalise that anguish can be both dealt with and survived.

Kindest regards,
Sergio Eduardo Nick
Father of two | Brazilian Psychoanalytical Society of Rio de Janeiro | Rio de Janeiro, Brazil

2

Michael Benn

Dear Parent,
I lost someone.

She was my best friend. She was like a sister to me. We promised each other in the event of the unthinkable that her teenage son, and the rest of her uniquely blended family, would join mine. When she died, my sizeable clan suddenly became an even bigger tribe.

Dinners became a bustling mix of different personalities and energies; a gathering of ten, with music, laughter and jokes. Other times meals were punctuated with solemnness, jabs, and the prickles of sibling squabbles and sulks. Sometimes friends and family would join us as part of our bigger extended tribe. I often pictured my friend looking on, imagining her appreciation of our lively table dynamics.

DOI: 10.4324/9781003385042-4

This carnival and chaos may sound romantic, but in reality, it is a handful. Parenting can feel like a claustrophobic struggle. To carve out space for emotional connection with each child and my partner has been overwhelming; not to mention finding time for myself. There are many moments when a parent feels like they are failing because there's not enough space to keep everyone in mind, or even one's *own* mind in mind. The reality of managing multiple children, each with their unique needs, desires and emotions, can feel impossible at times.

I remember when my adult son was little how we would spend time playing in the garden or making up imaginary worlds, how we would explore the veld and follow his daily adventures. With the big age gap between him and his siblings, he was essentially an only child until he was 15. I longed for that time when parenting felt slower and more engaged. For him, a lot of space was lost as he got more siblings. I feel like he had more individual focus in his formative years. This is in huge contrast to how my parenting world feels now – it is also a loss for me.

Trying to create good sibling relationships and helping my children manage this loss has been important to me. It is a loss that I know from my own history, having been a brother myself. I have seen that integrating siblings is complex and comes with difficult feelings. As an analyst I have also seen how sibling relationships come with complex dynamics and feelings, sometimes life-changing. So here, in this letter, I focus on four key areas that I have felt very present in this struggle of parenting siblings.

1. Finding space

When a sibling discovers they are not the only one, they have to share and learn to manage the terrible feelings of coming second. Sharing time and energy with a rival for the parents' attention is difficult. This can trigger complex and hostile feelings. There are multiple competing needs for space and attention, and for the expression of your own personality. The balancing of these needs is an impossible process to get right.

On our journey, the physical space within our home became symbolic of the emotional space we needed to create for our children. Managing who stays where, whose pictures adorn which walls, and who shares space with whom became part of a larger narrative of maintaining sibling relationships. At the fast pace that everything was changing, it became imperative to at least start with defining physical spaces.

This included sleeping arrangements, which changed over time. Some of the kids settled in faster and we had to rethink privacy as we now had teenagers. We played quite a bit of "musical beds" at night as they tried to find somewhere to feel comfortable. We had kids sleep on couches, kids sharing beds, and even kids and dogs sharing our bed. The dynamic nature of the sleeping arrangements was indicative of how tricky our new move was – both externally and internally.

Elsewhere, in my own mind, things have been shifting around too. During the writing of this letter, a creative parallel process unfolded which brought something to life for me. I was tasked with writing this letter for you dear Parent but was struggling. In fact, at one point, I had two distinct versions of this letter. Each version holding different qualities. The one letter, more raw, emotional, full of footnotes, colour coding, many "added in" bits, and subheadings: it was free-associative but also quite chaotic. In contrast, the second version I wrote was more dry and far more practical. It was focused on how to "do" things, almost systematised around functioning, work, paying bills, making lunch, doing homework, running groups, keeping things equal and fair, and maintaining routines. Like the beds at home, things inside me needed to shift around as well. My two letter versions somehow needed to be blended together to form one new letter, one that would strike the right balance, or find a way of integrating these two competing parts.

This allowed me to become aware of my need to function at a higher level than before. To run a big household and to manage work commitments had come at a cost of connecting with my own feelings of loss and sadness. Becoming conscious of my own loss allowed me to see my children and their losses more clearly. For me, finding this balance between these two letters – or these two positions inside me – came about by finding a third position. Finding this third space inside myself was also made possible because someone (my partner, family and friends) was able to recognise that I was carrying a lot and express their concern and love.

Finding space for your children is similar to the process of how we need to try find space inside ourselves. Our openness to finding ourselves is not just a self-absorbed narcissistic process. Feeling more allows an awareness of our many different experiences. By integrating these experiences, we can then connect in a more alive and authentic way with our children.

The different members in a family, and the complex internal states inside us, are not just there to be managed. They also need the time and space to be seen and expressed, so they can be contained, symbolised and integrated. A good relationship with another who can think about us can help facilitate this process.

Back at home, it has been interesting to watch dynamics play out as we navigate this new setup. Everyone has had to find their own way of being inside our ecosystem. Each child has had to create their own physical space where they can express their identities separately. A space for their own toys, pictures on the wall and, ultimately, their own character. A space to connect to their own feelings. It has been crucial to allow each child time alone, whether it was drawing, watching TV, reading on the bed or simply daydreaming. Having space to be alone allowed them to recharge, reflect and develop a sense of self that was independent of their siblings.

Time is another resource that is pretty limited around here. Spending time with all of the children is complicated. The most obvious way is to all eat together. There is of course no place like a dinner table to give us an opportunity to actively parent, comment and intervene. I found that managing sibling dynamics in this setting was helpful in facilitating the space for us all to connect with difficult feelings. This was quite robust at times!

2. Rivalry

One may have a fantasy of the dinner table being all warm and inviting – like something you would see in a Hallmark movie – with everyone who gets on well and loves each other. In truth parenting is about metabolising some really ugly behaviour and feelings between the children, and between yourself and the children.

It is complicated because it is not just about having everything be good and positive. There are extraordinarily complex feelings that exist between siblings, and it is better that they can be spoken about. Sibling rivalry between my kids has taken many shapes over the years. From full-on loud fights in the car about who was riding shotgun and (when they were little) who was going to untie dad's shoelaces. There were more subtle moments too, like whose question you replied to first, or whose gift was opened at what moment. All of this came under scrutiny. As they are slowly becoming older a lot of the battles have been channelled into Fortnite and chess games, or the dishing up of dessert, or some pointed banter amongst themselves. It is a lot more sophisticated now, just below the radar, but ever present and needing to be noted.

The kids themselves have started to learn how to acknowledge the complex feelings that exist between them – feelings of rivalry, jealousy and the struggle for individual identity within a shared space. I have noticed that my children and their peers at school have developed quite a sophisticated vocabulary to discuss their feelings. Words such as "jelly" are used to describe their feelings of jealousy, and it is done in a very clever humorous way that lightens these horribly embarrassing and painful feelings.

The difficult thing to figure out is whether that aggression between the children is part of some sort of playful dynamic, or if it has now escalated to a fight that requires intervention. Play can quickly slip into something mean. At that point, the parent needs to move from tolerating to confronting and setting boundaries. At these moments you are the referee, protecting them from each other's aggression.

Another challenge in rivalry is that of your own aggression. The competing needs within oneself, and within the children, and within a family, are not sitting passively. They may be active and at war! It is almost impossible to do this part of parenting right, and you are continually failing but trying again.

3. Loss

This letter is about parenting siblings in a large family, but it is also about loss and mourning. This loss is baked into parenting and sibling relationships. Even the only child carries the loss of not having a sibling. In a way we all share the primitive loss of not being at the very centre of a parent's gaze.

It is the loss of space and parental resources. The focus on one sibling means a loss for another. Each child in the sibling setup feels the loss. When a capacity for things to be seen is also lost, the ability to connect with one's feelings, wishes and desires is diminished.

Managing this loss is a key part of parenting and sibling relationships. Understanding each child's wishes and need to have space, to be seen and to have the gaze can vary. Ideally one would like to ensure equality among the children while acknowledging their differences all the time, but this is not always possible. For me, it has been about ensuring fairness in my actions as much as possible, while recognising their individual wishes and desires. In spite of best efforts, though, it constantly feels like one kid is slipping through the cracks.

This is a loss that goes with the reality of life. We can never have all our needs met, and we cannot meet everyone's needs. Parenting in some way is like the Velveteen Rabbit in that we become less shiny, less perfect, and more threadbare and real as we parent. But with this we also offer our children the option of finding something real within themselves and within each of their siblings.

In this area I am starting to see the beauty of these evolving sibling dynamics; sometimes beyond the competition there are brothers and sisters who look after each other. In this they discover their humanness.

4. The tribe

The loss for me as a parent is in realising that I am not able to be ideal. There is a limited economy of time and energy and that needs to be shared. We have to surrender and accept that we need others, a helping hand, a brother, a sister, a friend. We cannot plumb these depths alone.

With my children there is a constant intermingling and changing of sibling combinations that happen. They pair off or triangulate amongst themselves. They have a finger on the pulse of what is going on with each other in a way we sometimes do not. At any point if you ask one of them what is up with the other, they can sum it up in an instant. We have had to really lean into this specifically with social media. We allow them to monitor each other and let us know when something unhealthy is going on. They have an incredible gauge for what is appropriate for each other and will tell each other off whenever something does not sit well with them. This reminds you that your children are becoming part of that tribe. The siblings are also not just children but are there to support and find each other.

Our extended network of friends, family and close acquaintances have also played a crucial role in supporting us. The loss of our friend (my chosen sibling) highlighted the importance of maintaining strong sibling relationships within our blended family and our friendship tribe. I hope all my children will carry us inside them, as well as each other. Also, I hope they find a broader tribe around them. They can have the understanding that they are never alone and always interconnected.

One day my children will lose their parents too, leaving them to navigate life without us. And one day they too will have promises to keep. I hope, in preparing them for this eventuality, they have internalised the importance of having brothers and sisters, which will become even more crucial. They will need to rely on each other for support, understanding and companionship as they navigate the challenges of adulthood. But also, that they can find a tribe of siblings and friends that will support them in crisis. I hope, dear Parent, for you too, that you will do well enough in managing these complex things and will succeed in building good sibling bonds in yourself and in your own tribes.

Warm regards,

Michael Benn

Father, co-parent of a family of ten |

South African Psychoanalytical Association |

Johannesburg, South Africa

3

Harriet Wolfe

Dear Parent,

Andy Cohen's book is a welcome rarity. Psychoanalysts know how to speak clearly in the familiar – and private – setting of our consulting rooms and in conversation with our patients whom we come to know very well. We are out of our comfort zones, though, when we contemplate speaking publicly about intensely personal matters – like parenting. I hope, nonetheless, that I can contribute something to your experience of becoming and being a parent, particularly if you are considering adoption or have already taken the plunge. Over 30 years ago my analyst husband and I took that plunge. We adopted a newborn baby in an open adoption, namely one in which birth parents and adoptive parents make a very moving and serious agreement.

Adoption must be one of the most joyful, challenging and scary ways of becoming a parent. The gift of another's child

DOI: 10.4324/9781003385042-5

presents the adoptive parent(s) with an astonishing responsibility and privilege. The questions that arise include: Now what do I do? How do I be a parent? Who is this baby? Who am I now? These surprising questions are ones many new parents have. The birth of a baby is a terrifyingly marvellous event that can upend a person's sense of self.

Becoming a parent through adopting a child may be more complicated than other routes to conception and parenting, just as being an adoptee may be more complicated than sharing the biology and culture of one's biological parents. But these generalisations minimise the unforeseen in all parent–child relationships and the strange unpredictability of biological endowment.

For the purposes of this letter to you, I will use my personal experience to address becoming a parent through open adoption; navigating the sharing of information about adoption with a child in light of their developmental level and complex inner reality; managing our hopes for our child; and, last but not least, allowing love to be our compass.

I was a person who could not get pregnant when she remarried with someone who wanted a child as badly as she did. It was frustrating, disappointing and, after unsuccessful medical interventions, ultimately a sad loss we had to mourn. A first surprise that emerged was my husband's optimism that we could adopt. It had never seemed likely to me. Our route to exploring the possibility was joining a prospective adoptive parents' group in a residence for pregnant women, some of whom planned to keep their babies and others who wanted to pursue adoption. It was an important introduction to the emotional roller coaster of adoption.

We saw matches between birth mothers and potential adoptive parents that seemed made in heaven collapse, reconstitute, collapse again, and sometimes ultimately work out. The power of the giving and the receiving of a new life was evident in everyone's ambivalence, hopefulness and fear.

After an unsuccessful introduction to a young pregnant teenager who cringed at the sight of us (we were probably as old as her grandparents), we moved on to working with an adoption consultant who had a national registry of people seeking adoption. Through this route we met a couple who had lost their jobs and felt unprepared to care for a child. My child analyst husband was eager to know the couple who had created the baby. He welcomed this opportunity. Talking with the couple helped him better imagine the baby somehow — emotionally as well as biologically. I continued to be sceptical and, in retrospect, quite afraid.

How many pregnant women are afraid? I think more than we imagine. The process I went through in concert with our birthmother became a different sort of pregnancy, but a pregnancy nonetheless. The process resulted in an inner transformation though not a physical one. Through adopting one can still be a parent: nurture, protect, love and support a baby's development into adulthood. But what are the implications of this new life emerging from another's womb? What might it mean for the adoptive mother's sense of herself as a woman; for example, to her femininity, formed partly through her potential to grow life within her own body? It may be that the answer hangs on whether pregnancy is the sole domain of the uterus. In my experience, a person becomes, through the adoption process, pregnant with the possibility of a baby and, thus, authentically grows the experience.

Pregnancy is a psychic capacity as well as a physical one. This is true for both men and women. Speaking to the experience of a woman, as a little girl she intuits her body's interiority, the deeply generative space within, from which babies grow, and she gives birth thereby to the psychic capacity to be pregnant. The sense of interiority, itself imbued with possibility, is nascent in the young girl, and also in the young boy who wishes to father a child or create one in his own body. Such desires are part of every child's wishful, desirous experience.

Consciously or unconsciously, the little girl is swept into the feminine power of gestation. She carries the idea of her baby long before there is an actual baby to carry. When, as a woman, she adopts, she carries that baby in her mind although not in her body. Fatherhood through adoption is a similar psychic identification process that results in love and commitment to the child whom a person or couple will parent. Parenting fantasies are immensely powerful and are carried deep within us long before a child becomes ours, physically. These ideas linger on, as a parent and child live in the world together. They have a powerful effect on the relationship and how it unfolds.

My husband's and my choice of an open adoption reflected our shared commitment to transparency. Open adoption includes a commitment to ongoing contact with the birth and adoptive families. We both think a child deserves to know and to expect the truth. A child reads emotion in a way that reveals secrets, often those the parents don't know they carry. In analytic language, parents have secrets inside themselves that are unconscious stories, and they are also transgenerational. What we learn in our infancy and early childhood becomes inscribed in us as a mix of our unique selves and multiple identifications. There is a complicated set of emotional truths in each of us that reflect our experience of our parents and theirs of their parents.

We wanted our daughter to know as much about herself as we could share. This introduced developmental challenges that were interesting and daunting in different ways over time. What is the right level on which to offer information? This question has different answers for toddlers, preschoolers, sixth-graders, teenagers and young adults. In our first years as parents, we showed photos. Fellow adoptive parents told us how they created a picture book called "Sam's First Year". We made one for our daughter's first birthday. It began with a picture of her with her birthmother hours after birth, of the pilot who held the plane for us when we had trouble navigating the airport with a load of baby stuff and a six-day-old baby. This travel experience and the kindness of the people who staffed the hotel where we had stayed until it was lawful to leave the state with an adopted child were truly touching and early evidence of the bridges that an infant – a new life – forms with all sorts of fellow human beings.

Our daughter's book also illustrated first meetings with our families of origin and their friends – her entire extended family except for more of her birth family. We had offered her birthmother and birthfather tickets to fly to us for a visit but they remained distant. When our daughter was three years old her birthmother contacted us and said she was ready to visit. She told us we must not tell our daughter that she was her birthmother. We declined to do that saying we were not prepared to lie to our daughter. Her birthmother decided not to visit. She and her husband, the birthfather, did eventually visit when our daughter was six years old.

To show how much and how little we learn about our children's inner lives, I will tell you how the three of us approached their arrival at our house. We were in our family room, my husband and I in two chairs towards the end of a couch. Our daughter was lying on the couch on her stomach facing away from us. We were all quiet, waiting, a bit nervous and excited. She turned towards us and said, "OK Mom, OK Dad, what would you do if you got pregnant and you lost your jobs?" I opened my mouth and out came: "I'd get another job." This was a moment of automatic response that says volumes. We all have them in life. But we can't always explore them, especially with a six-year-old. I knew I'd made it obvious we would never give up a baby if we were pregnant and lost our jobs. We'd find a way to solve the problem. It was a complicated thought for a child who was trying to figure out why she had been given away.

I learned in that moment there was a lot in and on our daughter's mind that she could not easily share nor find words for. This process has continued over 30 years through more articulate verbal exchanges and also nonverbal ones that are experienced in our bodies or behaviours in ways that are familiar or surprising. As parents we get to wonder and sometimes recognise how the intergenerational truths of our child's family, biological and adoptive, enter into the complex adult she continues to become.

So how did we manage our hopes for our daughter? In my view, a parent's most likely pitfall is their own narcissism. It can take the form of a compulsion. We want many things for our child. Using ourselves as an example, we wanted the best of childcare as working parents; we wanted the best of education, the best of friends and the best of adventure. In short, we wanted for our child what we ourselves defined as bringing pleasure and success in life. The problem emerges when parents do all the defining, when they imagine they know for their child what is most important for them in life. Parents do know many important things; for example, about integrity, empathy, respect and decency. But often we think we know, without listening, what life choices are best for our child. We may fail to recognise what they think, want and imagine for themselves.

At the end of the day, parenting is one of the great joys in life. But sometimes life delivers the unexpected, including tragic personal losses, beginning perhaps with infertility and going on to include the loss of beloved relatives and friends. Uncertainty is a constant. In the big picture, the current state of the world is frightening. Climate catastrophe; extreme local, national and international violence; inhumane othering; and nuclear threat conspire to make us nervous about bringing a child into the world and anxious about their future safety.

At the same time, the wonder of being a parent reflects the upside of what it means to be human. Our children call our own selves deeply into question at times. They also enliven us, inspire us and remind us what it means to love and be loved. There are times when we really don't know what is best for our child. This is not just about parenting. It is about the lived experience of one's limits and how hard it can be to know the best way to help another person. When it is our child, the inevitable experience of being less than one's best self in moments of stress is particularly painful. The biggest challenge we face as parents is birthing a space inside ourselves that can gently hold all the losses, uncertainties, truths and disappointments, alongside a profound love and a deep respect for this most honourable task of parenting.

Warmest wishes,

Harriet Wolfe

Mother of one | San Francisco Center for Psychoanalysis | San Francisco, USA

4

Carol Richards

Dear Parent,

My upbringing *excluded* the dimension of being listened to as a child. In fact, I grew up believing that children did not have an opinion, and were to be seen, not heard. I remedied this in my own parenting style, but it was difficult and costly. Over the years, I have come to the realisation that parenting is mostly an unconscious replication, a repetition, of what we have been exposed to as children, unless we make a conscious and deliberate attempt to parent our children in the way we see fit and not based on unconscious and inherited parenting patterns.

I was born and raised during the 1960s, the heyday of the implementation of Apartheid in South Africa. I was consequently classified coloured. My parents were ardent conservative evangelical Christian fundamentalists who tried to be the best version of themselves. I discovered that their parenting

DOI: 10.4324/9781003385042-6

style in turn reflected the ways in which they had been reared, underpinned by their interpretation and version of Christian principles. This meant, for example, that my siblings and I had to be blindly obedient and compliant, with no option of engagement with the parental instruction given. There was neither space for curiosity nor entertaining differing opinions. The parental relationship was instructional rather than one which invited dialogue. The expectation or concept of feeling listened to as a child was foreign, in fact, anti-biblical. Back-chatting or "asking questions" or, worse still, challenging the opinion of one's parents deserved the punishment of hell, it seemed.

Consequently, I learnt from a very young age to not listen to myself, let alone my own needs and desires. According to the belief system of my parents, our responsibility was to ensure that our lives were Christ-like, which meant forgoing our carnal/fleshly earthly desires and doing what the other needed to have done in order that we may reach heaven one day. A dominant feature of the belief system of my parents was that heaven was a place where there would be no more suffering and, therefore, we should endure our current suffering.

To a certain extent, and with the benefit of hindsight, I can empathise with my parents for adopting their fundamentalist worldview with its emphasis on delayed gratification, premised on the sure expectation of heavenly rewards, only once you arrive in heaven. There was no expectation of earthly-based rewards. This was especially poignant given the visible suffering endured by my parents as a result of Apartheid.

My parents, like millions of people of colour, were victims of the brutality of forced removals as practised by the Apartheid system. The resultant economic hardships and destruction of self-worth and meaning were ramifications not dealt with by my parents. Furthermore, the dissonance not addressed by my parents was that the suffering caused by Apartheid was at the bidding of another interpretation of Christian principles, resulting in legislated racial segregation and economic suppression and dispossession of people of colour to the advantage of the God-ordained superior white race. This socio-economic and political background spurred on my quest to find meaning in this earthly life. As a result, my insatiable appetite for reading, learning and exploration deepened.

I was a sickly child and confined to my parents' home for most of my childhood years. Due to forced removals we lost our family home and lived as backyard dwellers for many years. Consequently, and miraculously, I developed a curious mind and a love for reading. My father was a school teacher and he encouraged us to read. My mother, one of nine children, had little formal schooling and worked as a seamstress in a clothing factory.

After high school, I completed a career as a professional nurse. I sought to satisfy my deepening curiosity about life through further formal studies in religion and later psychology. Eventually, after qualifying as a clinical psychologist and practising at a psychiatric hospital, I decided to delve into the writings of Freud as these had been excluded during my clinical training and curriculum by my professors. My curiosity caused me to privately delve into the forbidden Freudian writings and approach. In this way, I was determined to develop an informed perspective as to why Freud was supposedly not for me. The more I got into Freud the more at home I felt. My curiosity eventually spurred me on to become a psychoanalyst.

It was during this time of exploring Freudian literature that I learnt to truly listen and tune into myself, in order to explore what seemed to resonate with me and what didn't. By this time, I had two very young children, with very different personalities. They were implicitly and explicitly challenging me as a parent. The fact that I recognised that they were challenging me, and that I had a different response to my children compared to how my parents reared me, is itself evidence of a shift I had already made regarding how I desired to raise my children. I am not sure when that shift happened. All I knew is that I was *not* averse to my children challenging me and I had *not* threatened my children with hell and brimstone for asking their questions or "challenging" me. They were, after all, children, with innately innocent and curious minds.

On reflection, I suspect that my husband and I had created an atmosphere of safety that enabled the children to express themselves. This is, of course, a revisionist perspective. At the time, however, I did not have the theory or the words to make sense of what I was doing or saying as a parent other than the dominant voices of my parents echoing in my psyche. What I did know was that I did not want to raise my children in the way I had been restrictively raised. What I didn't know was how I would overcome this. My children would actually help me with this most important question . . .

Lesson 1 — I do not want to be a ballerina!

My first lesson in deep listening happened when my eight-year-old daughter told me she no longer wanted to do ballet. I hated this idea and vehemently opposed it! Sadly, here, I was listening more to my own wishes and desires for her to have this experience. My ideas and feelings were taking precedence and drowning out what she was trying to communicate to me, namely, that she did not enjoy ballet. My unexpressed desire to be a ballerina deafened and blinded me. I remember her heart-wrenching sobbing, which was unusual, given her tendency to self-isolate when she was emotionally vulnerable. This refocused my attention. She managed to utter that I was making her feel guilty about giving up ballet . . . I was astounded by this experience.

My daughter confronted me with the reality of how I had failed to listen to her fully. I was not attentive to her needs, nor was I able to process her feedback. Through this experience, I learnt that I was expecting my eight-year-old to listen to me fully and hopefully change her mind. This was a huge wake-up call. I needed to challenge myself to listen deeply to the other – whether it was my child, or my patient or my co-worker – and be fully present, putting my own needs and desires aside to truly hear what she/he is trying to communicate to me.

Lesson 2 – I do not want to be a medical doctor!

I have since had numerous opportunities to practice deep listening as a mother, but none as challenging as the one I'm going to share with you now. First some background. My daughter is the first one in my family to have had the opportunity to study medicine. It was a remarkable achievement for our immediate and extended family for her to be accepted as a medical student. It was an enormous struggle for my husband and me to pay for her studies, but somehow we managed.

It was now the fifth year of our daughter's medical studies. She was 22 years old and no longer eight years old. As parents we were in our fifth year of hustling to scrape together money to pay university fees so as not to jeopardise our daughter's future. It was during this critical fifth year of her studies that I had popped in at her student digs after returning from an exciting trip to Johannesburg where I received a prestigious award on behalf of my son who is an actor by profession. The minute I walked in, I could tell something was amiss. My daughter made each of us a cup of tea and then invited me into her room so we could meet in private. She'd hardly closed the door when deep guttural sobs wrenched through her body. I held her and waited. She was so bereft she couldn't speak. Eventually, after what seemed like hours, but in fact was only minutes, she managed to tell me through her sobbing that she wasn't sure whether she wanted to continue studying medicine.

In those moments, while the enormity of what she'd just communicated to me was still busy landing in my body-mind, I was somehow able to put into practice what I'd failed to do when she was eight years old. I said to her that I could sense how difficult it must have been for her to get to the point of sharing this news with me. She nodded, cried and then sobbed uncontrollably. She then apologised to me for having to bear this news and she went on to acknowledge how aware she was of all the sacrifices my husband and I were making to keep her at medical school for five years already. She apologised for letting us down, for disappointing us, for shattering our dreams for her.

I dug deeply and heard myself uttering the following words to her: "My darling, if medicine is destroying your soul, then you need to stop. I'd rather have you restored to full health and wellbeing, without a MBChB than encourage you to finish and witness your demise. I want to be here for you and support you in whatever way you choose going forward."

My daughter looked at me sadly and I could feel enormous gratitude in the way she hugged me goodbye. After warmly hugging my daughter, I got into my car that night and sobbed all the way home as I processed the cost of sacrificing for a future which she was no longer sure she wanted.

I needed to trust my daughter to listen to herself, to explore the meaning of her distress in the presence of her therapist and then listen some more. I held on to the hope and trust that she would find her way through a very challenging labyrinth without the judgemental voice of her parents. Imagine my surprise when, in time, she actually changed her mind and completed her medical degree. But she came to this decision without my needs in her way and was really empowered to make choices that were right for her, and which she could truly own as hers.

I would probably not have been able to put into practice what psychoanalyst Elizabeth Corpt (2018) invites us to do, had it not been for my own personal analysis. Corpt emphasises guidelines not only for proper professional conduct, but also overarching principles that shape our more intimate relations. She reminds us that listening is the bedrock of presence and a complex responsibility, with potentially violent outcomes if we impose our thinking on others. Furthermore, she invites the listener to be alert to the need for sharpening the quality of one's listening, especially when one finds one's attention drifting and being distracted by one's own inner dialogue.

Having had an extensive personal analysis which provided me with a dedicated space in which to feel heard, understood and process aspects of my unmet needs, I felt more enabled this time around, in relation to my daughter, to put into practice the act of deep listening, something which I too had been experiencing in analysis. Had I not been working through my own issues in analysis, I dread to think what I might well have said to my daughter. It is likely that my voice would have drowned out her anguish and that she would consequently not have felt heard by me.

It's not easy to honour and truly listen to oneself, especially when listening means being too attuned to one's own contradictoriness, ambivalence, conflicting desires and needs. Listening to oneself becomes even more challenging when it translates into being frowned upon, questioned and considered insane by those around you. However, from personal experience, I can confirm that it is so worthwhile. Most of the time it is fulfilling and our relationships with our children (and ourselves!) will be all the richer for it.

Warmest regards,
Carol Richards
Mother of two | South African Psychoanalytical Association | Clanwilliam, South Africa

5

Gohar Homayounpour

Dear Parent,

This has been quite a turbulent letter for me to write, as every time I wanted to begin, I found myself lost, clumsy, overwhelmed with immense affects and with absolutely no authority on the subject matter of parenting. I am usually a good enough writer and almost never this late for deadlines, for a short letter that as a psychoanalyst and a mother of two young girls I will attempt to write to you. I wish to write to you.

Maybe because when I am writing on any other subject matter, even the most challenging of topics, I feel a minimum degree of comprehension, a good enough level of confidence. But, when it comes to parenting there is absolutely no level of authority I can assume, for whatever you thought you knew, however you had promised yourself to be, all your fantasies of who you are or your child is and will become, one's steadfast

DOI: 10.4324/9781003385042-7

dos and don'ts will altogether evaporate into thin air the second you become a parent.

I remember the first day I held my firstborn daughter in my arms at the hospital and thinking what the hell am I going to do with her? My eldest daughter has almond-shaped, immense, black curious eyes, palpitating with the life drive, and eyelashes so long you can spend long summer days swinging from them. I wanted to stay in the hospital forever, marry the paediatrician (just because he was a paediatrician, at that moment any paediatrician would have done the job) to help me raise her and check on her, and answer all my questions. But to my surprise when I shared with Dr Philip my desire to marry him, he said, "I would never marry a psychoanalyst", and abruptly left the room . . .

Maybe what I was longing for in the fantasy of marrying my pediatrician was not just someone who would answer my medical questions, but a wish to have somebody who could claim to be a knowing voice on parenting, an authority on this most significant of matters. I was in search of Lacan's "subject supposed to know", despite having become disillusioned with such imaginary wishes in other areas generally and in psychoanalysis specifically. And yet this imaginary wish was again forcefully reawakened in me the moment I became a mother, when it came to a subject that I truly knew nothing about. Except, of course, having been a daughter myself, but alas that did not end up being an aid and, as it turns out, it often became the major obstacle. For indeed parenting is a transgenerational phenomenon. What does that mean? Well, simply said, it means that we are born into a heritage that we inherit from our previous generations, for good or for bad we are affected by how our parents parent us and they in turn by how their own parents raised them. I think it comes in handy to keep this transgenerational phenomenon in mind. To be aware of the seduction of transmitting the traumas of our previous generations to the next generation, at times endeavouring to master them for ourselves by, for example, being the active protagonists of our own becoming while making our children the passive recipients of it all, passive as we once felt as helpless, dependent children.

Today I have a hunch no one can claim such authority on parenting, but allow me to share with you a few things that over the years have been highlighted for me as a mother and a psychoanalyst, things that you might want to keep in mind and see if they can be worthwhile in transforming the most painful, ambivalent, scary, overwhelming, pleasurable, terrifying, enigmatic, intriguing, glorious and heartbreaking relationship of our lives.

Yes, I say heartbreaking, for, you know, Freud said we have children out of our own sense of narcissism, reaching for immortality, and he was absolutely right, listen to all of us saying "Oh, she has my grandmother's eyes, my own smile", obsessing over the adjective "My". Parents are fixated on these remarks and yet I think having a child is also one of the most narcissistically injurious events of our lives. I had fantasies all my life that I would be such a cool bohemian mother, the wise psychoanalyst mother, how I would judge all the mothers on so many things they did and back then I judged them with such ease. All my judgements came back to haunt me as soon as I became a mother, because karma is merciless, dear Parent.

When I think of parenting, I often associate to Schopenhauer's (2000) example of porcupines.

A troop of porcupines is gathering on a cold winter's day. In order to keep from freezing, the animals move closer together. As their bodies get closer, they feel warmer. But the more they huddle, the more they start to irritate each other with their quills. In order to stop the needling, the pain, they spread out, lose the advantage of contact and begin to shiver. This sends them back in search of each other. And on and on. The cycle repeats itself as they struggle to find a comfortable distance between entanglement and freezing, intimacy and distance.

Freud said every intimate emotional relation between two people which lasts for any period of time – whether it be marriage, friendship, the relations between parents and children, or siblings – contains a sediment of both aversion and resistance, which can only escape perception via repression.

In short, how do we attain the optimal distance with our children where we can enjoy the most warmth and the least amount of quills? Well, in my opinion, we can never arrive at such optimality, this is just something we can adhere to, and attempt to sort of survive. In the meanwhile, I recommend that you equip yourself for freezing temperatures and well-designed shields. Yes, parenting is something you just have to survive at times.

Something I have found particularly helpful is to give up power and control. I am not saying I have been successful in it at all times, but that the rare times it happens I find marvellous for all parties involved, and it is there that the possibility of pleasure and intimacy becomes reachable, touchable.

I find the wish for control and power struggles are the death of desire, pleasure and excitement, certainly in all relationships but maybe particularly triggered in the parent/child dyad. And this is so because of yet another painful, at times marvellous, and inevitable parenting premise, that our children are different from us. The wish for sameness is the death of the subject, but sometimes we just can't help ourselves, and the struggle goes two ways. Our children also have both the wish and the fear of becoming like their parents. The separation/individuation dilemma is a great deal more complicated than what we are told. This is intensified in adolescence as they struggle with their own wish to stay close, at times projecting it into their parents: "You do not want me to leave home, you want to keep me prisoner", a typical adolescent protest, which often has to do with fear of their own drives, and their ambivalence regarding separation and becoming. This certainly does not mean parents are not well-trained prison guards. This is all just to give a taste of how complicated and nuanced these matters are and, of course, any parent/child dyad is unique, hence no pre-made formulas are available.

It seems that the human condition is rarely wired to obtain the optimal distance, that we are all caught in the porcupine's struggle, in a vain attempt to find the desirable, if not the impossible: a perfect distance and an ideal closeness. These are the turbulences of intimacy, and in my opinion fully activated in the parent/child relationship.

Let me leave you with a few other small things that you might like to keep in the constellation of your mind as you are thrown into this impossible parenting adventure.

Do not lose touch with the supremacy of pleasure, the transience of things. I love the Persian expression that says, "This too shall pass", for you know the definition of trauma in psychoanalysis is when you have the idea that "This shall not pass". Trauma which is encapsulated in the belief that the situation we are in, or how we are presently feeling, is going to last forever, that it will always remain as such, that it will never end. Hence Trauma is defined by its timelessness, as there is no envisioning of a possibility of a beyond. I think this happens often for parents, it certainly has for me, where an internal sense of "things will turn out OK" is not reachable, where somehow you stop dreaming, or lose the capacity to dream.

One must have a notion of radical hope in general to have kids. Certainly radical hope is very different from hope, which is a very problematic term in my opinion. In a sense the notion of radical hope is one that is embedded within the capacity to dream, one maintained in spite of your heart falling to the ground. It is a "no" to the internal and external traumatisers, not out of a sense of denial, but because one does not let go of the capacity to dream, to become, not *despite* our wounds but *because* of them.

And, above all, to fundamentally believe that you and your child are not the centre of this world, that we are not that central, is the most freeing idea for us and our children. That is my wish for all of us as we attempt to do this impossible profession, certainly with no "subjects supposed to know" in sight, for all of us to be free in the name of the ethics of Eros and all its glorious derivatives.

And when you feel you are going absolutely crazy as a parent, know that you are not alone, that there is a psychoanalyst in a faraway land that is the mother of two young girls, age ten and four, who is right there going crazy with you.

Warmly,

Gohar Homayounpour

**American Psychoanalytic Association,
International Psychoanalytical Association and
the Freudian Group of Tehran | Tehran/Iran**

6

Florencia Biotti

Dear Parent,

This letter is not about giving advice on how best to parent. I cannot. Above all, I believe that the experience of becoming a parent is unique and differs parent to parent. You are even a different parent with one child versus another. What I can do is share my own experience and my learnings on this path, which of course I am still working on.

The invitation to reflect on my experience of becoming a mother led me to think about my "maternity" experience. I am not necessarily talking about maternity as the physical period of pregnancy. But, rather, this word holds what becoming a mother meant to me in my mind. In fact, I don't actually think of it as "maternity" but it leads me to think of "maternities" in the plural. Many maternities have inhabited me. Even long before becoming a mother. I mean, the mother I am today is

DOI: 10.4324/9781003385042-8

"inhabited", "accompanied", so to speak, by all these other maternities that have been with me, *in* me, all my life. Not all of them are pleasant, not all of them are wise. They have all effected the mother I find myself to be today.

When I was a child and someone asked me what I wanted to be when I grew up, I answered from a very young age: "I will be a psychologist and a mom". Of course, this musing was far from what I later discovered. But it makes sense that these two ideas were joined in my mind, although I didn't know why at that time.

I grew up, like all women born in the 1970s in Latin America, with a clear idea of what a mother should be at that time. In those days, motherhood was associated with tenderness, unconditional love and a mother's immediate infatuation with her child.

My maternal grandmother was the youngest of several sisters born into a humble immigrant family. A classic endogamic family. During my grandmother's youth in Buenos Aires, the streets were being asphalted. My grandfather was one of the asphalt labourers. He literally met my granny at the door of her house while laying the land. I always thought she had been so privileged because she didn't have to take a single step out of her house to find a husband. Of course, that is a child's version of a woman's life that was not so easy.

All of my grandmother's sisters were very dedicated mothers and homemakers, as they were expected to be at that time. In addition, most of the daughters of that generation have been almost the same way. As gossip would have it, my grandmother would "rest" from the chores of childrearing to watch soap operas or do something she enjoyed, leaving my mother in the care of the aunts. They were a team of women who worked together in this "motherhood business".

My own mother was the first professional woman in the family. I grew up in the midst of the team of women mothers that continued into the next generation. My mother belonged to it, but like my grandmother, she and my father took their breaks from the parenting role. Those breaks allowed me, when I was left in the care of these other women, to explore different styles of motherhood and femininity. I also liked to "spy" on family life in the homes of my friends and trusted neighbours, who sometimes looked after me for a while. In this way, I was nourished by all those styles, models of parenting, upbringing, and so on.

I grew up. I decided to study psychology as I had proposed to myself earlier on. While I was studying, some of my friends were becoming mothers. That idea was still far away for me. My fantasy about motherhood was either idealised or remained a question mark. I remember when a friend (who was a mother to a one-year-old and a newborn) once called me at work in desperation. She confessed that she felt as if she wanted to throw her child off the balcony! Of course, she was not going to do that. She just needed to tell me about these intense feelings that shocked her. I listened to her, although I didn't really understand what she was talking about. I was too young and had no idea how much work parenting could be. However, for some reason, I banked that memory, which I later discovered to be one of my first clues to my ambivalence about motherhood. I mean, my friend did love her children deeply but was also able to tell me about the hatred she sometimes felt for them.

The experience of becoming a mother myself was a long time coming. Longer than I would have liked. They were the first clues on a long road on which I am learning there is very little that can be planned and will go as planned. Fear, overwhelm and confusion did not take that long to come. I was eight months pregnant. I was sleeping badly. I was tired, nervous, scared, anxious. I remember waking up in the middle of the night and telling my husband, "I can't go on with this anymore". A few days later my first daughter was born.

I wonder if it was at that moment that I was born as a mother. Actually, when is a mother born? I have always loved babies and young children, and for that reason I thought I would have an easy time raising my children in the first few years of their lives. But one of the first things my oldest daughter taught me was that being a mother was not what I had fantasised about. It wasn't better or worse. Just different. And not nearly as easy. When I first saw her, I looked everywhere, but she didn't come with a manual! She was as beautiful as she was strange to me. Vulnerable.

Unlike my mother and grandmother, for different reasons, I didn't have the women's team gathered around me ready to take on their motherly duties. It felt strange to be a mother. My mind had yet to appropriate this new state. Excitement and a sense of poignant happiness were quickly overtaken by exhaustion. I loved this new version of myself, but I also missed the old one so much.

Babies and toddlers need routine. One day repeats the same as the next. If a certain routine can be sustained over time, it makes it easier for the mind to have a solid enough scaffolding to be able to cope with the novelties that life presents. It is common for children to ask moms and dads: "Will you tell me the same story again?" And it is also common for them to correct if a sentence has not been like the original one. So, the routine and the familiar favours the development of young children. You can have the feeling that the days are repeated one after the other: feeding, bathing, changing, sleeping, and then it starts all over again. At the same time, it is pure novelty, pure change. Today they hold up their heads, tomorrow they sit, crawl and walk. Suddenly the house is transformed, ornaments migrate to higher places, sockets need protection, corner brackets are placed on the pointed furniture. The landscape of the house looks different. Each achievement is a huge challenge for everyone in the family. The routine that was set up must be dismantled to invent a new one. And I have come to ask myself: where is the one I was, can someone give me back the life I had?

I wanted to resume my work as quickly as possible. Moreover, I liked meeting myself in my clinical practice. Though, it wasn't easy to leave my daughter in someone else's care.

Then, my second child was born. I was surprised that the experience we had gained as parents did not prove to be enough. A new child. We were new parents all over again with a fresh set of challenges. It reminds me of the game "Snakes and Ladders" I used to play as a child. The board game where you could suddenly land on the box that demanded that you slide all the way back to the start!

The baby years were then behind us. We survived! They were intense. With the most diverse palette of emotional colours, you can imagine. I had felt sad, happy, content, passionate, angry. Now, in the light of the distance that time offers, the memory is tinged with tenderness.

One day I had school-age children at home. The questions that arose were different. What they were discovering didn't depend only on what we as their parents could offer. The world for them and for us was getting bigger and bigger. Everything was expanding. Most of those questions that I was now asking myself were unanswerable. They were waiting to be invented one by one. I think this was and still is the case because the world has changed so much since I was a child. Social, cultural, technological and other changes have accelerated so much in recent years that my children live in a world that I never knew as a child. So, I have to prepare them to make their own way, to live, to unfold their full potential in a world which I am yet to know. I am learning to tolerate the uncertainty and the feeling of not knowing, which still threatens to invade me, often.

Fortunately, during this process of "maternities" I have felt a kind of self-confidence growing that assures me that I am oriented well enough. I want to say the important task, so to speak, has been developed quite well. My children are growing up, and so are we, as their parents. We are all in a state of constant transformation. This is a good sign. If there is movement, there is life.

My personal analysis was a refuge. A place where for a while everything calmed down so I could think more clearly. In addition, there I discovered, among many others, a tool that was fundamental for me. It is easier if I go behind my children than in front of them in every challenge. I mean, if I don't impose myself at various times or ways. It has yielded better results, and I have suffered far less frustration when I have tolerated waiting for them and allowed them to discover their own ways of solving difficulties.

At the time of writing this letter my oldest daughter is a teenager, my youngest son is on the threshold of adolescence. It is a time of life that has always seemed so turbulent, so complex. I often wonder if I can be a good mother of teenagers. Then I remember some reflections from my own analysis. Adolescence is sustained by childhood. If the mental and emotional growth was good enough in childhood, it will be a safe platform to brave the adolescent storm. If it was not, adolescence is a good time to repair that which was not so good.

I have surprised myself as I have transitioned into motherhood. I mean, I have had to learn to wait, to endure frustration, to contain my anxieties and anguish, to really get to know my own vulnerability. I am learning to tolerate myself, with all my virtues and imperfections. I make mistakes. Because how can you *not* make mistakes when you are a mother?

The opportunity that motherhood has offered me in terms of discovering parts of myself that I did not know has been wonderfully rich. When I started studying psychology, I had the fantasy that being a psychologist would give me knowledge that would in turn make me a better mother. However, it has been completely the other way around. Being a mother, letting myself go through all the emotions that this experience awakens, is undoubtedly, making me a better analyst.

Sincerely,
Florencia Biotti
Mother of two | Psychoanalytical Association of Buenos Aires (APdeBA) | Buenos Aires, Argentina

7

~~~~

Kristen Miller Beesley

Dear Parent,

I battled myself to write this letter to you. I struggled to get it "just right". This is ironic, since this letter to you is about the value of being just *good enough*, particularly as it relates to parenting. Despite the appeal of *good enough*, the social and cultural demands to be the "perfect parent" can join forces with our own critical consciences to make *good enough* sound sorely insufficient.

When considering what I'd like to write about in a letter to parents, from my position as a psychoanalyst and mother of three children, it didn't surprise me that the concept of *good enough* made the most sense. What did surprise me though was what happened in the process of writing this letter to you about *good enough mothering*. As I'd hoped to inspire you to be more generous with yourself regarding your own parenting,

DOI: 10.4324/9781003385042-9

I stumbled right into my own harsh internal critics. I will say more about this in a bit.

Good enough mothering is a psychoanalytic concept developed by paediatrician and psychoanalyst, Donald Winnicott. Though first developed by Winnicott to quite literally mean mothers, in its contemporary usage *good enough mothers* include fathers, step-parents, grandparents and other caregivers who are lovingly invested in a child's physical and emotional caretaking. The *good enough caregiver* adapts flexibly to the needs of her developing child, but she also recognises her separateness (she is not her baby and her baby is not her). This is crucial to allow the infant to slowly come to terms with their own separateness.

As a parent you know that even when you have done your best to prepare, children will always bring about the unexpected, both in novel experiences and in bringing about surprising feeling states. The primary parent is usually the parent with greater maternal capabilities. This parent must endure considerable emotional expressions from their children, who will at times express their feelings ruthlessly and without abandon. Parents are also tasked with assisting their developing child with the reasoning and problem-solving abilities on behalf of their child, yet at the same time they are asked to intuitively know when to step back and allow the child to work at it on their own. Oh, and all of this happens quickly, so we'd better keep up! Of course, dear Parent, you know this; yet I hope in this letter to offer some balm in the form of knowledge to protect from the inevitable chafing of your *good enough-ness* that parenting so often brings.

I fooled myself into thinking I'd somehow escaped the gruesome tribulations of mothering since I'd sort of easily slid into parenting my firsts (twins). While I can give myself some credit for my careful and thoughtful approach to parenting, I know that much of the ease had more to do with the good match between their temperaments, and my own personality and maternal style and the privilege that being an educated, middle-class, white mother afforded me. We developed our own rhythm, and we all thrived with consistency. They seemed to understand what I was conveying with my tone when I'd tell one that I'd "be right there", just as soon as I finished up something with the other. I developed other ways of soothing when my arms were occupied with one baby, yet my other baby needed me too. I rocked bassinets with my feet, held bottles with my chin, and discovered the joy of singing songs with nonsensical rhyming words, which soothed us all. And, in turn, they learned to trust that even if I couldn't respond immediately to their need, I would come, in short enough time.

My third child entered this party of three with a kind of energy I could have never anticipated. The *good enough* parenting that my oldest two and I were used to failed miserably when we went from our mostly balanced triangle to a shape-shifting rhombus. She didn't seem to need much sleep, she ate in dribs and drabs when the sun was up, and she was quite pleasant, but only when she was held on my hip facing outward to take in the world around her. As the sun set, she began her hours-long milk binge before finally passing out, only to wake every three hours to snack again. She didn't share my love of routines and schedules, or sleeping through the night, like her older brother and sister had. I was forced to become a different kind of mother, in real time. And even while exhausted, I was enjoying her rebelliousness and watching her tiny self-hood unfold. Despite my best intentions to consciously account for just how disruptive these changes were for my older two children, I hadn't recognised just how deeply these changes were impacting all of us.

Winnicott believed that a *good enough parent* begins by earnestly trying to meet all of their infant's demands in order to minimise their baby's frustrations. If the parent can register the infant's needs for food, warmth and safety, they can in turn respond accordingly by feeding, changing and soothing. The *good enough* parent works to not only respond, but to anticipate their infant's needs to try to get ahead of their frustration. The key to this is to know, *this is an impossible task*, and the *good enough parent* is bound to fail. Not only is this inevitable, but it is also psychologically crucial for the developing mind of the infant to experience these incremental failures. According to Winnicott, it is because of these letdowns that the infant begins to come to terms with the reality that they (baby) do not control the other (*good enough parent*). For example, if the baby fusses because of gas in their bellies, but their mother feeds them, or they call out and their mother doesn't immediately come running, the infant slowly come to terms with their separateness. "I do not control my mother!" *Good enough* mothering includes these kinds of valuable "failures", and it always offers the repeated experience of trying to get it right too.

With this said, our parenting "failures" tend to leave indelible marks in our memories. In both my personal relationships and professional work some iteration of the question of, "am I a bad parent?" will surface with shame when one encounters some aspect of themselves in parenting they hadn't anticipated, and especially when a parent meets some part of themselves they hadn't encountered before or they find they have unintentionally repeated something from their own childhood. With this in mind, I set out to write to you about one of the most memorable personal parenting moments I've experienced so far.

This particular memory is seared in my mind because it was both emotionally difficult and it seemed to mark a new challenge for me in motherhood. The accelerated pace made me suddenly and unavoidably aware that as a singular "I", I would be tasked with meeting the competing needs of "I" and "I" and "I" of three children all younger than three years old. I've sometimes mused that nothing prepared me more for motherhood than my years of being a server in a restaurant, not even training to be a psychologist or psychoanalyst, given the executive functioning required to serve, feed and tend to multiple patrons simultaneously – patrons, like children, who often believe they are your only priority. Not only does serving require significant organisational and planning capacities, it also challenges one's ability to receive and respond to the needs and hunger of others, and at its worst, to be on the receiving end of ruthless expressions of dissatisfaction. So, even with these experiences, and my psychoanalytic repertoire of knowledge, nothing prepared me for the emotional and visceral experience of this particular situation.

My infant daughter was about six weeks old, and my twin son and daughter were two and a half. The twins had just woken from their afternoon nap, and they were enjoying a snack next to me, while I was nursing their sister. My son spontaneously stood up, with his Sippy cup of milk in hand. As I think back, it plays back in slow motion, but in real time it felt like it occurred at warp speed. He brought the cup above his head, paused for a millisecond, and gleefully smashed it down on top of my infant daughter's head. She was physically and psychologically struck. I too was astonished. Having no idea where this pain came from, and of course absolutely no ability to understand why it occurred, she looked immediately to me. Her previously milk-drunk eyes widened with terror as she unlatched from my breast and let out a piercing wail. The utter helplessness I felt turned quickly to rage. When I looked over to my toddler son and saw the look of disbelief on his face, Sippy cup still in hand, I felt temporarily unable to think. I was overwhelmed with the immediate demand to try to remain calm enough to help both of my children with their very different needs, while also feeling the depth of fear and rage that had taken over me. I remember holding my infant daughter's head and kissing her forehead imagining the very worst scenario (later I'd see this as a way I'd adopted the intensity of his destructive feelings as my own): what if he'd hit her fontanel, her soft spot, and permanent damage had been done. Instinctually, and I can't really mark how I knew, I read on my son's face that he too was terrified and he needed me. These competing demands and my absolute uncertainty about how to respond led to a familiar foregone conclusion for me: this was, in fact, all my fault. I was a bad mother.

Returning to the moment I've described: I actually can't remember what I did or said after that, besides comforting my infant daughter, ensuring her physical injury wasn't too bad, and trying, likely hesitantly, to reconnect with my son. Do I think I did everything I could have at that moment? No, I absolutely did not. One, because I am a human; and two, because there isn't an "exact right" way of parenting. There were three individual minds, with three individual experiences (and actually four subjectivities, since my oldest daughter had observed the event and had her own experiences of it too). The *good enough* parent can look back, and without unnecessary guilt or shame or condemnation, try to make sense of what transpired and what else might be understood through the difficulties. We can try to do better next time by incorporating what we learned this time. We can understand our impact on our children, and we can know we can make peace with ourselves knowing we will never get it "just right".

All of what I've written to you so far sounds like a great learning experience, and one to share with you as an inspiration. So, why was it so hard to write? And why, when I finally wrote it out, did I unintentionally send an email to this book's editor that sat in my drafts, unsent, for three weeks before I realised she hadn't written back to me? As a psychoanalyst, I know that slips like this reveal anxiety and discomfort, despite all of my conscious efforts to push back on those internally critical voices. Psychoanalysis works from the model of the unconscious. While we may consciously strive for self-awareness, there is a human tendency to avoid difficult truths about ourselves and others. Our unconscious minds are by their very nature illogical, irrational and unregulated. It is the job of the other more developed parts of our mind to make sure we aren't ruled by these self-gratifying impulses, yet we know they are a part of us. For me, the slip of not sending the email likely reveals discomfort in sharing this very difficult story, perhaps worrying about your judgement of me or my children.

For my son, I'd imagine he was not consciously aware of how angry he felt towards his infant sister and towards me. Toddlers are much closer to their dysregulated and pleasure-seeking wishes, and learning to tolerate the delay in gratification. Looking back, I've wondered if his response was brought on by some awareness of having to hold his own milk cup and feed himself while she curled comfortably in my arms, nursed by me. As a toddler, he was newly faced with a world (and a mother) that asks for increased limits and rules and order, while I was so carefully navigating his infant sister's experiences and doing all of the thinking for her. As for my unconscious contributions, it's possible that I had regressed to a place of blissful ease with my infant daughter, and I had ignored the intensity of my son's rage because I wasn't in touch with my own anger in response to her demands. Tending to an infant, particularly one who sleeps little, is a particularly depleting experience and one that was likely impacting me in greater ways than I was aware. The terrible pain and shock my infant daughter felt were experiences that my toddler son was trying to communicate to me, and the suddenness of his action forced both of us to pay good attention to it. And, we all felt it. Deeply.

I hope this letter offers you some space to think about your own parenting tribulations, but from a position of helpful curiosity. I wish for you a loving and generous spirit as you navigate the pressures of parenting to facilitate a kindness with yourself, particularly during the times you feel most tested. From one *good enough parent* to another, there's always hope for repair if we can hold in mind that we are *good enough*, and of course our children are too.

With grace,
Kristen Miller Beesley
Mother of three | Michigan Psychoanalytic Institute and Society | Detroit, USA

8

$\Lambda\Lambda\Lambda\Lambda$

Heribert Blass

Dear fellow Father,

I have been pondering the transition from becoming a father to being a father. I am a father like you, and in the meantime also a grandfather. I am writing to share some experiences from my development as a father to a grandfather, in the hope that one or the other aspect may be of use to you in your own father-hood. To give you some idea about me: I am at the end of my sixties, married and I am a psychoanalyst for adults as well as children and adolescents. So, I am in regular contact with children, both privately and professionally, and this is a tangible source of joy for me, despite sometimes bringing unavoidable stress.

In thinking about you, I ask myself from what psychic starting point you have become a father – or would still like to become a father. Have you carried the desire to become a

DOI: 10.4324/9781003385042-10

father within you since the beginning of your adult life? Or
did you already feel it as a child and teenager? Or have you
approached this wish rather slowly and at first felt more misgivings, doubts and fear of this step? Furthermore, I am also
thinking of your social position and partnership. My internal
questions might sound too direct, but I ask them for a reason.
For example, I wonder whether you are in a heterosexual marriage or partnership, and whether you became a father through
your sexuality with your female partner, or whether you may
have become a father in the context of reproductive medical
assistance? Or are you not a biological father, but a "social"
father in that you have adopted a partner's child? Or are you an
adoptive father together with your partner, be it heterosexual
or be it homosexual, if you are living in a homosexual partnership? I ask these questions because I know that there are many
ways to become and be a father, and I would like to address you
in your specific version of fatherhood. And at the same time,
I also want to tell you that, from my perspective, if you have
decided to be a *committed father* to your child, the basic features
of fatherhood are more or less the same from a wide variety of
starting points.

The fact that you are reading this letter and other letters in
this book tells me that you are definitely a committed father
and that you, along with your partner, want to be lovingly
there for your child. However, as I know from my own experience, it is not always so easy to put this plan into practice.
I would like to tell you about a few aspects that I consider
important. Firstly, there is the happiness, but perhaps also a difficulty, that with the birth or arrival of your child, the previous
relationship of two becomes (at least) a relationship of three.
Even as a happy and proud father, you now have to share your
partner with your child, and especially after the birth of your

child, you may have to take a back seat in your partnership for a while. This also requires a renunciation from you and, if necessary, even a temporary renunciation of your sexual needs. Of course, this should not last forever, but the arrival of your child reshapes your partnership: it may well be painful to no longer feel like Number One. However, this does not mean that you become unimportant and insignificant as a man and father – on the contrary! It is precisely when you are ready to accept this change in your position from an exclusive relationship of two, and realign yourself in different ways within the new family triangle. Once you accept and adapt, you will then be able to gain new significance as a protective, committed father to your child and once again be a loving sexual partner within your adult partnership.

I suspect that you don't want to leave the care of your baby and physical contact with your child solely to your partner as a mother. Surely you want to hold your child yourself, change his diaper, possibly feed him, and, if necessary, get up at night to comfort him. You know yourself that this can also be exhausting, despite all the joy. I would like to make two comments about this.

Firstly, I feel it is a great cultural and societal advance that we as men participate in the care of children much more today than was common in earlier decades. Nevertheless, you should not be too worried if you should also feel resentment or anger at some point in view of the many changes in your life. Such feelings are understandable and almost unavoidable, especially when stress levels rise sharply – this applies to mothers and fathers alike. However, one's own inner work consists of noticing these angry feelings without taking them out on one's own child. In tense situations, I myself have repeatedly been helped by the knowledge that my child is not intentionally trying to annoy me. A baby is completely dependent on its parents, and when it cries, this is a message or request for help to eliminate its physical and mental discomfort. Their primary helplessness sometimes makes our children's crying and screaming become very fierce, and this can create physical and mental tension within ourselves. This tension is a sign that the message has reached us. It should not be a reason for guilt, at least not if we manage to decipher the call for help and translate it into a calming action.

At the same time, I would like to ask you to distinguish that you as a father should not be a duplication of the mother. I do not want to diminish your commitment, but it seems important to recognise that the physical contact of your child with the mother through breastfeeding is usually closer than with you. This perhaps painful recognition of maternal primacy is something we as fathers have to manage. But I am not saying that the physical contact between you and your child is unimportant – in fact your child needs the physical contact with you and your emotional presence to a great extent, but as a father rather than as a second mother! As a father you are *different* from the mother, and this *otherness* is vital for your child. So, take care of your child physically, but do not try to compete with the mother: stay yourself!

Now I hear you asking: "What do you mean specifically by that?" Here is my response: As a tender and receptive father, you can nevertheless play with your children differently than mothers do. This does not detract from your tenderness. Your child needs both similar and different experiences with mother and father for his development. I follow here study results of developmental psychology, but also my own spontaneous actions as a father. Of course, I also held my babies in my arms, but I also played with them a little more riskily at times, lifting them up with my arms and catching them again, or spinning around my own axis with them. Such behaviour is more typical of fathers, although mothers can do it too, of course. The point here is not to spread rigid gender stereotypes, but it is indeed the case that such "kamikaze play" (Herzog 1982) is more likely to be practised by fathers. I tell you this because I want to encourage you to be careful, but not too anxious, with your child. Your child will enjoy romping around with you, it is fun for him – hopefully for you too – and if you don't overdo it, you will also give your child confidence in your holding abilities in case of danger.

Now you may say: "So far, so good. That may be easier with babies and toddlers. But what about when my child grows up?" To that I can say that some fathers don't find early interaction with their child so easy, because they can't yet communicate with each other in words. This makes it all the more important to empathise with your child's possible feelings and your fatherly balancing response to them. And your efforts to find an *emotional balance* in your response to your child will also be crucial in further development. This emotional balance will become especially important in two mental areas that will challenge you in your contact with your children: firstly, there is the area of angry and resentful feelings on the part of both your child and you that can potentially become very fierce. Secondly, there are feelings of love that are so magnetic and intense that they *almost* feel like romantic love with an adult – I say "almost" because, in fact, paternal love for your own child is not romantic love, even though your child admires you as a father and desires your affection. I attribute these different feelings sometimes to the aggressive and sometimes to the erotic realm. Aggressive and erotic feelings exist in both sexes, and accordingly conflicts and challenges can arise in contact with both your son and your daughter, especially with the onset of their teenage years. Nevertheless, experience shows that situations of struggle and rivalry are more likely to occur with adolescent sons, while some fathers are frightened by their daughter's developing femininity – sometimes a father's own inner struggle against the seductive illusion of romantic love leads to excessive severity and then also to sometimes hurtful struggles with his own daughter. Conversely, fearful loving feelings towards one's own son can also be held in check by excessive harshness.

Now you may say: "That all sounds very odd – they are my children after all, all these feelings have no place here." To which I would like to respond that you are absolutely right in not wanting to act out these adult feelings in your interactions with your children. At the same time, however, it is part of your developmental task as a father (together with your partner, of course) to open up mental and emotional space for your child and at the same time to help him or her find boundaries. This is why it is so important that you both participate in conflictual disputes and both honour and protect the growing sexual maturity of your children, both sons and daughters. The best way to do this is to be ever mindful of your own inner reactions, and to move between allowing intense feelings and limiting assaultive actions. With your son, in particular, a conflict can arise because first he wants to be similar to you as a role model, but then he also wants to be different from you in order to develop his own personality. He admires you and at the same time questions you. This mental conflict could become very violent, and disputes sometimes arise between sons and fathers whose sharpness is reminiscent of a duel. In order to recognise the strength and efficacy of your son or daughter, it is important that you face up to the conflict and do not avoid it. On the other hand, your son or daughter as well can only really accept your setting of paternal boundaries if you keep a benevolent attitude even during tense anger. Instead of a duel, ensure a "tender fight" (Stierlin 1974). A duel usually ends fatally or with psychic damage, whereas a tender fight will more likely lead to mutual respect, appreciation and recognition of reciprocal boundaries. Similarly, I like the advice of my colleague Stefano Bolognini (2008) – a fellow contributor in this book – according to him every father should dance a waltz with his daughter once in the course of his life: but only once and only in public! This beautiful metaphor poetically sums up the fatherly task: as a father, you encourage your daughter's erotic development and at the same time protect her from boundary transgressions and violations. As with aggressive emotions, it is important to feel and allow your own erotic feelings as a father, but not to translate them into encroaching actions. I call this the "anti-incestuous position" of the father (cf. Blass 2017).

Let me close with two recommendations: don't give up on remaining present as a father, especially if you are questioned by your children during adolescence. Your children need a balanced response from you. And do not try to deny your own ageing process by rivalling youthfulness with your children. Accept the generational difference that exists. In this way you will remain significant for your children and, should you become a grandfather, for your grandchildren. We are all mortal, but by acknowledging our own limits and the generational succession through our children and grandchildren, our chance of leaving a constructive legacy and being remembered vividly beyond our deaths increases. Dear fellow Father, I wish you a fulfilling life with your child or children and your whole family.

I send you my warmest regards,

Heribert Blass

Father of three, grandfather of five | German Psychoanalytical Association | Düsseldorf, Germany

9

∿∿∿

Maria Lival–Juusela

Let everything happen to you: beauty and terror.
Just keep going. No feeling is final.
"Go to the Limits of your Longing",
Rainer Maria Rilke, 1905

We are never so defenseless against suffering as when
we love, never so forlornly unhappy as when we have lost
our love object or its love.
Mourning and Melancholia, Sigmund Freud, 1917

Dear Parent,

In an essay from almost 40 years ago, journalist Ellen Cantarow called having a child a decision to forever have your heart go walking around outside your body.[1] The vulnerabilities we take on when we try to conceive and when we

---

1 Original reference not found.

 DOI: 10.4324/9781003385042-11

become parents are tremendous. And they're tremendous, simply because we love.

When my kids had just turned three and one years old, I entered what would become my second psychoanalysis. At first it was a twice-weekly training psychotherapy, as I was in training to become a psychotherapist.[2] But the therapy quickly turned into a lifeline, as my younger child – my daughter – continued to miss her developmental milestones. As time went by, the doctors we saw stopped playing down our concerns and instead began to share them. Our daughter had been born with some complications and for a long time that was the given explanation: "She will catch up after her rocky start", we were told. But in my bones, I had a nagging feeling that wouldn't leave me alone. I was a second-time mother, who knew what it felt like to drift in and out of musical spheres with a nursing baby. I knew how to listen to wordless language, how to connect through gaze and in play, how to sense my baby's feelings in my own body and how to respond in turn. I had found myself easily falling into the rhythms of being in love and exhausted and sensitive to the needs of my first baby, then toddler. When my second child, our daughter, came along, I was expecting the music to be different – she was after all her very own little being. But I wasn't expecting silence, for there at times to be no music at all, for her to tune out so extensively. She would come and go, smiling serenely in connection and then suddenly not responding at all, and all the more, as her main dancing partner in life, I wondered at this cut-off tune, panicked at the way the music sometimes just seemed to stop. It took us far into the second year of her life

2 Where I am from, therapists need to have their own therapy, at least twice a week, to learn more about the ins and outs of their own psyche and to embody the experience of therapy.

for the doctors to catch on. It was a huge relief when they finally did: a response of something I didn't want to hear, but which at least felt truthful. "She may have a developmental disorder", they told us gravely. It was much too early to run any cognitive tests and the main genetic ones, for Down's Syndrome and a couple of other fairly common disorders, had come back negative. "We just have to wait and see", they told us.

Teetering on that edge, between desperate hope and desperate grief, was almost unbearable. Some days I would hang on to the thought of everything being fine, other days I just knew it wasn't. It was, needless to say, a crashing wave of grief that I had to learn to surf. I wanted very badly to learn how to surf, because as the mother of two very small and still very needy people (and with quite a bit of psychoanalytic training on hand) I knew the option was highly undesirable for all of us. I couldn't afford not to mourn, couldn't afford to give into the siren song of melancholia that some days tugged at my feet, calling me to just give up. I fought it with all I had, because I knew how much my family needed a mother whose own music would continue to play.

The way I did that was through submerging into my own analysis. Instead of twice weekly, I began to drive across town four times a week, to lie on a couch and allow myself to be held through every feeling that welled up and every defence I used to block the seemingly unbearable. I became intimately acquainted with my own refuges into rationality, into actions, even into guilt, which, painful as it was, still carried the magic wish for it all to be my fault, so I could then figure out a way to undo it (this, deep in my unconscious, made perfect sense). With unending patience my analyst walked me through it all, always gently awaiting me, as I weaved through my own defences to how much it hurt to accept the truth. To remain with the truth without dodging.

In an article about mourning, psychoanalyst Jonathan Lear (2014) speaks about our human need for a mourning environment. Part of what it is to be a mourner, Lear writes, is to recognise that one is at the grief-stricken limits of one's understanding. This implies being *at a loss* about what to do, feel or think. Lear's point is that when we are at a loss, we are helpless in a sense. We need help and the help we need most is with *meaning* for what might otherwise be an unbearable and incomprehensible disaster.

How does one find such meaning? Historically, cultural and religious rituals have provided the frame for a mourning environment. But there are many losses where there are no given rituals, and perhaps this is most true for losses that are ambiguous. In my case, I was certainly at a loss about how to navigate my conflicting emotions of intense worry, hope and longing for the satisfactions of mothering my younger child in a predictable way. According to Lear – and this is certainly what I have found in my own experience, both on and behind the couch – psychoanalysis, with its own set of unusual rituals, can become such a mourning environment, a space one retreats to from the daily demands of life in order to experience and express one's feelings with another. The analyst becomes a companion and a witness to one's testimony. "This is what life did to me", one cries, and the analyst's steady presence verifies, "Yes, yes, it did". Unlike in life outside the analytic room, the analyst's task is *to bear* the mourning of another, without trivialising, denying or sugarcoating it. By accompanying the mourner as loss is experienced in all its emotional complexity, echoes of earlier losses, fears and separations surface as well. And somewhere on this unusual journey, some meaning may begin to form, as the unconscious meanings we assign to our losses become more apparent. Accompanied by another we may eventually be able to reorganise that meaning, and by doing that, to belong to ourselves all the more. We become able to integrate into ourselves those truths and experiences that we previously held at a distance, simply because they hurt too much to handle.

Analysis gave me a space to listen to my own tones of deep sadness. "No one ever told me that grief felt so like fear", C.S. Lewis (2013/1961) once wrote. He continued to describe the physical resemblances: "The same fluttering in the stomach, the same restlessness, the yawning. I keep on swallowing." In essence: mourning hurts, physically hurts. Gradually, however, I began to learn that to the extent that I could stand that pain and meet my own sadness, it would every so often give way to an inner expansion, to presence and to more fully experiencing the many satisfactions that my life continued to afford. Slowly, slowly, I began to inhabit my own unbearable reality with more courage. And then came the first inklings of hope that reality, while deeply sad, wasn't really unbearable. I began to realise that, afraid as I was for my daughter, she was far from unhappy. She was different certainly, but also, I began to realise, just as she should be in that very difference.

Dear Parent, in 1839 the phrase "the apple never falls far from the stem" was first introduced into the English language by the transcendentalist philosopher Ralph Waldo Emerson. It gradually morphed into the commonly used phrase "the apple doesn't fall far from the tree", an expression we use to describe how children inherit their parent's characteristics and traits. Interestingly, this wasn't what Emerson originally meant: he was referring to the tug that often brings people back to their childhood homes, reminiscent of nostalgia. But perhaps the transformation of the phrase says something about a wishful fantasy often embedded in parenthood: that of our children resembling us. Perhaps this is related to the nostalgic tug to go "back home" that Emerson wrote about. There is an inherent self-centredness in this fantasy – we may just be hoping for the ease of keeping our metaphorical apples close at hand, of not having to be challenged by them rolling off too far. If our children are a lot like us, they verify the life-choices we have made. They pay us a compliment; we may unconsciously feel – or even demand. One of the big developmental tasks of parenthood may just be acknowledging this possible wish within ourselves enough so that we don't task or burden our children with it. To let them be who they are, even when we wish we could protect them more from their own destinies. Maybe especially then.

Innately my daughter seemed to have within her a sureness of her own right to be exactly who she was. In that, she became my guide, as I slowly began to discover the ways I hadn't always afforded myself that same right. And to breathe easily again as I realised, that while her still, soft music hadn't always been perceptible to me, she seemed to have heard every note of the protective love which had surrounded her. While I had been afraid of what life was asking of us, my daughter had not.

When she was four years of age, we finally received her official diagnosis. In cases like these, we were told, it's like looking for a needle in a haystack. Nonetheless we were granted a series of deeper genetic tests, while warned not to expect much. To everyone's surprise, an answer was found. An unusual genetic mutation showed up in the tests. It had a name, a descriptive profile and a small worldwide support group on Facebook. It was definite now, and I remember receiving that defining phone call: the waves of grief-mixed relief running over me. This was no one's fault, there was no one to blame, this was just biological evolution, a trickster in the wheel of life, dealing us, among so many others, a set of genetic cards we hadn't counted on. It was nothing psychoanalysis could or should solve, no "refrigerator parents" to analyse, no way around it. It just was. But what psychoanalysis *could* do was exactly what I had been working with. Psychoanalysis could help me mourn and accept the facts of my life. It could help me towards deeper levels of intimacy and authenticity within my relationships. It could, especially, when faced with hardship, help me turn my pain into suffering, and suffering, slowly, into a kind of fearlessness.

Over many years, the deep grief my psychoanalysis helped me work through also showed me my own capacity for profound joy, that most vulnerable of feelings. With every developmental gain our daughter made, my gratitude was palpable. I no longer felt entitled to any of it. Would she walk? Would she talk? Would she ever dress herself? In the beginning no one knew, and so each gain became a gift, a reparation of something I had feared was broken beyond repair. In some ways: yes, it was. But life is full of brokenness, I learned, and brokenness need not be feared. The only fears, ultimately, are guilt and shame. The fears of all fears: those of not being loved in the brokenness we all, in our own uniquely diverse ways, share as human beings. Dear fellow Parent, on this awe-inspiring journey of loving our children just as they are, I wish you courage and tender companions.

Warm regards,
Maria Lival-Juusela
**Mother of two | Finnish Psychoanalytical
Society | Helsinki, Finland**

10

~~~~

Ntshediseng Tlooko

Dear Parent,

I am writing this letter to you at 3:21 am, while I wait for my daughter's bottle to cool. You can lay judgement upon my decision to formula-feed my baby, because condemning mothers for the choices they make has become the democratic prerogative of modern society. A condemnation that is birthed at the infancy of a pubescent girl's life. Perpetuated through lifelong disapproving narratives such as, "What was she wearing?" and "What kind of mother is she?"

Women are precociously taught that they do not have any autonomy over their bodies, minds and life choices. They are conditioned to outsource their decision making to the favourable gaze of society and if they display any form of autonomy, it is criminalised. Therefore, by the time a woman gets to motherhood she has lost most of her autonomy, making her

DOI: 10.4324/9781003385042-12

susceptible to society's denunciation of her maternal choices. Leaving her powerless and at the mercy of the wisdom of Mom Influencers on Instagram. You are probably wondering, dear Parent, why I am being so defensive at the outset. My defensiveness is likely the result of three sleepless nights, due to my baby's teething cries, mixed in with my own raw emotions about being a mother during these chaotic times. It is also my way of preparing you for what is to come in this letter.

Motherhood has become increasingly difficult and complicated, as Tsitsi Dangarembga states in her book, *Black and Female* (2022), motherhood used to be the natural task of feeding and washing a baby. And if that failed, the mother would strap the baby on her back and continue with her work, while the baby eventually fell asleep (Dangarembga 2022). Now, however, a mother must not only perform these instinctual tasks, but also talk in full sentences to the baby right after birth, respond to the baby's slightest wince of discomfort as well as be careful to not overstimulate the baby, otherwise they will get an incurable sensory illness. The pressure to become the perfect mother is insane and impossible. A pressure that makes mothers feel that they must be the daily-freshly-baked-wholewheat mother, who lives in servitude to her children, because she is terrifyingly conscious of how much her mothering will affect the entirety of her child's mental health. Oh, and dear Parent, did I mention that all this insanity is meant to be done before your snap-back gym class and right after your 7 am board meeting?

Motherhood on its own is quite difficult, even without the freshly baked bread and Instagram narratives. Bringing life into this world stretches one in unimaginable ways. A mother's stretch marks and dark rings serve as markers of her constant expansion. An expansion that women should have a right to opt into or opt out of. Furthermore, birthing a melanated child into a world that will never accept them, requires an even greater expansion. An expansion that not only creates cellulite, but also forces the mother to reckon with the terrors of her own skin. As a black mother, pregnant for the first time, I knew I was not ready for that reckoning. I understood with my first pregnancy that to be a black mother to a black child meant more than just feeding, soothing and decreasing stimulation. It meant liberating myself, so I may raise a liberated child. It is for this reason that I aborted my first pregnancy.

In *Beloved*, Toni Morrison (1987, p.95) stated that, "Freeing yourself was one thing, claiming ownership of that freed self was another." I knew when I fell pregnant the first time that I was not ready to be a mother. I was still a compliant woman, unliberated and shackled. Similar to Sethe, Morrison's protagonist in the book, I knew that if I was not free, my children would not be free. Sethe decided to kill her children rather than let them be captured into a life of slavery. She only managed to kill one of her children, Beloved, and was upended from killing the other three. I repeat, if the mother is not free the children will not be free. It is the enslaved mother who has not taken full autonomy of her freedom who in the end lives in servitude to the judgemental gaze of society. I knew at five weeks pregnant that I was not ready to be a mother, as such I knew that I would fall prey to the imprisonment of motherhood and I did not want to unconsciously teach my child to always be enslaved.

Sethe killed her beloved child out of love, for she knew what it was like to live in slavery, and more importantly, Sethe knew what it was like to be free and she wanted to give that to her children. Sometimes a mother's love liberates her children from the perils of the world. To be born is to live in this world, and as a marginalised body living in this world, it is sometimes better to not have been born at all. Being birthed black in a world that will never accept you is a difficult birthright to inherit. And as the mother of that black being, I knew I owed it to my child to have some form of ownership over my own existence before bringing them into this existence. As I would be the one guiding them, teaching them and helping them, as they navigate the struggles of marginalised life. Freeing myself, and claiming ownership of that freedom, was in part an act of freeing my child and helping my child claim ownership of their freedom.

Let us remember, dear Parent, that to birth a child also means you birth a mother and the best gift I could give my child as a mother was freedom. Yes, one is never completely free, but a mother who knows enough of her own freedom can free herself from the constant shackles of oppression over and over again, as many times as necessary. Being constrained to a life of mothering when you did not willingly choose to do so is a very harmful bondage on both the mother and the child. I have lived the experience of being born to a mother who did not choose to have me. An experience that left an indelible ache in my heart. One that no amount of psychoanalysis could ever wash away. It is an ache that I must live with. A grief that will always haunt me. A clemency that I must constantly find inside myself. I therefore did not want the same for my child and knowing that you are not ready to be a mother is a good enough reason to not be a mother.

My mother was 16 when she had me. She fell pregnant when she was 15 years old. A gestational fall that tragically changed the trajectory of her young life. Her simple, yet all-consuming, adolescent troubles were erased by one act of pleasure. She did not know what she was doing, neither did he.

Pregnant beneath her black pleated "jim dress", she gave birth to me during her third term school exams. She did not have the freedom to choose whether or not she wanted to become a mother. The accelerated development that was imposed upon my mother as a consequence of sex meant that she would have to forgo the narcissistic enjoyment of youth and figure out how to breastfeed while doing her homework. As a result, I had to be raised on the back of her mother's spine to afford my mother an opportunity to finish school. By falling pregnant at 15 she did not have the opportunity to mother me the way that she would have liked. In having a child at 16, she also gave *her* mother another mouth to feed.

Many black teenagers growing up in Apartheid in the 1980s did not know that they could get pregnant from having sex. Sex was a taboo topic in my young mother's house. The conventional six-year-old question of the origins of babies was handled like hot coals: dropped very quickly and not to be touched again. The subject of menstruation was treated in the same vein. At the first sight of blood, you were handed cloths to absorb the leak and sternly told to stay away from boys. The reasons thereof were quite unclear. And Bantu education, being the only formal education at the time, was only limited to the making of domestic and factory workers. An adolescent growing up in Apartheid South Africa was therefore deprived of knowledge. Denied a knowledge of self, an understanding of their own bodies and given no options. My mother therefore had no choice but to become a mother, because of a single night of sex. You may ask, dear Parent, why my mother did not heed the stern warning issued at menarche. To that I will respond with the hope that you still remember and continue to be in touch with the intense and rule-defying love of adolescence. The hormonally infused desire of adolescent yearning that threatens to render you senseless. And the simple joy of having a crush on someone. For my mother was in love with my 18-year-old father. A short-lived love that resulted in my existence, but a love nonetheless. Perhaps my mother had an unconscious wish to bear my father's children. At times teenage love lulls one into a belief of an everlasting love. I am sure she had fantasies of marrying my father. Looking at his pictures as a young man, he was quite charming and, knowing his personality, he definitely mesmerised her. Tales of their courtship were filled with burgeoning passion and numerous secret encounters. She wanted him and he wanted her. Romeo and Juliet were barely 14 years old when they decided to die for love. As fictional as the characters may have been, they captured the essence of young love. To therefore be sentenced to the hardships of motherhood, while yourself still a child, is a punishment that did not fit the crime.

My young mother's life was short and complicated. Being a mother at such a young age resulted in an unfulfilled life, filled with strife. She was forced to give me up to my paternal grandparents. A difficult decision that she never really made. As a young mother, growing up in oppression, your only wish is to provide your children with a life better than yours. To love them is to sacrifice them. As Sethe tried to explain to her Beloved child, that she sacrificed her because she loved her (Morrison 1987). My mother made the greatest sacrifice for me. She gave me up to my paternal grandparents, not knowing when she would see me again, yet holding on to the belief that I would grow up to one day write her story. A loss that plagued her life until she died at the early age of 37. What more could she have been if she was given the freedom to choose?

My mother loved me, this I know for sure. Just as much as I loved my first baby and that I know for sure. It is because my mother loved me that she certainly wanted more for me. She knew she did not have the internal and external resources to give me the life that she wanted for me. She made a sacrifice, the kind that many mothers would make in her position. To be a good enough mother is to know your limits. To know when you are not capable and recognise when you need to hand over to the village. To know that you are not ready and recognise that a termination may be saving both you and your child. This knowledge is borne out of a mother's love.

A good enough mother, as psychoanalyst Donald Winnicott (1965) puts it, is a mother who is responsive to her infant's needs and is able to be sensitive and adaptive to her child's developmental needs. The reason he says the mother must and can only be good enough, instead of perfect, is because the mother *will* fail the child and it is these regular and developmentally appropriate failures that give the child the ability to be resilient in an imperfect world (Winnicott 1965). I knew at five weeks pregnant that I was not even capable of being good enough to my child. There was still so much work that I needed to do internally to be ready to be a mentally free mother to a black child. I knew from my parents' inability, as well as their wisdom to know their inability, that I had an obligation to do better as a parent. It is because I loved my child that I knew he or she deserved more from me. As Steve Bantu Biko said (1978, p.92), "If one is free at heart, no man-made chains can bind one to servitude, but if one's mind is so manipulated and controlled by the oppressor, then there will be nothing the oppressed can do to scare his powerful masters."

You may be wondering, dear Parent, why I would write such a personally revealing story given my profession. To answer you, I will employ the words of Audre Lorde (1978, p.32), when she said, "when we speak, we are afraid our words will not be heard nor welcomed, but when we are silent, we are still afraid. So, it is better to speak remembering we were never meant to survive."

Yours in freedom,
Ntshediseng Tlooko
Mother of one | South African Psychoanalytical Association | Johannesburg, South Africa

11

Daniel Jacobs

Dear Parent,

Giving you advice seems a risky business, particularly as we are strangers. I have no idea of the ages of your children, where and how you live or why you chose to read this book. I do remember, however, the result of well-meaning advice given by strangers to my wife when she took our first-born to a nearby supermarket. She returned home in tears. Shoppers felt their duty to advise: "Put a sweater on him, he's freezing to death!"; "Clip his fingernails or he'll scratch his face"; "He looks like he's cross-eyed. Has he seen a doctor yet?"

I feel in no position to give advice. My children would most likely agree. In fact, I try to refrain from advising my adult son and daughter, who are now parents themselves, about their child-rearing practices. That's if I want them to continue

DOI: 10.4324/9781003385042-13

talking to me. So, instead of telling you of my successful and unsuccessful ventures in parenting or giving advice not specific to your situation or culture, I will leave you with 12 epigrams, culled from my own experience that, in one way or another, are related to parenting. Decipher them for yourselves; find meaning in them or not.

1. My grandson, when asked what he wanted to be when he grew up, answered, "Taller than my father."
2. My parents spoke Yiddish when they didn't want me to understand them. I felt like a foreigner in my own home.
3. I felt that way again, when they argued in earshot.
4. At my Bar Mitzvah, my father couldn't read a word of Hebrew.
5. A four-year-old told me, "If you have a baby, you are tired for the rest of your life."
6. When my mother came late to pick me up from school, I wondered if she wanted me.
7. My father asked me when I was an adolescent, "Do you need to wear those eye-glasses all the time?"
8. When we played catch, my 12-year-old son threw the ball so hard it stung my hand.
9. We watched our son, age 21, descend the stairs of a Paris Metro. Alone, he was starting on a trip around world that lasted a year.
10. When our teenage son was hanging with delinquents, I took him on a trek to Nepal.
11. My daughter and her partner consider marriage "too bourgeoise". Having a child is not.

12. Our five-year-old daughter, going on a week's vacation with her mother without me, said sarcastically "Thanks, Daddy."

Best of luck with your kids,
Daniel Jacobs
**Father of two | Boston Psychoanalytic
Society and Institute | Boston, USA**

12

Kateryna Alpatova

Dear Parent,

The birth of my first child fell at the beginning of Russia's full-scale invasion of Ukraine in 2022. In this letter, I want to think about some of the things that I have been struggling with since the beginning of war. And while most of you will never know what it's like to face the realities of raising your child in a real-life war situation, perhaps we *can* think together about the more ordinary conflicts that get evoked inside us when we have children of our own. Living your own motherhood during a time of war is an overwhelming experience that is hard to describe in familiar words. How does one describe something unthinkable? Extraordinary experiences create flooding feelings of overwhelm and chaos. I think about how difficult it can be for us to find the words to label the primary experiences a baby projects into us in the hopes that we will understand and

DOI: 10.4324/9781003385042-14

pronounce the treasured solution: "you're scared" or "you're hungry". The moment that feeling is named, relief comes. Why? Because there is a bond between mother and infant, where the mother has the strength and experience of recognising her own feelings, and that lived experience can then bring calm to her child by offering words in place of the frightening inner chaos battling the baby at any given moment.

Of course, this requires the mother to have a reasonably good internal balance. In my case, I found myself caught between extreme infant experiences; my own emotional state (as a new mother) and the surrounding dangerous environment (a world at war). I was thinking about how experiencing an external real threat conflicts with the need to have an internal space in which to contain a child and give him or her room to gently develop.

When a mother is overwhelmed by her own experiences, there is not enough room for the child to "become". I am particularly aware of how important the "onion" concept is to a child's development: how each layer envelops the child, then the mother, father, grandparents, friends and acquaintances, the environment and so on. And each layer provides safety and space for the infant's development. This is an experience that every parent faces, in a war situation however, it becomes most acute. War destroys the perception of the world as a good place. Therefore, there is this painful feeling that you have brought a child into a world that is neither good nor beautiful. What feels essential, though, is that you need to find good things to pass onto your child! So, in my experience, the supportive environment played a very important and obvious role in restoring my faith in the world. I went into premature labour at 29 weeks and my son was born weighing 1.5 kg. I remember my terror for his life, as well as the suffocating experience of my own failure as a mother who was not able to save space for my baby's development. The first reaction of my husband and my loved ones upon hearing that the baby was in the incubator and my life was not in danger felt congratulatory! I remember my shock, because my state of mind was very far from the anticipatory joy of welcoming my son. I often think, what would have happened if my loved ones had not been there for me? If they, like me, had been flooded with guilt and the experience of failure? I think this is one of those forks in the road of life and a sense of how different my experience of mothering and motherhood, and therefore my interaction with my child, would be if my personal issues of guilt were not set aside. To look at the baby based on your own experiences of guilt or failure is to see the baby poorly and to colour the relationship in a certain way. It will require the baby to adjust to the proposed model of communication. We do a lot of work within ourselves, trying to see the world as it is, without colouring it with our own inner dilemmas, because it is the openness to the new dynamic that empowers the mother to welcome the child as he or she is.

Support for the mother is essential, especially at the beginning of parenthood. The constant challenges of growing a child will accompany a parent daily, and it is important to remain in touch with creativity and the ability to be flexible and adaptable. The luxury of not noticing time or being sheltered is already less available when you become a parent!

The beautiful challenge a parent encounters is how to face both external and internal reality in its entirety. We are not only encountering nature's ability to create, but we are also experiencing our own remarkable participation in this process. It is no wonder that the birth of a child is often called "a miracle"! Facing these existential questions of life and death, experiencing the passage of time, and participating in the changing of one generation to the next, is extremely provocative. And the arrival of a child confronts us with these profound questions of reality, as well as revealing to us our own inner world that then responds to the external changes that have taken place. This is not an easy experience for anyone!

Parenthood is, on the one hand, a basic natural process for all of humanity. And at the same time, it is experienced as an extraordinary challenge and an enormous responsibility. It is a challenge for every parent to experience negative feelings about their child. We have internal guides that dictate to us what is allowed and what is not and how we should adhere to ethics and morality. Sometimes these reference points are excessively cruel to us and cause a terrible sense of guilt. When this is the case, it is very challenging to connect with and transform our destructive feelings into something reasonable. It was a revelation to me how much a child opens up contact to these basic experiences of love and hate, as well as experiences of time and life and death. The parent comes into contact with a fragile, tender creature and feels the extreme importance of what is happening, and the enormity of their own responsibility in it all. At the same time, the child demonstrates a powerful force of nature and drive to develop – the child grows, develops its relationship with its parents and the world at large – and this conveys a strong embodied message about the structure of the world.

I think every new parent is surprised to discover how they are both still themselves and yet incredibly changed. That we have feelings inside us, that are buried between and through the onion skin, and while they may catch us off guard, if we are brave enough to fight it out *inside*, we can learn many new things about ourselves. Things we never thought we would, could or should know about ourselves. Such a creative act as childbirth manifests our capacity for creativity and love, care and intimacy. Even in the midst of internal warring worlds. We are actualising our capacity for bonding, but at the same time we are also developing it. It seems to me that we do not simply reproduce our experience as children, but we have the opportunity to modify it, already being an active participant in forming a new relationship with our child. One that survives . . . in spite of hate.

I hope, dear Parent, that my words offer you some solace on this challenging but exciting journey. And that you can see how this intimate discovery begins by really appreciating how we battle with ourselves internally from the moment the baby is inside us. This ordinary fight will reawaken during stressful times and may go unnoticed at others. The trick is not to be taken by surprise by those sudden attacks.

Warmly,

Kateryna Alpatova

Mother of one | Ukrainian Psychoanalytical Society | Kharkiv/Poltava, Ukraine

13

Arthur Leonoff

Dear Parent,

What can I tell you that you don't already know? I have no special expertise when it comes to parenting, so I approach this task with the humility of one whose reflections arise mainly through the prism of personal experience and, of course, through helping others. It is in the afterthought of my senior years that I can consider what it means to parent, to be a parent and, perhaps, what it has meant to be parented. Roaming through the wash of time provides a transgenerational lens, having grandparents to becoming a grandparent; a panoramic view of the parenting cycle that crystallises into a condensed image of what it means to be a parent.

It takes a long time to grow a child, and, in any case, children grow themselves. We nurture, attend to their needs as best

DOI: 10.4324/9781003385042-15

we can, provide, cajole, communicate, discipline and love, but ours is a supportive role along the way to their becoming who they are and who they are not. It has always seemed to me that the micromanaging approaches of parenting books imply too much control of outcome, as if children are constructed by what parents do, what they say, or not do or say, along the sojourn of childhood. In the rearview mirror of retrospection, the optimal attitude is one of curiosity and respect: "Who are you? I am glad to meet you. I look forward to knowing and accompanying you on the voyage of who you become and are becoming."

It is not that parenting styles, philosophically positive and affirming, do not matter. Neglect is always harmful and parents who retaliate, shame and control their children through guilt leave a residue that is visited daily in every analyst's consulting room worldwide. Parents, though, tend to be combinations of types: authoritarian when they feel they must manage like choreographers, permissive when they feel they mustn't, and willing guides when they feel knowledgeable and confident to allow the child to emerge in their own rhythm and timing. To emerge as a being-in-the-world that will start with us as parents but will extend well beyond our years.

Parenting is a long and fascinating play in many acts. We certainly get to applaud and to offer important commentary and productive advice and input, but a child is always their own person, not a mouthpiece for a parent or blank slate to be filled by parental projections. This is not to say that parents do not serve as models for their children, but the overall effect is unpredictable, as influence is refracted through the child's temperament, subjectivity and family context. Ironically, what the parent wishes least to transmit may be what appears conspicuously in their child. Indeed, transmission across the generations is unconsciously mediated with each new subject constructing their own amalgam from self-other bits into a unique mosaic. Families are more than the sum of their parts. They are living systems, necessarily open to the world, alive with change and absorbing influences from past generations, re-partnering parents, other individuals and other families, all impacting how members relate to each other and how they understand what it means to be a family unit.

Whatever expectations I had of being a parent, I could not imagine the reality of three girls under two years of age when twins arrived in addition to a very young singleton. Of course, the optimal scenario, a boy and a girl separated by three or four years, distributes the load on the parents and provides an extra degree of difference between siblings. They can have their own space for development while having each other and their parents. Optimal for sure but there is no one configuration or guarantee of anything.

Parenting is initially a hardworking partnership, as much physical as relational. It is enough to care for and nourish little children and somehow carry on with life. I recall vividly the weekend strolls around the neighbourhood in the very early morning, twin-stroller and tricycle in procession. Later, the bike rides, feeding the chickadees in the Canadian winter forest, camping and fishing, cross-country skiing, and long summer holidays doing special things. These outings characterise what parenting first meant to me with its articulation of family life and being a dad.

When I mentioned no guarantees, this includes children with special needs or challenges that also come within the territory of parenting. Every family has some share of unforeseen complexities and challenges that arise at some point in their children's development. In my case, there were some health issues in the children, a mother stretched to her physical limit and a steep adjustment from one little child to three. To add to the difficulty, my mother became ill and died. My parents lived elsewhere but were involved and a major support for all of us. I have no doubt in retrospect that her death added to the burden and left us with less resources to cope with our complex family situation.

Of course, life complexity is the norm and families need to adjust to factors internal and external that impact on them. I learned how essential it is to maintain a strong communication between the couple, to talk together, to mourn when losses intervene, and to find a space and time for oneself. I also came to understand the importance of repair when missteps occurred, or hurts arose as they inevitably do between parents and children. Of course, this included apology but is something more elemental, a human connection at a most vulnerable moment that acknowledges pain caused by one human to another. This is essential.

The shadow of our own parents is ever present as we step into parenthood. Sometimes it arises as a cautionary tale of what and who not to be. Other times, it is an ideal, a beacon to which we aim, or, most likely, somewhere in between. We carry these images consciously and unconsciously, introjected tendencies, reactions, behaviours and emotions, that reflect our own childhood experience of our parents in their role as parents. We also take our cue from how the parents functioned together, their capacity for co-participation, conflict resolution, how they configured the notion of family, and each other. This includes how they interacted with our friends, school life, activities and, also, how they were involved in the wider community. This underscores that families are a microcosm of the world, and they offer an important lesson in engagement and participation beyond themselves.

My own parents had different strengths that were not always along traditional gender lines. They were each committed to their surviving mothers and siblings when I was young, and this left a lasting impression. It mattered then that I resided and raised a family far away from where I was raised and where my parents lived. I suspect that this is common among academic and professional groups who relocate to pursue education and job opportunities, which takes them away from their families of origin. Having family in the same community and involved on a regular basis is an important benefit that I missed.

So, what did it mean for me to be a father and a father of daughters? For one, concepts such as patriarchy never seemed very important, at least from my perspective. Father-hood merged into parenthood, two adults coming together in desire to create a family. Of course, one was the mother and the other the father, traditional and heteronormative, but in practice there had to be sharing and overlap of roles with too much to do in any case to manage otherwise. My impression is that families that insist on an outdated notion of patriarchy and a rigid division of labour create problems for themselves and their children. A father of daughters is best advised simply to be a parent and not overemphasise gender differences. Same-sex parenting couples achieve this complementarity of roles, same but distinctive, without gender difference in the equation. This would seem to me to be a good model to follow.

This does not mean that gender is irrelevant, but I cannot say how it mattered to each of them. In my view, the Freudian notion of the Oedipus complex, based on a social construc-tion of the early twentieth century, relies too much on rigid distinctions between mothers and fathers and relegates "the father" more to a symbolic presence rather than a caregiving participant in baby care and everything that follows. It is not applicable to modern families where rigid gender distinctions lessen the capacity of the couple to respond in real time to family needs. Also, children need to elaborate their own identities, including gender, as free of stereotypes as possible to optimally meet their developmental needs.

It is a complex issue then how fatherhood is constructed in a family of daughters. There is the enormous satisfaction of caring for a family, providing and nurturing, but there is a degree of difference, and this means that the father is always somewhat "other" to a feminine circle, which was not something needing to be resolved or remedied in any way.

What gets underestimated in families is what happens between the siblings rather than between children and parents. Twins, for example, have a complex relationship. They know each other *in utero* before they know their parents and their attachment to each other can equal what they share with parents. They have their own dynamic and this can get complicated by developmental and other differences. The relationship to singleton children is also complex, as is the relationship of singleton child to them. In my case, the older daughter pushed to separate from a young age and was precociously outgoing and accomplished despite the less than two-year age difference. The twins were less ambitious and stayed closer to home. Establishing close friendships with peers in early adolescence complicated their own dynamic.

Parents want so much from their children, at times to reclaim lost dreams or to undo significant and sometimes painful disappointments in their own life. None of this though is helpful to their children who must chart their own path forward. The parents' own psychological and psychotherapeutic work is aimed at getting out of the way as much as possible so as not to burden offspring with unfinished business, old wounds and unresolved disappointments. Parents who take this task seriously help to free their children to live their own lives.

Children are exposed to multiple influences, well beyond their parents, that can be significant in their effect. For instance, parents of the children's close friends, especially as teenagers, can be very positive and supportive influences. On the negative side, untoward influences can arise from unexpected corners. As an example, a neighbour befriended one of my children who enjoyed the attention and exclusivity. The neighbour had lost a daughter to a chronic disease. However, when our daughter passed the age at which her daughter had died, the woman abruptly withdrew her interest. It was a confusing episode. Parents must be present in children's painful moments, not just their joys, including when the nightmare intercedes and crowds out the dream.

Complex issues arise inevitably and are hard to predict. The phantoms of history have an uncanny way of looming large. This is especially true of trauma. As a Jew, I was only dimly aware of the impact of the Holocaust on my own family growing up. It was avoided. I recall that my mother did receive a cheque from the Polish government of the day as reparation for stolen property. Later, a great uncle visited and brought with him a drawing of a family tree illustrating all the relatives who died in the Warsaw Ghetto. There were many. Somehow, this unprocessed history impacted greatly on my children in ways that I would not have expected.

In conclusion, family life is a tableau to be painted anew in every configuration. There is no standard format or definition for being a mother, father or child for that matter, and family will likely never live up to the idealised images from cards and media. "Family" is best seen as a verb; a dynamic process that must be more than its constituents, a launchpad for giving children to the world and trying to make it a better place. Surprisingly, this process continues long after children are raised and have their own families. They still come to us for love and nurture, which we try and meet, to then give them back once again to the world.

Respectfully submitted,
Arthur Leonoff

Father of three, grandfather of five | Canadian Psychoanalytic Society | Ottawa, Canada

14

Ashis Roy

Dear Parents and especially Fathers,

In this letter, I share my experience of being and becoming a young father. As you read this you may realise how the experience of a father remains unknown, especially in the initial phases of infancy and childhood. I hope this letter speaks to the unknown parts in fathers and the unknown parts in mothers, about fathers. I hope it facilitates conversations between these parts, about this beautiful and struggleful process.

Being a parent is an ongoing process. As I look back and look forward this letter is going to be a permanent point of reference. Even though psychoanalytic training had taught me to be caring, attuned and sensitive, the unknowability of this experience was unparalleled. Psychoanalysis focuses on how our childhoods and pasts leave us with unfulfilled wishes and desires towards our parental figures. Also, it makes us recognise

DOI: 10.4324/9781003385042-16

how we didn't have the maternal or paternal attunement that we desired. Regardless, it makes us see that there is a loss of love and a longing for parental love that we still desire in our lives. As an analytic practitioner I was used to being a kind of "substitute parent" to my patients, but when my child was born, I had the chance of comparing that knowledge with what it felt to now be a "real" parent. My relationship between my analytic training and my new set of lived experiences was going to be reborn with the birth of my son.

The birth of my child felt like a rebirth of a part of me. An unknown not yet part of me was born once again. It was a new way of feeling connected – with a new set of desires, emotions and anxieties. My internal world was full of questions: Was I taken care of as a baby? What was my early childhood like? Will I be a good-enough father? What should I do to get it right?

Everyone asked: how does it feel to be a father? I didn't have a response. I felt the question was premature. It felt as though the question itself was wrong. And then a colleague helped me articulate it. She said, they should ask you how it feels to be a mother. As I processed this more I wondered, how is it for a male parent to be a mother? Prior to becoming a father . . . can I be a mother? More than order or discipline, my young baby needed someone who could sense his hunger, distress, and soothe him. Being able to provide these maternal gestures was tough. My maternal self that could sense and respond to his inchoate distress was yet to be born.

The initiation into the complexities of pregnancy and labour were so new for me that it took me a long time to understand it. Even as I engaged with it a part of me didn't want to think about it. With all the attention and emphasis on my wife I felt that there were hardly any spaces where I could articulate my questions. Psychoanalysis helps us understand how the father feels left out when the mother is carrying the baby in her womb because he feels that she is preoccupied with someone else and feels outside this bond between the mother and child. My teaching papers on feminism and psychoanalysis helped me see how pregnancy was also a transformative experience for women in which they felt very powerful, especially while giving birth to the child. Witnessing labour was traumatic for me but it was an act of power for my wife.

Reading about the cultural practices around labour in India helped me see that in some parts of India there was a cultural practice in which husbands would also retreat from their lifely duties and go into a space that would prepare them for labour. This process would help them be closer to what their wives would undergo as an experience. Videos of water birthing that I saw in the Lamaze classes also helped me see that labour can be non-medical, with the entire family participating in the process. Although this created an intellectual frame for understanding what was going to happen, there were few spaces available to understand the internal fears that I would experience. In retrospect, I feel that the absence of a language around these fears for the male parent makes it difficult for him to participate wholeheartedly. I observed in myself loneliness and alienation from the world even as I supported and helped my wife through her ups and downs.

Watching my wife go through 17 hours of labour was draining and traumatic. Thankfully we had a doula who was gifted and trained in taking care of mothers who were in labour. Her attunement to both what was happening in my wife and in me was remarkable. She knew how and when to help my wife in the different stages of labour. Her intuitive knowledge was sharp. Amongst all the medical professionals that we met she was the only one who would make sure that what I was feeling was also important. She created that space in between my wife and me.

When our son was born, I thought my wife would pass out after the excruciating labour. I was surprised and relieved to see the look of joy on her face. For several weeks after the birth of my son this experience of seeing her in so much pain stayed with me. I thought I was trained to deal with mental pain, but this experience gave me newfound respect for other professionals like our doula, whose capacity to be attuned to pain was a gift that I don't have. This agonising process of labour came to an epiphanic end when I told the doula that he would be born closer to the time of my birth. He was born a few minutes after the time that I was born. As he grows up and looks like me, I feel like I have been reborn. As if life is giving me another chance!

When I learnt that my wife was pregnant I remember that apart from experiencing mixed feelings of delight and anxiety I also felt the weight of becoming a father figure who would be idealised by his son and who would have to carry the weight of feeling idealised. Although most of my humanities-oriented university education made me think that the male–female relationship was filled with power, psychoanalysis brought to my attention that it's the adult–child relationship that is the first hierarchy we are born into. Dependence between the child and the adult is full of power negotiations.

Such a big part of being a father is to support the mother. The psychoanalyst and paediatrician Donald Winnicott brought to our attention how society needs to support mothering. For the mother to feel connected and attached to her child, her mental and emotional well-being is important. In India, almost everyone in your household and extended support system feels excited about being with a child. Bringing up my son in a nuclear family wasn't easy. Although we had nannies who tried to be mothers, taking care of a baby who was born a few weeks earlier was a difficult task. Our nannies would help but they would also abandon us quickly. I would marvel at their capacity to feel attached to the child and then at their capacity to detach themselves. And it was exhausting to change and make new attachments when you felt so fragile. It was interesting to see how the nannies had children, but they didn't know much about being attuned and would often behave mechanically. I am in awe of my wife who was able to tune into his wordless needs and whose intuition and instinct became our guiding force. I was in awe of the fact that despite being in a helpless situation herself she was able to connect with him so deeply. Retrospectively I realised how this connection helped him feel more secure within himself and he wasn't afraid of new surroundings or of meeting new people. He never cried in unfamiliar situations. I hope that young parents are able to realise the need to provide a safe environment for the mother which subsequently transforms into a secure connection between the child's inner and outer world.

Trying to be a parent myself, I realised that I had to face immense anxiety and helplessness, especially when he was young. And also, that even if I loved him, I couldn't force myself to do things, so I had to trust others when I was helpless and not knowing what to do. I remember feeling so anxious about not knowing how to soothe him. My son was born slightly early and was underweight. Care in the initial weeks and months was driven by the need to make him survive. I inferred that suckling at the breast was the first element of work that he had to organise for himself. As my wife worked tirelessly, her own mother's presence was a big support for her.

As he grew older, I could relate to him more and I became more conscious of what it means to become a parent at an older stage in life. I started thinking that when I would be 70 years old, my son would be 30 years old. This instilled a sense of regret. The fact that life is limited grew upon me with a more definitive awareness. I wished I had become a father earlier. I hadn't yet pondered over the limitedness of my life. It seems to be a new state of being that needs a home inside me.

Even as I write this it fills me with sadness. Although I have friends who have become parents later in life, none of them shared a similar preoccupation. In urban India, later marriages are more frequent, and I guess this is an unarticulated question that many would carry within themselves.

As I look back at my anxious self that was scared of becoming a parent, I feel surprised at the way I feel with my son and the joy and happiness he brings to my life. He feels like a friend with whom I can be open and expressive. I join him in his coos and every new sound that he makes every day. I am happy to find in myself many parts that are childlike that make my son feel that I am his friend or at times his twin! It's a precious feeling to go to bed waiting to wake up to be with him the next day.

Warm regards,
Ashis Roy
Father of one | Indian Psychoanalytical Society, Kolkatta | New Delhi, India

15

~~~~

Liliana Castro

Dear Parent,

Although I became a mother for the first time seven years ago and for the second time five years ago, the journey to motherhood began in the preceding years while I was in my personal analysis and deepening the relationship with my husband. A wish and internal space to become pregnant developed gradually, together with the desire to build a home and create a family together. In this letter, I would like to share with you how the personal work that a psychotherapy and psychoanalysis encompasses allows us to increase the space for our inner freedom to dream our life in several domains: love, family, work and relationships. The contact with our powerful unconscious inner lives can lead us to a mind expansion which will allow us to change and grow and enrich our own personal projects and lives.

DOI: 10.4324/9781003385042-17

The desire to be pregnant and become a mother was something that grew gradually along my analytic journey. Let us consider the idea of time and space and how we make way for a baby. Although a pregnancy lasts for around nine months, actually it all starts a long time before this . . . in the form of the *wish* to become a mother. This time is also related to the idea of a space being created simultaneously in the parent's mind and literally when pregnancy happens inside the mother's body. A baby can germinate gradually in the mother's or couple's mind with thoughts, desires, feelings, fantasies and aspirations (both known and unknown). This creates a thinking and feeling space inside the parent's mind, making room for the baby to arrive. In this way, a womb might not be the only place where babies develop and are born.

As a human being grows inside, this space expands from an internal space in the mind . . . to an internal space in the body . . . to a fusion of spaces of the baby and the mother . . . to a space in the father's mind and in the family's imagination . . . and eventually after birth to an expanding space in the environment, with a new room for the baby. Here the baby is embodied in the house, a space that also transforms to receive him and his presence. This space is both psychological and physical and can become very dynamic as the baby and parents' new lives unfold.

This comes to life for example in the "nesting" that moms and families do when a new baby arrives as they prepare the room for the baby. The baby's room is filled with a crib, a change table, toys, books and blankets. A literal room at home is being created. But this also mirrors an inner room in the "mind's house". But here, instead of household items, this inner house is being furnished with thoughts, ideas and feelings about the new little tenant and who these individuals will be to each other in days, weeks and years to come. In this way, this room is both "transformer" and "transformative", allowing multiple interactions and a simultaneous change and development of everyone inhabiting these new spaces.

This negotiation of "space and mind" play out with older siblings who need to adapt their own space to accommodate the new brother or sister, bringing with it strong emotions and challenges for the child who (until then) "occupied *all* the space"! I remember when my second son was born, my older son of two-and-a-half years (who slept in his own room) came into our room in the middle of the night, holding his blanket and teddy bear. When he saw this new little baby boy sleeping in his parents' room he asked – with a mix of surprise and anger – "What is happening here!?" as if he was demanding an explanation for this new space which was now being taken up by his brother, with his exclusion.

When he was originally presented with this new baby brother, he looked at the baby and nonchalantly mentioned: "OK. I have seen him. I am going to play with my toys" and promptly began bringing many toys to the living room, "filling up the space" with *his* play and *his* toys while giving only a few seconds of attention to the new baby as if to say, "this is *my* space with *my* toys and in time, you will have to conquer *your* space too".

As a new life begins, evolves and develops, the people, and the spaces around him, also unfold and expand in multiple directions. This space can also be seen as a playful space for imagination, exploration, adaptation, freedom and a common space for the family to work things out. Here several roles are played out and developed together. It can also be a space for disruption, doubt, uncertainty and strong emotions that can hopefully be metabolised and integrated together.

So, we see that this creation of this space can entail both a physical space in the world as well as an inner space, in the mind, big enough to hold all the thoughts and feelings about the new family dynamics. In addition, it can relate to an earlier space and time, reminding each of us of the period when we were the babies or the children interacting with our own parents, who are now in a new role as grandparents. These multiple spaces become inhabited with many people (negotiating new roles and old ideas) and this interplay across generations can become very rich and lively, but also challenging or threatening as transgenerational histories collide. My father-in-law bought a doll in Paris (on one of his trips abroad) and gave it to his pregnant wife. But then a baby boy was born: my husband. So, they held onto it in the hopes that the doll would finally get an owner, but then their second child was *also* a baby boy. When I eventually got pregnant, they wished the doll might finally get her chance but then I too had a baby boy and, later, another boy was born into our family. And so, this doll is still part of the furniture, and everyone laughs that the poor girl is still waiting.

Returning to the baby's room, it's a common practice to decorate the nursery in pink or blue or yellow (either polarised or neutral). Traditionally in nice, soft and calm tones. Interestingly we keep out the harsh colours. Perhaps inside the mother's mind this happens too, she usually only makes space for nice, soft, palatable thoughts and doesn't allow the harsher ones in. So how do we allow for more intense, less appetising spaces inside ourselves in relation to our children? My experience was that the presence of their father and other family members contributed to this expansion. I learned to deeply value the company and presence of my husband along this journey. He taught me how a good sense of humour can lighten some difficult moments. His serenity, balance and support have allowed me to integrate my family growth with my professional development while maintaining my own hobbies, interests and studies.

But what happens when there just isn't enough space? How can this space, inside our minds, contain *all* the feelings and experiences the new baby is going to bring? And how can more space be created? My personal analysis made more emotional room; by giving me the time and space to think all my thoughts – the good, the bad and the ugly! Analysis helped me get in touch with my emotional wounds, with my own childhood, with my real and imagined parents, with the parent I idealised to be and with the parent I am in the real life. I learned that infancy and our own parents' histories are activated many times in the parental journey. Allowing ourselves the time and inner space to get in touch with those emotional challenges is a privilege that analytical work can allow. Our inner child is in a certain way reborn with motherhood and presents along the way, permitting us to converse with our own infantile world in all its beauty and turbulence. It is in these conversations with ourselves, in the presence of a considered listener, that space opens and calm is found.

In the beginning I had this idea that I would teach my kids a lot of things, but I am finding out that the learning is mutual, and they are the ones who constantly teach me many lessons. When I asked my youngest son "What are parents for?", he rapidly and very confidently replied: "For nothing!", showing his conviction of the inutility of parents and – in contrast – the importance of his own will and desire. Somewhere he still experiences himself as "the king of the house" and is gradually learning the limits of reality. But in his childish wisdom, he actually touched on an important idea: each child has the unique potential to develop and flourish in ways which are very different from the aspirations or projections of the parent's desire regarding each son. The same question ("What are parents for?"), was asked to his older brother who gave the very different answer of "You tell me!", returning the question to me. This is also interesting as it calls on our responsibility and role as parents to be aware which kind of parenthood we are exerting. So, it seems that a further challenge of parenting is making space for new ideas – their ideas!

It was amazing to discover how unique the relationship is, that you start developing once you find you are pregnant and all the myriads of emotions and ideas that come along the way as your children grow. No one is prepared for such an emotional challenge and adventure, boiling in all its dimensions, erupting through your personality and life as you experience everything changing! All the certainties and rules you used to live by seem no longer true or look fragile and useless. You are now faced with several new tasks and duties as well as with the richest and most intense connections you have ever had: the unique relationships with each one of your kids! Fasten your seatbelt and enjoy the ride! No one prepared you to become a parent and to forever change to a new version of yourself!

My children are also teaching me that while that I am still partly "the woman of their lives", gradually other girls are entering their space. My five-year-old was telling my mother-in-law how much he loved his mother, and she then asked him "What about your father, do you love him?" and he answered, "More or less". Another time, when he saw his new baby cousin he mentioned that "she is even cuter than my mommy" and then my husband laughed, saying that I had lost my place as his favourite. Another time, on Valentine's Day my younger son brought a card with two hearts. I assumed the card was for me, but it was actually for his five-year-old girlfriend at school. The good news . . . is that they still want to live with me!

I remember my eldest son asked me, "Will I live in this home forever?" I told him "Maybe no, you will grow up and can have your own house" to which he demanded "No, I want to live here forever". However, on another occasion when he was frustrated over not getting what he wanted he said: "I am taking all my toys and things and I am going to live in another house!", remaining seated at the front door for a while. One thing we can know for certain is that life with kids will never be boring. They occupy a lot of space – in house and in mind – spaces we are honoured to inhabit. I have discovered that this space and the uniqueness of these relationships are ours to discover, nurture and develop gradually. There are different times, needs, temperaments and personalities (for both parent and child), so there are no generalisations which apply to everyone. I have found the need to listen to my inner voice and intuition and follow the unique rhythm of each relationship, according to each child's developmental needs. Time and space to dream and develop together are an ongoing process when building a home and a place inside ourselves, for imagination and creation.

Take your time and find your way together. We are always failing, but we end up learning that it's OK. In time we all find our best way to put love into action. There is always a storm on the horizon, either close or distant and the biggest challenge (as someone said) "is not waiting for the storm to pass but learning to dance in the rain". I guess that my sons really encouraged me to become a good "rain dancer" and, over time, I have come to enjoy both the dance and the downpour!

Children accept parents as we are and love us with all our imperfect bodies, minds and ways of applying parenthood.

Hopefully we too can accept our limitations and respect the temperament, nature and personalities of our children, helping them to develop and flourish. And may all this happen in vast spaces, both internally and externally.

Warmest regards,

Liliana Castro

Mother of two | Portuguese Psychoanalytic Society | Oporto, Portugal

16

∧∧∧∧

Barbara Stimmel

Dear Parent,

I am a mother. When I think of who/what I am, this reality is first to mind, always. Although the word mother implies "woman" of course, for me it refers also and profoundly to a transcendent sense of self that developed in relation to my two sons. It is not that their existences validate mine; it is not that I had no sense of identity before their births; it is not that I exist because they do; or that I would cease if, perish the thought, they do.

There are of course other aspects to my identity – too many to list. But the one I am including now is psychoanalyst, through and through. I mistakenly thought my professional knowledge, experience and commitment somehow would protect me from all those moments of motherhood that lead to mistakes, regrets, guilt and often shame. Yet, ironically, recognising and accepting

DOI: 10.4324/9781003385042-18

my failings allows me also to experience that of which I am so very proud. Dare I say "pleased as punch" to have participated so profoundly in the safety, security and sustenance of two marvellous men?

However, I am not writing to you as one psychoanalyst to another, such as in the professional literature; nor am I writing to you as a psychoanalyst to a patient. I am writing to you as a parent with a particular profession, as each of you has your role(s) in life. I am writing to you, mothers and fathers who, having traversed many different pathways, have/had children in your care.

So why even mention my career choice? Paradoxically, and hopefully to help you become increasingly comfortable with what you have done and felt that you would give anything to be able to undo! My aim is in sharing not specific mistakes, rather the range of human imperfections that we cannot avoid possessing and that are rectifiable in some instances, and for-givable in many. And interestingly enough, much that I am thinking to say to you transcends the relationships between mother and son(s), as in my case. And that is because I am thinking of how challenging it is to live with others in all contexts. Of course, being a mother is unique but so is each identity we carry. So why participate in this collection if I'm not going to lend "words of wisdom", and I'm not going to teach you how to analyse yourself and your dreams in relation to yourself as a parent? What do I have to offer? What will I share? Just this . . .

I passed many milestones "late" in life – undergradu-ate college degree, advanced degrees, professional licensure, full financial independence, marriage, motherhood. As you might imagine, there was intersection among these pursuits and accomplishments; these overlaps were daunting yet doable, tiring but thrilling. Therefore, my children were born in years that were not focused solely on their creation or their care. When my husband placed the PhD hood over my head and onto my shoulders, I looked out at an audience and viewed my two very little boys as they were viewing their parents doing something very strange. While this was a puzzlement to them, for me it was the amazing reality of what one can do when she loves inexpressibly her family and, yes, her own dreams. That love carried me through the integration of marriage, motherhood and mind expansion.

Sadly, though, there were many prices that my children paid, and not just then of course.

Simply and inescapably, I had needs of my own that interfered sometimes with my thinking, and more importantly with my feelings, about them. As a result, I continue to work through the guilt, shame, sorrow and regret that are unavoidable elements of parenthood. I know this is not new to you, I cannot imagine how it could be. But perhaps if we consider the human condition in its vast complexity, you will find it easier to accept your inevitable errors and shortcomings. Certainly, the hardest typically to tolerate is anger, disappointment and conflict with one's child.

My adorable, lovable, wonderful, perfect(??) first child would not ever sleep; I mean never, not at night, not at nap time, not in the carriage, not in the car, you name it, I tried it. At one 2 am moment, I simply lost it, as they say. I went into another room, shut the door and cried at the top of my lungs. How could I be angry at this little person who just wanted to check everything out, constantly, who wanted to read books at midnight, who wanted answers to his complex questions VERY bright and early, whose remarkable curiosity and creativity had no surcease? I couldn't, I shouldn't, I wouldn't!

Ha, the last laugh was on me of course because for some amazing reason he didn't actually need that sleep, I did! And we all know what sleep deprivation equals: torture (remember Guantanamo Bay). I would not be angry at him for his "cruelty"; instead, I would love him "to death". One day, when just two, I had put him in his little cot for an afternoon nap at the beach on our summer vacation. He was talking up a storm, dictating stories, singing and laughing, when he called out to "my good mommy", imploring me to take him out of his bed and play with him on the sand. I sat under his window, listening, trying not to listen, reading or, rather, trying to read, reminding myself how much I loved him. No, I was not angry at him in the moment! No, I did not wish I were on a boat in the bay! No, I was not moving to Australia, alone!

One way to counterbalance this powerful wish that my child conform to my temporal rhythm was to focus on his precocity that brought such delight and wonderment. Little children are so often entrancers and I was hooked. Undoubtedly, he benefited from my intense pleasure in him and his capacities; but I was blind to the pressure to perform inherent in my awe that was subtly and extremely painful for him. This failure remains one of my most profound errors as a mother.

Almost four years later, when my first child was no longer expected to sleep much, and when I had actually caught up on mine(!), my second sweetheart was born. He was certainly not second in my heart, but I assumed I now knew so much as a mother that I would not have to spend as much time fretting and figuring things out. After all, I was experienced and both my children are boys from the same genetic pool, getting ready for the world in the same uterine environment, listening to the same male voice playing the guitar for them while gestating – you know, they were brothers! Although I have several siblings and should have known better, imagine my utter surprise when this little baby slept regularly, reliably and for long periods. Wait a minute, what's going on? Should I worry that he stays asleep for so long and then plays quietly in his crib?! He sleeps through the night and he's only six months old?! He's not climbing out of his crib at 11 months and running around our home?! He's sitting quietly as he absorbs and clearly thinks about his little friends on the page and wonders also, Are You My Mother? Is this little introspective, watching, wondering boy really ours?

He was so different to his brother that I found whole new aspects to motherhood that were unique to my relationship with him. This too is no surprise to any parent of more than one child, such that like all the others, I too was new at this. My son needed my awareness that I was in new territory; his, not his brother's. I moved from worrying to wondering at the mystery of it all. His way of developing, his manner of moving through life, were magical to watch. At nearly two he had not yet spoken much, really hardly at all, and he showed me new ways to be with a baby that age: we developed an unspoken communication that was definitely ours, different to the one he developed with his father and, most startlingly, with his brother. He was remarkably responsive, understood everything he heard and that occurred around him, always where he needed to be – ready to eat, read, play with his pets, fight with his brother(!). He understood language and emotions well; he knew when things were worrisome or exciting, ordinary or an adventure. I was able to appreciate his perceptiveness and comprehension regardless of the absence of words – and that helped me understand how bright and wonderful he was, too – and that he would be just fine.

Yet his "non-talking" remained so puzzling that by the time he was two and a half, I confess I was very worried; what had

I not done right and worse, what had I done wrong? These intense feelings that I tried very hard to ignore led me to indulge him in ways that kept him perhaps too close, in ways that still haunt me. Yet another profound error as a mother . . . I came to understand that clearly, I was turning my anxiety towards my beloved son and his "silence" into a form I could tolerate; intense involvement.

Of course, I spoke about his speech development with his paediatrician during our regular visits; he reassured me repeatedly that he was growing beautifully. At the last visit I ever spoke with him about this, he laughed when I expressed my worst fears, saying, "He's a prince and he knows it; he'll speak when he decides the time is right!" And so he did. Soon after, he was sitting with his father's oldest friend while his parents were away at work. At the tender age of three, he regaled him with full, complex sentences that were filled with feelings about the unfairness and obvious mistake of having been born second! He had been musing, suffering, maybe plotting(!), these several silent years. Thus, while I was worrying about the pace of his development, he was way ahead of me in his understanding of life, its complexity and certainly its intrinsic disappointments.

In an analytic session one day I "confessed" the sin of my anger towards my two little sons at moments. My analyst laughed, somewhat akin to my children's paediatrician. What was funny about failing fully as a mother? She posited that, as special as they were, their "perfect-ness" was not only a burden on them, but it helped protect me from my need not to know or feel something truly unavoidable. I came to admit, and finally accept, that I could hate being a mother, and barely above a whisper, tell myself that I could even at moments hate my children. Therefore, although there was much to explore from my childhood on, that was really beside the point in this moment.

Rather, I allowed myself to think of other pretty important people I had wished gone from my life at moments; starting with my parents, my partner, my siblings, and the pattern goes on. Finally, after much walking on hot coals, I allowed myself to know that all of them, and yes, even my darling sons in turn, and most powerfully, sometimes hated me!!

One of Freud's most important theoretical papers, "Instincts and Their Vicissitudes", tackled the intertwined nature of our strongest feelings: love and hate. And in so doing, he posited that indifference, the absence of feeling, at times is the true antithesis of love. The Nobel Prize Laureate, Elie Wiesel, was even more definitive when saying "The opposite of love is not hate, it's indifference." And Taylor Swift, that musical phenomenon, sings, "It isn't love, it isn't hate, it's just indifference." Psychoanalysts, prose geniuses and pop stars all get it – and so too should we parents.

Thus, I was helped by the knowledge that my exhaustion, disappointment, perhaps even dislike and hatred, all existed in the grip of great, undying love. It helps to remember that the conflicting emotions and experiences that we parents cannot escape – ambivalence, in other words – are intrinsic in all human relationships, This vexing, aggravating state of affairs arises especially, and always, in our attachments to those we love so very strongly and deeply – our children.

Hoping this helps in turn,
Barbara Stimmel
Mother of two | American Psychoanalytic Association | New York, USA

17

Joan Raphael-Leff

Dear Parent,

Entering the "land of the parents" sets you on a lifelong journey. Paradoxically, one that is unique to you and yet common to all humankind. It may seem that no one has ever been through the multi-layered tangle of feelings as you become a baby-carer – until it strikes you that everyone in the world must have had someone care for them, otherwise they could not have survived babyhood.

But survival is not enough . . .

The most distinctive feature of this journey is the *asymmetry* of the travellers: one is little and dependent, the other large and all-powerful. How parents negotiate this stark inequality differs. Though who is small and who is big isn't always so easy to discern and this is the contradiction that I would like to think about here with you.

DOI: 10.4324/9781003385042-19

One of the first challenges of early parenting is developing an awareness that the infant's perspective is not the same as yours, and this is a crucial element in this complex process of early interaction. Seeing the world from the child's viewpoint helps us to understand and tolerate differences in temperament, needs, responses, passions and pace. But this capacity is heavily influenced by the reflections we each bring from our own personal experience of being parented.

Each of us was brought up differently, and the practice, features and quality of parenting we ourselves received influences the care we provide. Carers differ even in the same household, and their give-and-take interchange with the baby will vary according to their own subjective perceptions and beliefs about the needs and attributes of babies. One may put the newcomer in pride of place, while the other insists s/he needs to adjust to the family's lifestyle. Believing that the "wise" baby knows best, one parent may hope to follow "instructions" by listening intently, while another, convinced that adults know best, looks to "experts" (or the internet) for advice. Yet another parent may feel confident to rely on their own intuition, hoping to be flexible enough to co-operatively negotiate each new happening as it occurs.

Clearly, the variety of baby-care practices also reflect the way each carer deals with their own anxieties. For instance, co-sleeping can have many meanings. It may meet family needs or mitigate the adult's sleep deprivation or facilitate on-call breastfeeding. But it may also stem from fear of the baby's fragility, or a carer's dread of separation, or anxiety about being found wanting. Similarly, a routine may be set to increase predictability, or to provide continuity among co-carers. It may serve as a safety framework, a means to ratify threatened authority, a regulatory regime to promote discipline or "tame" a baby deemed "wild". In many ways, we are unknown to ourselves and often do not understand our own motivations. All we know is that parenting can be bewildering and calls out our deepest emotions.

But why *are* infants so frightening?

I think it is because dependency has the capacity to evoke in us latent memories of a time when we ourselves were helpless. We may try to escape from our own anxieties by negating the child's fears, and projecting our own onto them. Sometimes it may feel safer to treat the baby as a pretty doll than to engage with her frantic desire to be understood. And other times we find obtuse ways to deny this and let off some steam. I remember seeing a viral YouTube compilation of "laughable baby moments" where a father kept jiggling his young child's lips; another clip showed a mom withholding a piece of cake. On one level it seemed funny – the ten million views proved that – but also disturbing.

If you watch these "cute" videos closely, many "hilarious" interactions are less amusing once you recognise the adults' misuse of their greater power.

A power differential based not only on size and strength but also *need*. The baby is totally dependent on the carer, whom she trusts to share vital resources and loving approval. And absolutely reliant on these to build not only a healthy body but self-esteem too. So, it is devastating when a beloved provider takes delight in tantalising – tauntingly withdrawing a precious object just beyond the child's reach. In this social reality of virtual relationships with anonymous others, by "sharenting" on YouTube and other platforms, parents may unwittingly use their children to play out some undigested internal scenario of their own (while leaving an internet trail that cannot be erased). Looking beyond the joke, we recognise that teasing can be terribly cruel, and often reflects the adult's desperate attempt to defend against their own frightening emotions. But shaming and derision is as hurtful as if someone told you to shut up or stop showing off when you were trying to explain a complicated idea. Similarly, when a parent deflates the excited infant, by disrespectfully wobbling her cheeks. Or pokes fun at the unsteady toddler's determination to stay upright, forgetting the momentous achievement involved in becoming a biped. Most importantly, babies and young children learn through feedback – and do not understand mockery, irony and sarcasm.

That said, one way to negotiate this complex task begins with self-awareness and compassion. If you *are* open to learning by switching perspectives, your exchange with your baby will be a most rewarding conversation. It is not smooth sailing. We know the problems that arise when communicating with someone who does not speak our language. Gestures and guesswork help. But even in our "mother tongue", the most difficult part of an interchange is grasping what the other person really means. So, trying to understand a pre-verbal baby may seem especially hard. But when the other lacks words, *empathy* is what enables us to intuitively consider their mind.

While absorbing each other's "language" we are heavily reliant on *feeling* our way through it. Luckily, since once you too were a baby, you have the basic vocabulary of feelings – your nerves tingle with the baby's fears, and proxy hunger clenches your stomach. And the innate capacity for what is called "motherese": a form of repetitive sing-song baby-talk we find ourselves intuitively using with little babies. Even more luckily, *you* do have the words to voice, reflect, name and soothe the baby's feelings, as well as your own. So, you may find that your side of the conversation often consists largely of a running commentary on your life together and the feelings that are aroused in you both. Inevitably, it is a conversation redolent with misunderstandings and mismatches, known as "rupture and repair". The repair part involves saying sorry and making good your mistakes. Readiness to acknowledge blunders may also involve undoing unrealistic preconceptions you hold about yourself or the baby.

So, if authenticity is a most important factor in parenting, another is readiness to be receptive. Ask yourself: are you open to imagining what the world is like to your child? Do you usually observe and listen? Wonder and try to understand what messages s/he is trying to convey? Are you curious to discover *who* s/he is?

Perhaps even trickier – who *you* are becoming? This highly challenging experience of caring for an other also facilitates self-discovery. Parenting can be transformative.

As noted, drawing on intuitive understanding relies on an openness to your own feelings as well the baby's. This is a tall order at any time. But the visceral nature of baby-care makes for a rare form of receptivity. Parental understanding is much affected by *unconscious bodily arousal*.

For instance, the baby's crying is intensely disturbing. Of course it is. Cries are *programmed* to disturb us. They are a warning. Because babies are as yet unaware of danger, parents must be protectively vigilant and often spend the first months in a state of high attentiveness. Like the alarm one feels at hearing a siren, crying is a signal that someone needs help. Similarly, as we become more attuned, we are alerted by whimpers or even more subtle expressions of need. Naturally, confusions arise, because we are not only helpers. We were once babies ourselves. I remember being caught off-guard when bathing one of my babies. The distinct floral smell of a particular baby-soap instantly catapulted me into the past . . . to a time when that soap was used on me. Bringing back with it long forgotten sensations.

So, if by its very nature, parenting re-evokes our own earliest feelings, how does that happen? In my work with new parents around the world, I realised that the parenting experience is a unique conduit. When the infant cries, our own infantile emotions are "contagiously" aroused. I suggested that not only raw nonverbal emotions reactivate our own, but the often-overlooked exposure to sensory stimuli during baby-care. The unmediated contact with *primary substances*: aromas and textures that are specific to early life - baby pee, poo and posset. Also, perhaps, highly evocative odours of amniotic fluid, and our own postnatal sweat, vaginal excretions, smell and taste of breastmilk . . .

In my view, what is relevant here is that the sensory triggers we experience during early parenting were deeply encoded in our sensual beings when *we ourselves were tiny infants*. It is these very evocations of our own infancy that guide our intuitive understanding of what the baby is going through. Ironically, if personal feelings are unprocessed, they can also get in the way of truly listening. Intense arousal can be deeply disturbing. When old issues arise unbidden, they can surprise us with their visceral intensity . . . the jitteriness of a heart pounding with primary emotion. Suddenly we may feel inexplicably bereft or furious, bewildered by powerful sensations of grief or fear, unbearable shame or disgust. It is terrible to have these painful moments! But reactivated emotional and sensual experience grants you a "window" to greater understanding of what your baby is going through. If, at that moment of arousal, the world seemed to you chaotic and unbearable – imagine what it must feel like when you haven't a clue . . .

Arousal in parenting is thus a double-edged gift. Not only does it provide an inkling of what your baby might be feeling but it also leads you back to the baby inside yourself. If you are willing to "go there" – to that strange zone – and wonder what might have evoked such strong feelings in you in the first place, the bonus is new self-awareness.

People will tell you this is the hardest job you'll ever do. They're right. It is very hard to meet so many needs and feel so many conflicting emotions all at once. Hard to admit to being less than perfect in a world of unrealistic expectations. Hard especially for mothers to pursue career ambitions when contemporary work conditions often conflict with the needs of babies, which have changed little since ancient times. So much of parenting relies on heartfelt improvisation and flexible compromises. But fortunately there are many exquisite rewards. Those quiet moments of sheer joy and amazement on meeting the serious gaze of a newborn or receiving an unexpected smile, a curious or knowing look. Times of great intimacy, when the warm little hand on your nape reaches places inside you that nothing else can touch. Or times of hilarious fun. The seduction of an infectious giggle or side-splitting full-blown laughter over a game as simple as peek-a-boo. And times of absolute wonder when you decipher the first words and realise the immensity of the process of a human mind-in-the-making.

And yes, sometimes, baby-care can be exasperating. You may feel exploited with so little time to call your own. Or find it hard to fathom what on earth makes your baby cry so interminably, especially at midnight when you desperately need to get some rest. During such frantic times it is hard to remember that the little human being in your care is *not* winding you up. She is in the grip of intense feelings – pain or hunger.

Overtaken by innate survival emotions of fear, anger, sadness or panic, and still *too little to self-soothe* while feeling so frustrated, shocked or completely lost.

In fact, what your infant has no words to say, is that she or he just craves what any of us really want deep down – security and *compassionate recognition.*

In conclusion, entry to the "land of the parents" is challenging but offers you a singular privilege. Direct connection with another mind developing in the emotional give-and-take with your own. But it is not a one-way street. Look into yourself! Your own mind is growing too.

So, although the nature of the primary exchange is asymmetrical, this can be a reciprocally rewarding relationship of mutual enjoyment. It can grant you the genuine satisfaction of functioning in a deeply meaningful way, while simultaneously feeling trusted, and giving your baby a foundational feeling of being safe, loved and valued!

Warm regards,
Joan Raphael-Leff
**Birthed four and mothered more, with eight
granddaughters and one grandson | British
Psychoanalytical Society and honorary
member South African Psychoanalytical
Initiative | London, England**

18

Johanna Velt

Dear Parent,

So many things come to mind that I don't know where to start. You're going to receive a thousand pieces of advice from the moment you enter this (not so) wonderful world of parenthood . . . and even before! From the moment you tell the people closest to you that you're expecting a child . . . that's it, you're going to be entitled to all the little pieces of advice: do it like this, do it like that . . . The adult version of the "don't do this, don't do that" of your childhood. In the end, everyone wants to infantilise you and tell you what to do. That said, you're still hungry for tips and recipes of all kinds. Hence the plethora of books, programmes, podcasts, etc. on the market. I myself have given in to this tendency to want to gather as much knowledge as possible to become the best mother I can be. In a way that was barely disguised when I was pregnant, like

 DOI: 10.4324/9781003385042-20

when I got a university "baby diploma" (yes, yes, it exists, don't laugh). A very serious diploma, in fact, aimed at health professionals in the field of perinatal care, and actually not specifically geared towards pregnant mums like me at the time. And so, wearing my child psychiatrist's cap and my maternity tunic, I set off to discover what a baby is . . . at least in theory! But I was to learn what you no doubt are already learning; that no matter how much you prepare, nothing prepares you for this, and that's just as well! Because you're going to meet a being who is you but not you at the same time, who is and who isn't what he will perhaps be one day, who will take unexpected paths from you and it's precisely because he will manage to take these new directions that you will have accomplished your thankless job as a parent.

Birth and the periods that follows are certainly the most disorientating moments for a parent . . . but that's not all. I think a lot about a later pivotal phase in my children's lives . . . which I'm still experiencing with my youngest – one which is full of surprises, both good and bad. I'm talking about adolescence . . . Ah, adolescence! Alone, or with my children, or in sessions with my teenage patients, or simply former teenagers, I spend my time marvelling inside, observing, imagining and remembering that awful and delicious time of puberty. That in-between time when children negotiate not being a child anymore and not yet being an adult either. What I see in my practice is that adolescents are often strangers to their parents. Parents have a completely different image of them than what they have of themselves. It may sound like a platitude, but there have been many times when I too have thought that I didn't (or no longer) know my children once they became teenagers. I've been caught off-guard at times when they've expressed choices and thoughts that weren't necessarily oppositional "in reaction to" or "against" their father or me. I was discovering that they were beings with desires and thoughts that I simply hadn't thought of. A few years ago, when it came to enrolling my daughter in secondary school, her father and I had thought of two possible options close to his work or mine, and therefore more practical logistically. But my daughter said she wanted to go to a completely different third option, which we hadn't thought of at all . . . which is funny and curious for an analyst like me. With hindsight, I smile at my naivety: my daughter wanted to do a sports-study course and pursue a career in sport . . . like her father! She was driven by desires (to resemble/get closer to her father) and not by the mundane logistics of domestic commuting!

Now other thoughts come to me about adolescence: my discovery of the adolescence of others in the hospital when I was an intern, and my own adolescence of course, as I also moved from one life stage to another – from student to doctor. I said earlier that this time of adolescence is both awful and delicious, and it's true. It's delicious because it's full of possibilities, but it's awful because these possibilities are also uncertainties that can be terrible, even the most banal ones: grades, a friend who betrays you, another who doesn't look at you or looks at you too much, breasts that grow too little or too much, the same goes for hair, etc. My encounter with adolescents in psychiatric hospitals was a turning point in my career. In France, if you want to become a psychiatrist, you have to do four years as an intern in a psychiatric hospital, including at least one year in child psychiatry. In the university hospital where I studied, the triage was quite clear-cut: either you loved child psychiatry, or you hated it. I hated it at first. I used to tell my colleagues that I crossed out little sticks every morning, like a prisoner, to count the number of days I had left before I was "released".

After three months, I stopped counting. Looking back after 25 years, I'm now a committed child psychiatrist. But it did feel like I was in prison with those hospitalised teenagers. They can be violent, of course, but that's not what terrorised me. Unlike the agitated adults I had to deal with in emergency or inpatient wards, I was dealing with these almost-children, while I too was an almost-version of myself (as an intern, I was still flirting with my twenties).

This vacillation between childhood and adulthood is not the only vacillation to which the adolescent refers you: the vacillation about identity and sexual choices in particular is really unnerving. We're talking a lot about this today with transgenderism and all the related debates. But back to the point, dear Parent. You're probably not an analyst yourself. That said, your teenager or future teenager will probably confront you with these tough questions too. And maybe even before . . . I remember one of my son's little friends telling me at the age of six that he could be in love with a girl or a boy, it was all the same: "like Dylan's two mums who are in love and there's no dad". That's right! How stupid we are! Now you're a bit trapped! It's becoming more and more acrobatic to explain that baby boys are born in cabbages or baby girls in roses, or that it's the stork that brings them . . . Although! In the end, these explanations that children come up with about birth fit in perfectly with the newer gender theories that seek to do away with the idea of the sex difference altogether. The search for an explanation of birth is what allows the child to discover who he is, what sex he is and is not, that he does not have everything, that not everything is possible and that he must therefore make certain renunciations and certain choices. Modern gender theories do just the opposite: they suggest that everything is possible; you can be either sex, it's up to you, you can have/be both, or sometimes one and then the other. But over and above the possible physical consequences (gender transition involving surgery, and therefore irreversible mutilation of the genital tract, which means the impossibility of having children at a later date even if the original sex is restored), the thing that begs the question is . . . not to ask questions! But, dear Parent, if there's one thing your child will confront you with, it's questioning. You're going to have a field day, from evening to morning, especially around the toddler years:

Him: "Say, Mum, why is Tom going home and not staying in the park?"

You: "Because it's bath time."

Him: "And why is it bath time?"

You: "Because there's dinner time afterwards."

Him: "And why is it dinner time?"

You: "Because we're hungry."

Him: "And why are we hungry?"

You: "Because it's normal, because that's how it is . . . well, I don't know!"

[You're now exhausted, you're thinking about the meal you must still prepare when it would be so practical not to have to bathe or cook or put the children to bed, all after a day's work . . . No, but what an idea to have had children, you hadn't thought of all that . . . and then you add:]

You: "Well, we have to go home too."

Him: "And why do we have to go home?"

You: "Because it's bath time

Of course, your child will also ask you questions in much more subtle ways, without even realising it themselves. You'll be asking yourself questions quite simply because you'll naturally be putting yourself in their place and going through all the stages of becoming a "grown-up" with them, in your imagination. And that's normal, that's what you're there for. Except that putting yourself in his place in your imagination doesn't mean taking his place either, which would risk preventing him from becoming himself, in other words from really asking himself questions. So, I come back to my little diploma on the baby or other bookish attempts to understand the baby. I wonder – I'm sometimes asked – if being an analyst, and in particular being an analyst of children and adolescents – helps you to be a parent. I think it does. But I also think it doesn't. Somewhere in between. For me, at least. To paraphrase a great analyst, D.W. Winnicott, who was first and foremost a paediatrician, and who inspires me a great deal in my daily life as an analyst, I'll lastly say that being a parent isn't something you learn from books, it's about developing the ability (sometimes more or less innate) to listen to your child, that child, and to find what's best for *him*. This is my wish for you, dear Parent friend.

Warm regards,

Johanna Velt

Mother of two | Paris Psychoanalytical Society | Paris, France

19

Stefano Bolognini

Dear Parent,

With these 2,000 words I am going to talk to you about something unromantic and damned true: our very human difficulty in separating from our children, over and above our idealistic pretence of being perfectly open-minded parents.

I am not a mother, so I am skipping over the fundamental scientific chapter about the ultimate original separation, which is childbirth.

Instead, I am referring to all those successive micro-separations that I have experienced in later times, as a father, sometimes together with their mother, sometimes alone; and which are usually mentioned with righteous pride exclaiming: "My son did this!", or with reductive obviousness bragging, "Yes, he went to school, and then he went abroad, and then he got

DOI: 10.4324/9781003385042-21

married, and so on . . . what's so strange about that? That's normal, isn't it?!?" Here, omitting the complexity of how the parent's experience evolves beyond the enchanting initial symbiosis (the relationship between two different living creatures that live close together and depend on each other in particular ways, each getting particular benefits from the other), first as a child and then later as a parent with our own children.

Here, I will therefore speak of ambivalence and the complexity of separation, of satisfaction and pain, of trepidation and relief, of enthusiasm and melancholy: knowing full well that it is part of our human nature to tell things – to others and to ourselves – by defensively selecting the pleasant things and overshadowing the unpleasant ones.

Scene 1

Our son goes to kindergarten, and then to school. He detaches himself from us. His mother was anxious, I felt more resolute and firm, albeit with an underlying restlessness. However, we were afraid of our son's ease in separating. Perhaps we were responding to the fact that it actually went well enough and while we felt some relief, we also noticed the sudden weight of his absence. It took some time to realise that this separation affected us as much as it affected our little boy. That came as quite a surprise. By association, I am reminded now of a very fusional patient of mine who in the days following the start of her son's school, with whom she had been in full symbiosis, immediately found herself a lover, replacing the lost total union with her son with that new intimacy.

Scene 2

Our teenage son goes on holiday for the first time without us. This is usually presented to the other parents with smug complicity and ostentatious confidence, saying boldly "Well, of course: at this age they don't want to come with us anymore, they go with their friends", and I was not an exception, playing this down also in my own mind with these comments . . . meanwhile backstage the entire family were reassuring each other with phone calls (of course this part wasn't shared with acquaintances). An ambivalence nags below, "maybe he could have waited until next year . . .", and we try to tell ourselves a sweetened but basically inauthentic version of our situation, such as "finally a holiday alone!", with unsuccessful attempts to deny the pain of detachment.

Scene 3

Our son has a girlfriend. This time is characterised by an extreme ill-concealed parental curiosity, ambivalence and evaluation of the possible new entry with a creeping, not innocent, temptation to criticise. But here comes the anti-separation countermeasure, socially and culturally very common in our Mediterranean countries: in short, in the last 20 years, there has been here a frequent strategy of intra-family encompassment (especially on the part of mothers, but with the silent connivance of fathers) by allowing the two young people to use the bedroom with the door closed, in order to include the new arrival in the family symbiosis, long before the child's real separation from the family and before the establishment of a real independent life for the new couple. This is the main trend. Have we, my wife and I, been able to avoid this (also widespread) way of procrastinating our son's separation from home, from us? The answer is unequivocal: *no*.

Scene 4

However, the clock is ticking, and natural developments are not long coming: our son gets married and goes to live elsewhere. At the wedding, we, the relatives of the bride and groom, classically are moved and have reddened or frankly teary eyes. Asked why, we reply that we "weep with joy", i.e., that we are so happy about the event, which will permanently separate us from our son, and that we are in fact overwhelmed with positive emotion. While that is certainly true, there must be more to it than that: tears always testify to grief, which is defensively denied. Joy and heartbreak inevitably coexist when there is a separation, which also highlights the ageing of us the parents, which in itself is an unpleasant thought.

Of course, the difficulty in separating is almost never only of the parents: even children, beyond appearances, often struggle to truly separate from home. They often take it for granted that their parents' front door is always open for them in the usual symbiotic way, and if anything, they have the impression that they are adding one more living option, when they leave, without losing the previous one.

Scene 5

Rituals producing awareness. My analyst, an elderly Mittel-European gentleman who had travelled extensively between the two world wars, told me of an archaic custom in pre-communist Muslim Albania: the traditional marriage rite required the bride and groom, witnesses, relatives and friends to go to the mosque, but the groom's mother had to remain at home, waiting.

At the end of the ceremony, the officiant would suspend the ceremony: the groom and only the witnesses had to go to his house of origin, and in front of the witnesses, the groom had to slap his mother repeatedly and theatrically, as a sign of repudiation and of definitive and proven separation from her. Then, all together, everyone, including the mother, would then return to the mosque and the marriage could then be officially sanctioned. Then followed the wedding feast, which was naturally attended by the mother, thus ritually disavowed, symbolically abandoned and rendered inoffensive (at least in theory).

Today, however, it occurs to me that for the sake of parity an equivalent (although hopefully less brutal) ritual should also be adopted to represent the dissolution of many very tenacious and undeclared extreme father–daughter bonds; knowing, moreover, that in many cases these theatrical gestures can do little, in fact, to truly dissolve visceral ties that struggle to leave room in depth for new investments in new figures. As always in human affairs, real evolution does not proceed through the unrealistic rule of "all or nothing", but through partial, progressive and qualitative transformations of ties; and apparent radical solutions to previous ties must always arouse realistic suspicions.

An example? Here it is:

Scene 6

A son has just married or moved to another town. Reacting immediately one (or both) parents empties the room in which the young person had slept until a few days before and turns it into a study or something else, magically and surgically making all signs of the former presence of the departed child disappear. No sign, no void, no mourning: nothing has happened, "no problem!".

At the opposite extreme, we are all familiar with situations in which the son's room is kept forever intact, with his books, his objects and even his childhood stuffed animals awaiting his eternal return or even as a denial of his detachment: these are the impressive mausoleum rooms, which strenuously deny the painful separation that has taken place.

How did I, a psychoanalyst with such a curious and observational attitude towards others, deal with this in my own life? Well, in retrospect, I could perhaps say that I am average: when my three children left home, one at a time and over a period of a few years, their rooms remained the same – including their personal belongings – for some time, say for a year or two; then they became progressively "secularised", in the sense that they became bedrooms that could be used by guests (including them, of course) but with few personal items left; finally they became a conquest ground for the grandchildren, who live in other cities with their parents. Now they are "family rooms in grandparents' houses", cosy but not museum-like: even occasional guests can sleep there without the impression of occupying someone else's room.

But let us return to the subject of the difficulty of detachment from children.

Greek tragedy, an inexhaustible reservoir of myths, archetypes and valid models for describing the relationships and fantasies of mankind through the millennia, has presented us with the character of Antigone and her father Oedipus, who did not let her evolve independently as a woman but who, blinded, used her as a guide and support, the true "stick of his old age" when he exiled himself to Colonus.

The subject of parental possessiveness is rather rough and difficult to deal with even within the framework of Freudian biography: Freud discouraged many suitors who aspired to the hand of his young daughter Anna (whom he himself analysed) and who – as was the custom at the time – asked him in advance for permission to court her, asserting firmly that "Anna did not think of these things". He made her his handmaiden and the most trusted custodian of his science, and Anna in turn filled that role with conviction, not marrying and having no children.

At the same time, it should be noted that there are also parents who detach themselves from their children in a truly dissociative manner, withdrawing their affections from them in the "all or nothing" mode and experiencing them as completely external individuals to the point of extraneousness.

Is it possible to detach oneself from one's children after having loved and raised them, experiencing the natural physiological pain of distancing but without disassociating oneself, without lapsing into melancholy, without seizing them affectively or blackmailing them with the threat of the accusation of ingratitude? Maybe my following association can help.

Scene 7

I am reminded of a sequence from a very famous docu-film, *Born Free*, based on the true story of the lioness Elsa, raised by naturalists George and Joy Adamson in Kenya in the late 1950s. Elsa and her two sisters had been adopted by the couple after only a few weeks of life, having lost their mother.

The two sisters were then entrusted to the zoo in Rotterdam, while Elsa grew up in full symbiosis with Joy, more or less like a pet. Joy, however, raised her with the firm intention of preparing her to return to the wild and to survive by hunting, which she managed to do, while also dealing – like her adoptive parents – with the hesitation and pain of mutual separation. As reported in the book *Living Free*, Elsa surprisingly reappeared of her own accord three years later, bringing her three cubs to the Adamsons' home, at a time of particular danger to them due to the arrival in the area of other aggressive lions and some poachers.

Elsa brought her three cubs, one at a time, to the home of the Adamson "parents", entering through an open window on the first floor after climbing the tree in front, because they were absent at that moment: she trusted, and knew, that the little ones would be welcomed by the "grandparents"!

This story, which became world-famous, moved me deeply and made me think that the door of the parents' house should always remain open for their children, especially in case of need, even and especially if the process of separation has taken place positively, in a harmonious enough manner, with healthy natural pain and without any defensive anaesthesia. Just like the windows in the Adamsons' house and the doors in a parent's home, *inside* ourselves we should also leave an opening for all the complex feelings that separations generate in us.

And with this final consideration of appreciation for the life of our most intimate affects I take my leave, hoping to have intercepted common experiences that can be shared by all of us.

Warm regards,
Stefano Bolognini
Father of three, grandfather of five |
Italian Psychoanalytical Association |
Bologna, Italy

20

∧∧∧∧

Alan Sugarman

Dear Parent,

For some, becoming a parent is something they have looked forward to for much of their lives. In contrast, others find the idea daunting and have many fears when they contemplate parenthood. Regardless of whether you fall into one of these camps or somewhere in between, my experience is that all of you want to do the very best job you can. No one sets out to be a parent thinking, "I want to put in a minimum effort." The very fact that you are reading this book speaks volumes to how much you are trying to be a good parent. It also suggests that you are realising that this is hard work.

I remember the all-encompassing sense of responsibility with the birth of my first child. In the blink of an eye, all my subsequent actions and decisions were made with his well-being in mind. Job decisions, relocations, what house to buy

DOI: 10.4324/9781003385042-22

and so on kept his happiness in the forefront. After all, infants are quite helpless when they come into the world. At the outset, they seem incapable of anything other than eating, sleeping, crying and going in their diapers. To be sure, each newborn has a unique temperament or personality. But we then shape that personality as we try to help them develop into happy, well-functioning adults.

It is the process by which we do that that I will emphasise to you. You have probably read some, perhaps much, information about child development. It may seem quite complicated if you never studied it in school or paid much attention to children. And as an academic and a clinician, I can describe all the details involved in development ad-nauseum. But there is one facet that I find most important. All the details involved in the developmental process can be boiled down to the one essential fact that children grow from being extremely dependent on their caretakers to being self-regulating and capable of succeeding in the world by themselves. They learn to do this from us. It is via internalisation of our ability to regulate them that self-regulation develops. Being capable of managing one's own feelings and impulses is crucial for success and happiness. Academic psychologists have demonstrated that children who can delay gratification do better in life than those who easily give in to their immediate impulses. Being able to wait, weather disappointment, tolerate frustration, and so on gives children an emotional strength that makes them less vulnerable to all the stressors and challenges that life throws at them. Two prominent child psychoanalysts, Jack and Kerry Novick (2010), talk of the need to build "emotional muscle" throughout development.

This emotional muscle is what occurs as self-regulation is internalised. I'm sure all of you, as did I, will say unequivocally that you want your children to be independent, successful, happy and emotionally strong. And I believe you. Unfortunately, however, my personal experience raising my two children, and treating children, is that our very love and desire to protect them from unhappiness and danger too often undermines our efforts to build emotional muscle. This conflict occurs because building emotional muscle requires some pain as the muscle is stressed, just as building physical muscle requires stressing it and causing some pain as fibres are torn and forced to regrow bigger and stronger. Because we love our children so much, it can be difficult to cause them pain. Keeping in mind that some pain now will prevent far greater pain later. In addition, there is good pain and there is bad pain. I do not advocate pain for pain's sake or believe that anything that does not kill our children makes them stronger. Any of you who have become interested in physical fitness know the good pain that comes from your muscles having been strained and forced to grow. It even has a name: delayed onset soreness. Even when it's intense, this sort of pain feels good and brings a sense of satisfaction and a job well done. That contrasts with injury pain that hurts in a different way and means we did something wrong and hurt our bodies.

The same distinction holds for psychological pain that promotes emotional muscle. Your child feels some pride at being a "big boy/girl" after doing something that they had feared or found difficult. They know that they have survived something that frightened them; this survival promotes a sense of mastery over anxiety that holds them in good stead. This feeling of internal strength looks and feels quite different from injury pain that leaves them sobbing, clinging and even more fearful for the next time. That pain is like the time I tore a rotator cuff bench pressing and needed two years to regain upper body strength. Our challenge as parents is that it's difficult to distinguish between the two types of pain when our child is fearful (perhaps even crying) about attempting some new challenge. None of us enjoys feeling that we are traumatising our child.

As a result, too often we shy away from setting limits or creating expectations that are necessary for our child to internalise capacities that keep them growing emotionally. What sort of limits and self-regulation am I thinking of? These days, separation and being able to tolerate it are near the top of the list. The advent of the two-career parental couple has given rise to various fads like the "family bed" or "attachment parenting" wherein the importance of child–parent bonding is taken to an extreme that ignores the reality that attachment or bonding exists in a dialectic with separation and independence. When either dimension of this polarity becomes everything, insecure children are likely to ensue. My suspicion is that our guilt that we are not spending enough time with our children, or our fear that we are bad parents, makes us vulnerable to such advice with its message that separation and saying "no" leads to unhappy children who grow into miserable and unsuccessful adults. Ironically, following the advice of these so-called experts is far more likely to lead to such outcomes. I have been struck by the number of children brought to me for consultation whose parents never leave them with a sitter for a few hours at night so that the parents can go on a date. Not surprisingly, these children have never been left for a weekend, never attended a sleepover camp in the summer, or had a sleepover at a friend's house. Or the parents will only leave them with family relatives who the child knows extremely well. Or they wait for the child to fall asleep before going out. Their reluctance to see their child cry prevents them from thinking about how their inability to cope with their child's negative emotions is inevitably passed down to their child.

Usually, such parents are notably reluctant to allow their child to cope with separateness and being around less well-known adults acting as caretakers. A variety of parental fears usually lie behind this reluctance: fears of child neglect, child abuse, separation trauma, the child feeling unloved, and so on. Too often, however, the child interprets these concerns as meaning that the world is unsafe or that they are not capable of tolerating uncomfortable emotions. They become fearful, anxious, demanding children who try to modify the environment to avoid negative emotions. I have treated children who slept with their parents as late as 14 years of age. It is not surprising that these children were reluctant to separate enough to go to school. Nor did they study for class because they were so afraid that they could not learn, having never been required to do difficult things. Instead, the strategy for managing this anxiety that they had internalised was to avoid situations that made them anxious.

These outcomes can be minimised by teaching our children to regulate their feelings and behaviour by themselves. Limit-setting does that. It reassures them that someone is in charge. Children are afraid of their emotions for many reasons. A significant one is that their feelings are both extreme and often confused with real actions in the world. For example, young children don't just feel angry, they feel hatred and rage. And giving vent to these feelings feels like they are physically attacking or hurting someone, exacerbated by their awareness that their emotional control is precarious at best. For these reasons, children need to feel that someone is in control of their feelings and impulses. After all, they know that they can't control them. Unless their parents demonstrate control, the child goes through their day worried that they could lose control and cause some serious mishap. This worry easily generalises so that it is common to see children worrying about a myriad of dangers when they feel that neither they nor their parents can control their feelings.

Our dilemma as loving parents is how to demonstrate this control in a way that helps children learn to regulate their inner states. That is what I mean by internalising self-regulation. This brings up the complicated subject of discipline. Many of us react negatively to the word "discipline", because we equate it with punishment. But I am not advocating punishment. Far from it. I am advocating the teaching of self-control. Children don't learn when they are afraid. We can help our children learn self-control by requiring them to do so, not by frightening them. It begins with our demonstrating that we can regulate them. That means we must set limits and make clear what we expect.

The first step in doing so is for us to be in self-control. Something I learned very quickly as a parent was not to avoid a problem. Waiting until my child had ignored my request to do or not to do something several times only increased the likelihood that I would be angry when I finally dealt with the problem. By that time, the opportunity to teach was lost because hearing the anger in my voice frightened him too much to think about anything other than making Daddy's anger go away. Or he might cry or regress to a tantrum. I had to oversee my own feelings before I could teach him. Doing so proved to be easy after I learned never to make a request more than two times. Once he ignored my request a second time, I used the advantage of size. I would simply pick him up and move him away from the problem situation. Or I would carry him to the bathroom and say that we were not leaving until he brushed his teeth. The point is that I forced him to comply. Now, I don't want to give the impression that I am advocating being a bully. I did my best to be gentle and loving while exerting control. It was easy to do that when I wasn't furious that he had been ignoring me for some time. It is crucial to remember that we do not want our children managing their impulses simply because they are afraid of us or of getting in trouble. Self-regulation works most smoothly when it comes from their loving us and wanting our approval. That is very different than fearing our disapproval. Living up to internalised ideals fosters self-esteem. Trying to avoid the pangs and guilt of a punitive internalised conscience undermines confidence and self-acceptance.

The easiest way to navigate the distinction is to use the magic of words. Words are crucial to children. The more that they can put feelings, impulses, urges and the like into words, the more they can manage themselves. These words do not always need to be spoken by your child. Receptive language develops before expressive language. So, it's important, even crucial, to always be explaining and talking to children from the beginning. Just because they can't speak doesn't mean they can't understand or think in words. Words and thinking are major tools for self-control. That's why I would always explain my reasons for whatever limit I was placing or requiring. And I would always give him a chance to ask questions about it or to even protest verbally. It was important that he understood the necessity of the rule. But that did not mean that he could refuse it because he did not agree. Parenting is not democratic. He still had to control his behaviour the way

I wanted unless he was able to persuade me with words that I was wrong. And it is important that we remain open to such persuasion. Bright children may think of something we have overlooked. Unless they do so, however, they need to see us as benign dictators.

Furthermore, our dictatorial ways need to change as our children mature and develop. The older they get, the more say they should have. But limits can still be necessary. My older son obtained his driver's licence when he was 16 years old. Despite being a cautious and thoughtful teenager, he received one traffic violation and had two minor auto accidents in his first few months of driving. I felt both worried and irritated by what seemed like a sudden burst of poor judgement. Reflecting on it, and what I knew of him, I realised that he was not an adolescent who behaved recklessly. It seemed far more likely that something was interfering with his attentiveness. So, I explained to him that I was worried that he was not paying sufficient attention when he was driving. I then said that I had been thinking of ways to get his attention. Just talking about being more careful did not seem to be working. Therefore, his mother and I were taking his car away from him for one month. I stressed that this was not meant to be punishment, that I just wanted to grab his attention with something tangible. Not surprisingly, he tried to negotiate exceptions a few times during that month. But we stood our ground. Over 30 years later, he has never had another traffic violation or auto accident.

In conclusion, firm but loving limit-setting, accompanied by words, is the best formula for promoting the sort of emotional muscle we want in our children. My experience is that acting in this way is usually more painful to parents than it is to our children. But it does seem to help them to become the happy, successful adults we hope them to be.

Best regards,

Alan Sugarman

Father of two sons | San Diego Psychoanalytic Center | San Diego, USA

21

Martina Griller—Mushel

Dear potential Parent,

They fuck you up, your mum and dad.
They may not mean to, but they do.
They fill you with the faults they had
And add some extra, just for you.

But they were fucked up in their turn
By fools in old-style hats and coats,
Who half the time were soppy stern
And half at one another's throats.

Man hands on misery to man.
It deepens like a coastal shelf.
Get out as early as you can,
And don't have any kids yourself.

DOI: 10.4324/9781003385042-23

This Be the Verse by Philip Larkin powerfully wraps up the feelings I had about parenthood as a young woman.

Growing up in Vienna in the 1970s, I observed adults around me who had been deeply affected by the Second World War in Europe. There were men and women who had been wounded – physically and emotionally. Some were crippled, some blind, many of them angry and unhappy. I remember riding the tram as a nine-year-old when an old man suddenly shouted at me to get off the tram and walk because I was "young and had healthy legs". The war generation I knew didn't seem to like children. They were scary and unpredictable to be around. I shuddered to think what it must have been like for their own sons and daughters.

Needless to say, they didn't have an easy time of it either. Many of them had started off as their families' greatest pride: the Nazi party awarded a special decoration to mothers, who delivered a great number of babies. Young "Aryan" women were spurred on to supply a multitude of "soldiers for the Reich, and mothers of future soldiers". Adolf Hitler himself issued a unique award as an incentive. From 1938, a *Cross of Honour of the German Mother* was given to those who procreated on a large scale. There was a third-class Bronze Cross for birthing four or five children, a second-class Silver Cross for six or seven, and a first-class Golden Mother's Cross to honour those who produced eight or more descendants in the service of the German Volk. Proud parents took photos of their offspring arranged from left to right – like organ pipes – from the tallest to the smallest.

But after the war the system lay in ruins, and mothers struggled to feed so many hungry mouths at a time when food was scarce and many fathers hadn't returned from the battle field. Among all the horrors committed in Austria, the devastation and shame that was left behind, the former "organ pipes" were shoved aside. National Socialism had wrought so much damage and destruction, murdered so many people and left so many traumatised victims in its wake that the perpetrators' progeny was the least of anybody's worries. Once a source of pride, they fell out of favour. As far as post-war priorities went, children were relegated to the back of the queue.

Vienna's "Russian zone" was occupied by traumatised soldiers, whose families had suffered the Wehrmacht's raping, pillaging and killing during the war. Now they reciprocated and victimised Austrian women and girls in return. While children went hungry and received poor medical care, they also faced a lack of emotional capacity from their terrified mothers.

Left to their own devices, toddlers played in the rubble mounds of bombed-out buildings, where they came across valuables, or shoes, or clothes, or torn-off limbs, or dead bodies. In the face of all that deprivation and trauma, they learned never to complain or "make a fuss", to not add to their mothers' already overwhelming burden. Eventually, they perfected the skill to not only keep quiet about their physical and emotional needs, but also to not know about those feelings in the first place. They became masters at "not being difficult" and "getting on with it". The German journalist and author Sabine Bode wrote about those silent children in her highly insightful book titled *The Forgotten Generation*.

And then they grew up and had children "of their own". Here it was, the first word I struggled with: why did our parents "own" us? As much as this concept felt disturbing, it did make a lot of sense in a world in which husbands all but owned their wives. A married woman needed her husband's permission to apply for a job. She also had to submit to her husband's sexual demands, which he could obtain with or without her consent. Austrian criminal law did not penalise rape "inside a marriage" until 1989.

In such a world, a child must needs be their parents' property. Additionally, grandparents, teachers, priests, nuns, uncles and aunts turned out to have rights over us children. Complete strangers – like the man on the tram – could abruptly reprimand us, threaten us, or hit us, while our parents refused to "kick up a fuss", as it would "only escalate things". They explained it was best to "let it go" and decide that "it wasn't a big deal". Childhood felt like a prison, in which adults held the keys.

And a considerable number of those adults were still Nazis. My take on it was that some people were clearly "superior" and held a lot of power. They were allowed to be cruel to others, who were "inferior", while nobody was going to step in. Being weak meant being a burden on a society for the hardy and able. And being small spelled living at the mercy of big people's whims. At school, I heard that, "Like in the wild, the old and the sick must be weeded out, to leave enough food and territory for the healthy and strong; that's the way nature has designed it. Only we humans allow ourselves to be slowed down by those who contribute absolutely nothing to society, while they occupy our space and consume our resources." I was still a child, contributing "absolutely nothing", and worried about my right to even be around.

It was in this context that I promised myself that I would never grow up to be a parent. I believed that people who had power over other people – and let's face it, who has more power over another human being than a parent has over their child? – would inevitably abuse it.

What would this mean about me in the role of guardian? Would I turn into an unpredictable, dangerous authority figure, whom children would fear and hide away from? No. I was determined not to pass on the trauma inherited from those before me. The concept of "man hands on misery to man" appeared so inevitable to me that I vowed to be the last link of this chain, to not hand on anything to anyone, and remain childless.

What changed my pessimistic misgivings was the experience of my own psychoanalysis. Here was a person, who listened. A person, albeit from the Forgotten Generation herself, who was curious about feelings, who asked about them and wanted to explore them. In the context of this treatment, I learned to look at painful truths, not past them, and not the other way. Tears, far from being an unnecessary "fuss", were allowed as part of the human experience.

This opened a door into a new world, in which the difficult, the painful and the horrible all had a place alongside the beautiful, the pleasant and the ordinary. Hate could be explored as much as love, and nastiness as much as kindness. Nothing was off-limits, everything mattered.

For me, it set in motion a fundamental reparative process. It made room for the weak and vulnerable parts of myself, it did not seek to eradicate them. Unlike the disfigured people's limbs, which had been cut off and buried, silenced emotions could be resuscitated and felt. Analysis allowed me to hope for and believe in change. It also encouraged me to trust my own goodness. I discovered that despite my burdensome heritage of cruelty, murder and war, there was something in me that could be generative and productive, and helpful to a new generation.

My analyst's sincere care served as a template and taught me to hear and nourish the frightened child within. It was through psychoanalysis that I found the courage and the wish to become a parent after all.

I was told that during pregnancy, the mother-to-be all but "turns into" that precious, fragile human being she is busy growing in her womb. And when I was pregnant, people did indeed treat me differently. I was told what not to eat, not to drink and not to do; strangers were full of advice and felt entitled to touch my belly. A pharmacist refused to sell me regular aspirin; he never asked whether I meant to ingest it myself or buy it for somebody else. It was an eye-opening experience to be infantilised in this way; I cannot say it was pleasant.

My daughter's birth proved to be a life-changing event. I felt utter disbelief at the sight of this little human, who seemed to have arrived from a different world. Overcome with bottomless joy, I was also transported to another unknown side of myself. Baby in pram, I walked through a parking garage one day; a car sped past, the driver revved their engine, and the noise of squealing tyres echoed all around us. An unprecedented raged washed over me; like a protective rhino mum, I was prepared to charge anyone who might endanger my calf. In that moment, I realised that a new level of vulnerability had been born along with this infant, a deep fear of loss, and a novel courage. Over the following years, I often noticed how I stood up for my daughter in situations in which I might have backed down in the past.

But there was another aspect connected to our intimacy: when she was hungry or tired, wet or in pain, her cries reached inside me and evoked feelings of helplessness and overwhelm.

It was as if her fear of starving or her painful colic triggered an urgency I believed never to have felt before. Except, of course, I had – we all have felt it – as babies ourselves. The psychoanalyst Wilfred Bion (1962) wrote about the concept of containment: just like adult birds have to swallow and predigest food, in order to make it suitable to feed to their chicks, we human parents are called upon to take in our babies' deep unconscious emotions and existential anxieties, metabolise them and reintroduce them in a suitable form. On some days, we lean into the hefty task, at other times we get overwhelmed and want to back away.

Particularly in the first year of her life, the immediacy of my daughter's needs sometimes rattled me and made me terrified of failing her. I was grateful to receive help from my partner, from nurses, midwives, cousins, aunts and uncles, friends and acquaintances. In Africa, people say it takes a village to raise a child. This makes so much sense when you think of how many people it takes to make a mother. Luckily, we were surrounded by a culture of loving adults, who doted on my baby, supported my efforts and made us feel safe.

Seeing my daughter growing into an adult, I am struck with the headway we have made since the cultivated muteness of the Forgotten Generation. Her emotional eloquence would have been completely unthinkable for myself at her age; and even more so for my parents or grandparents. I hold that psychoanalysis has helped me to consciously experience life's ups and downs, on the outside and inside.

These days, I read Philip Larken's poem differently. It sounds sad, rather than quippy. While there will always be misery in the world, I no longer believe it has to "thicken" from one generation to the next. If we make an honest effort to address our own pain, it may allow our children to discover for themselves what is painful, and what is pleasurable, for them.

I wish you all the best on your road and hope to have contributed a little bit of thought material to whatever decisions you will choose to take.

Warmly,
Martina Griller-Mushel
Mother of one | South African Psychoanalytical Association | Johannesburg, South Africa

22

Patricia Harte Bratt

Dear Parent,

It was never my dream to become a parent. As the eldest of five sisters whose mother wanted many children, but was much a child herself, I imagined a different trajectory in life. This might have seemed a contradiction to those who knew me early on since I specialised in working with children and adolescents. What I can share now is that along with my son, the parents of my younger patients and their children taught me much about being a parent.

My early professional experiences were with kids in the criminal justice system, clinics and, later, in my own practice. Those children were gems, covered in emotional grime, longing to be discovered despite their aggression and venom. Slowly, painfully I learned that to make any headway, I had to develop positive relationships with the parents.

DOI: 10.4324/9781003385042-24

My mind was still locked in a defiant, authority-rejecting mode, left over from adolescence. But it became clear that without parents' alliance, the chances of gains for the kids were slim. Parents needed the same empathy, compassion and boundaries as the children they brought to my office. I needed to get to know and respect them as individuals struggling with their own issues, doing the best they could. This path was difficult, shifting away from my anti-parent attitude, but helped me entertain the idea that having a child did not mean that becoming a parent automatically put me in opposition with kids. I, and my children, might be able to enjoy parenthood regardless of mistakes made. My kids could thrive, while I tried my less-than-adequate best. Years of my own therapy, and clinical supervision of the patients I saw, also helped unlock mental doors.

So, I took the jump. Pregnancy was a lovely, healthy time. We lived in New York City, worked, took long walks and anticipated the baby. About six weeks before our due date there was a problem. We tried getting in touch with the obstetrician, but he was away. Finally, we drove uptown to Columbia Presbyterian and stood in a waiting line for some time, not knowing we were in the wrong place. My husband asked for a wheelchair, the attendants noted my condition and rushed us to the proper floor. The baby was in distress, I was fading. A C-section was ordered, and we waited for a surgeon to arrive. For the week of recovery in the hospital, I functioned in a kind of trauma denial mode, frightened and relieved at the same time.

During that frantic afternoon when the baby arrived, our car radio was stolen from outside the hospital. It got replaced, and later that week, the new one was stolen on another city street. Should all this have been a warning of things to come?

We were far too busy with our baby's sudden arrival to let that scary idea surface.

Watching as my son made his way through infancy and toddlerhood, I was often surprised by how much older than his age he seemed, even though a preemie. He was active and inquisitive with a barrage of questions and early comfort with autonomy. He would climb from his crib and turn on his favourite video, *Dumbo*, in the middle of the night. One day we found him feeding oatmeal to the VCR in case it was hungry. He was insatiably curious to explore and know. There was an afternoon when he asked for some additional toy while we were out shopping. I said we had already spent enough for that day. He didn't complain, but shortly after I found him climbing on the kitchen counter taking a cup from the cabinet. "What are you doing?" I asked, stunned to see him there. He wasn't yet three, a most dangerous age when children can move faster than you imagine. "I'm going to work to make some more money", he answered. "What? Work?" I asked, baffled. "I'm getting a cup to go to the corner, like the man who's always working there, and people will give me money too." It was said in complete innocence. I wasn't sure whether to laugh or cry. The logic of his plan made such sense, from his experience. It didn't consider that someone would also have to take him down in the elevator and stand on the corner with him. Or did he picture himself in a stroller with a cup held out? I hugged and lifted him from the counter, reminding him of the rules about climbing. It was a pivotal moment for me, recognising this was just the beginning of my wonderful child growing and challenging all my resources and doubts around parenting.

Fear and a profound sense of inadequacy about how to be protective, and yet encourage the explorations of an adventurous kid, overwhelmed me. It reminded me of my own escapade, when I was just a year older than my son was then. I wanted to work, have a business, make money and play with my neighbourhood gang. With no sense of the scope of my plan, I began taking letters and magazines from our apartment building mail cubbies and created a game of "selling" it to the other kids. We'd hand pieces around, pretend reading, exchanging, and later return them to the mailroom. This scheme didn't end well when the authorities came knocking on our door about someone lifting social security checks from seniors in the building. I was caught, literally red-handed. My parents, who I later thought of as strong disciplinarians, set a good model for not crushing a child's creative and social impulses. There was an aftermath, but it mainly involved talking and exploration. That day, my son's sag of disappointment when his begging-cup plan was foiled triggered memories of my mail adventure echoing through me from across the years. Children need supportive emotional room to thrive. His antics were a visceral reminder of how crucial it is to encourage a child's problem-solving, inventive behaviour without a judgemental attitude.

On the heels of incidents like the begging cup, we decided to move out of the city which was then in a stressful and somewhat dangerous period. I'd already explored options for opening another practice and affiliating with an analytic institute in New Jersey. We bought a home and found a good preschool nearby. It was an experiment, moving from a city we loved and navigating school, work and commutes. The overlapping schedules and travelling meant that my son joined me at many institute meetings, listening to our discussions as he played with Legos or matchbook cars.

One day he told me there was a problem at preschool. His teacher was mean and yelled too much at the children. He said that if someone didn't do something fast enough, or wasn't paying attention, she would raise her voice and "make consequences". I asked if that happened to him. Not really, he said, but it upset him to see other children feeling bad. It wasn't clear to me whether he was giving me a warning about a message that might be coming from the school, or if he was genuinely trying to work out a problem. He so rarely complained it seemed something to explore seriously, if diplomatically, with the school. I asked if it would be good for me to bring it up with Ms. Y. He said "Yes", and I agreed to go in early for pick-up, and explore things with the Director, as a chat without making it too formal.

That afternoon, walking into the building, I realised how nervous I felt approaching this woman. She had always been welcoming and friendly, so why the anxiety? Some back story: I had gone to several elementary schools, as my father got promoted and the family moved. In each, I was faced with authoritarian, punitive adults who both terrified and angered me. All the old feelings geysered up whenever I approached school situations now for my son. No matter how successful I was, or how many degrees I had, there was always that shy little girl lurking inside.

On this day I walked into the Director's office, said "Hi", and asked if she had a couple of minutes. She laughed, smiled and gestured for me to sit. "I know what you want to discuss, and your son already brought it to our attention. He said you planned to come in today, too." I was shocked. She continued. "He asked if he could have a meeting with me, my Assistant Director, and his teacher. There was something he wanted to talk about. This was a first for us, but we said sure." We gathered during lunch, and he started by saying that Ms. X probably has things on her mind, and it makes it hard for her when the children don't listen. He feels bad that she needs to raise her voice and then some kids get frightened. He thinks if she could yell less the children would listen more. Ms. X agreed she has had some upsetting things on her mind and will try to be more thoughtful. While she told me the story, we saw my son walking out as class ended and she called him into her office. She thanked him for his thoughtfulness and courage and said her door was always open to him. I felt incredibly fortunate that the Director and school welcomed the self-assertion and self-advocacy of their charges.

Well, dear Parent, you can probably imagine how shaken, bewildered, proud and leery I was, sitting in the car with my little whirlwind after that. I asked if he'd thought I might forget to speak with the Director or say the wrong thing. I wondered, too, if there was shouting or raised voices at home we should be talking about. "No", he said. "I thought that's what you do when something's not going right at work. You have a meeting, talk about it, and solve the problem." He got a little nervous and asked if it was OK that he spoke with Ms. Y. I just looked at him and reassured him I would always try to listen to and respect his ideas and was glad he had talked with me about it in the morning. Inside, my anxiety about parenting, about dealing with school officials, about possible denial of the impact of charged conversations at home, stampeded wildly.

The incident was a further induction into emotionally appreciating the dilemmas parents face in the quest to raise their kids. The balancing act between one's past surfacing and the child's needs of the moment can be torturous. For parents with stretched resources of all kinds, it must feel like life is happening to them rather than living it. There is no time to think through the problems that can jump up, ambushing you at many moments during the day. Things might have gone any way with my son. He could have acted up at school, lashed out at the teacher or not talked to me. It could have happened no matter what I'd been doing or how hard I'd been trying, except that I was raising a child to talk before acting, when he could. He was learning to address anxiety in a constructive way, not letting it fester.

It felt embarrassing, yet tinged with optimism, that it took a child listening to bring home this fundamental logic to me. Children "hear" their parents, and the parents in my office have three-dimensional lives that are heard, experienced and incorporated by their kids. Knowing a parent and helping them adapt to life's demands may be the best route to helping a child. For my son and the adult "children" who shuttle their kids to my office, I need to mindfully put myself off stage and listen to their emotional realities. We all bring our inner child, our younger selves, with us wherever we go. Without talking, or opening up with ourselves about unprocessed old wounds, everyone's flying blind. We cannot know what drives our behaviour or interpretation of experiences. It's one of the many essential things I learned from my son along the way. It's important to listen to the wisdom of children and have compassion for parents whose younger selves may need to be heard, too.

Warmly,
Patricia Harte Bratt
**Mother of one | Academy of Clinical
and Applied Psychoanalysis |
Livingston, New Jersey**

23

$$\wedge\wedge\wedge\wedge$$

Katy Bogliatto

Dear Parent,

I'm writing you this letter with the thought in mind that I would have loved to have received such a letter when I became a mother. So, this is written in acknowledgement of an important moment in a woman's life: when she becomes a mother. Similarly, I also have in mind fathers, and mothers in same-sex families, who have not necessarily experienced pregnancy themselves, with the wish and hope to help you think about what is going on inside your partner's mind as her body changes. The process of becoming a mother is a crucial moment of transformation, at the origin of an intense, long and constantly evolving life experience, that really changes one's life, and it has changed mine too! Knowing that other women and mothers have gone through similar emotional turmoil, helps one understand and persevere, even though each one of us will have a unique experience. But above all, having

DOI: 10.4324/9781003385042-25

the opportunity to lean on other's experience helps to keep in mind that regardless of what you may feel and think, you are not alone and there is no reason to feel ashamed of your feelings, or of what is happening in your mind and body.

I personally remember how I felt at the very early stage of my pregnancy; my first impressions of astonishment, followed by a sense of relief when one of my friends shared her fears about the forthcoming delivery of her child and her wishful thought of wanting her pregnancy to continue forever, given that she felt in such symbiosis with her baby. I could really identify with her, even if thinking about the delivery was not a topic I had yet considered! But it made me feel part of a "womanhood" and "motherhood" also signified the importance of sharing and talking to someone you trust!

So, my wish in this letter is to share some thoughts about my experience more specifically on the beginning of motherhood: the pregnancy period – a time marked by important psychological changes in the woman – and the first few months after having given birth. A time marked by the meeting and discovering of the baby as an individual with his own mind and competencies. Indeed, to link the thought of becoming a parent to the experience of "parental function" – in the sense of linking the wish to do the best you can for your child to experiencing the feeling of accompanying your child through life – is not so easy. This is a complex thought and task to achieve.

I remember my two pregnancies vividly, their similitudes and their differences, and the continuous feeling of discovering an unknown inner field of emotions with each child. But of course, the first pregnancy was the one that opened the path to parenthood, this particular period of discovering and experiencing what becoming a mother for the first time meant. I remember my first thoughts and emotions, at the beginning of my pregnancy, it felt like I was taken on a roller-coaster adventure. I found myself facing so many opposing emotions all arising at the same time, from happiness and joy of bearing life, to worry and fear about the uncertainty of the outcome and of not being able to grabble the enormous responsibility and changes that were to come! I remember trying to contain them as best I could: an array of emotions, thoughts, ideas, wishes, fantasies and dreams covering such a large span; feelings I was not prepared for, some of which I recognised myself, and others where I was left wondering where these ideas came from!

Suddenly, I found myself feeling more emotional than I was used to, in contact with a strong need for protection – for both myself and for the growing baby in my body. I was craving protection from the outside dangers that were physically in the world, but also from the inside dangers of my own emotions and thoughts. I felt a strong need to lean on my husband and close friends. I felt the importance of being surrounded by a supportive, friendly and safe environment which mirrored and recognised my becoming a mother and who showed interest in the baby to come. Opening a space for my baby to arrive and to be welcomed into the world.

Paradoxically, I also progressively became more conscious of the need to forge a kind of space that created a distance between me and my environment (family, friends and profession). There was a craving to create my own bubble of calm, security and intimacy in order to feel and process what was happening inside me, privately. Listening to classical music allowed me to process the feelings and sensorial waves that ran through me, giving me time to daydream and process imaginary scenarios of different kinds, some with happy ideas and other more fearful ones. I found myself in need of sleeping with a soothing bedside nightlight, just like when I was a child. I needed the contact of a warm and gentle light to soothe my internal emotional upheavals and nightmares! Fortunately though . . . things soon calmed down . . .

Looking back at this period, many memories come to mind, with their attached emotions and sensations. As well as the gratitude I have towards close friends who have been there for me at crucial moments, when confronted by the enormous psychological, relational and bodily changes that a woman goes through during pregnancy and the first months of a baby's life.

Indeed, being pregnant marks a shift in a woman's adult life in many ways. In particular with regards to her family of origin. Just think of the impact when announcing your pregnancy to your parents and close family: your sense of identity broadens, passing from "being the daughter of" to "being the daughter of *and* also mother of". I remember the excitement I felt when I announced my pregnancy, condensing different thoughts and emotions that I unfolded and subsequently understood. This is a crucial moment, opening up a new life cycle for women; on the one hand announcing that you are going to access and share the field of parenthood as your parents did with their own parents – which means that you can trigger and test *their* parenting functions – and on the other hand it also means that you are also "pushing" your parents to adapt their positions in the generational line: pushing them into the position of grand-parent. At the time, I was so happy to become a mother that I didn't grasp the domino consequence it would provoke, witnessing the concomitant arousal of ambivalent emotions and reactions in the elders, and also being confronted by their need to process what it meant for them: this sudden change in their generational position, and all of a sudden to have to access a grandparental position and function!

Pregnancy is also a period when you progressively discover new sensations from within your body while your body changes and adapts to your baby. As your baby grows, you'll progressively recognise his movements, for some this will be calm while for others it can be more intense. You'll of course project different scenarios, meanings, and create an emotional climate around what is going on inside you and your baby. Nevertheless, the mystery and creativity of life taking place in your body can also be an overwhelming and fearful experience. You progressively realise that you cannot control what is happening inside your body: a baby is growing, moving inside you and paradoxically completely dependent on you and your lifestyle.

I remember wanting to protect my baby from everything, including my personal feelings, emotions and thoughts in order to allow the baby to develop with all his singularity! While at the same time imagining and projecting numerous wishful dreams and ideals onto my child. Paradoxically, it didn't occur to me that my baby would have his own ideas about his life! In my imagination it was as if the baby and some intimate part of myself weren't differentiated. These thoughts coexisted with opposite ideas that an independent human creature was developing within me. These conflicting ideas and scenarios were negotiated alongside all the unknowns and uncertainties of what the reality of the encounter between me and the baby (with its own feelings and fears) would be after birth. Indeed, I also had to face a hidden side of pregnancy, eagerly waiting for every ultrasound appointment, giving me the opportunity to see the baby and to hear the gynecologist assure me that everything was going well. These moments helped me get back

171

in tune with reality and connect with better scenarios, leaving behind the more nightmarish scenes.

Unlike my friend, who wished her pregnancy would never end, the more I approached the predicted term of my pregnancy, the more eager I felt to meet my baby, to meet the "real baby" and to finally be able to hold my baby in my arms! So eager that one evening my husband and I went to the maternity hospital thinking that it was *the* moment . . . only to be sent home a few hours later, after having walked up and down several flights of stairs which failed to bring on delivery!

Fortunately, the delivery went well for my baby and me. I vividly remember the first exchange of gazes, my baby's wide-open eyes, looking straight at me and feeling struck by a vast array of emotions that I couldn't name, provoking tears of happiness in me and in my husband just next to me. It felt as if I was going to melt from tenderness, love, fright, fear . . . in front of this tiny, helpless and still unknown little baby I was holding in my arms.

The following months after the birth of a baby are marked by the importance of the reciprocal interactions between the baby and his parents. It's an unknown field of relationship and mutual exchange to discover! In this newly bonding relationship, you may feel bemused having to face so many unknowns. You will need to find how to answer and adapt to your baby's needs. This is not an easy task; often there is only opportunity to take minimum care of oneself, for example slipping in time to shower, while the baby is sleeping or in a rare moment of calm!

During this period, all my senses, attention and thoughts were turned towards my baby; I just wanted to do my best, but it wasn't so easy. Holding and handling my child, cuddling him, breastfeeding him, putting him to sleep, finding the best position to help him "burp" after his meal, to soothe his crying . . . and so many more moments! Sometimes we managed to tune into each other while at other times it was not so easy. Gradually, though, things became better and better. As I said earlier, during the first months of life, all my attention was turned towards my baby and his needs, I even remember thinking that I couldn't imagine going back to work. I could not imagine that my baby could survive with me being too far away. All I could think was that the baby needed me, his father and his known family and a friendly environment! Fortunately, as time passed, my baby grew, and we managed those first important separations. A moment where I realised my child's capacity to manage his own life moments, with their pleasurable and more difficult moments, without me. Meaning that whatever I do, think, feel or project onto my baby, I can only be there, just by his side, accompanying him to live his own life as best he can!

Many years have now passed since I became a mother, experienced two pregnancies and given birth to my two boys. Family life has evolved with its inherent joys and sorrows. Nevertheless, the early stages of motherhood, of taking care of a baby in total dependency of the other, is a unique experience which not only transforms you but is unforgettable. Indeed, becoming a parent confronts you not only with the idea, but *also* to the reality of being responsible for the other!

Warm regards,

Katy Bogliatto

Mother of two boys | Belgian Psychoanalytical Society (IPA) | Waterloo, Belgium

24

Lauren Segal

Dear Parent,

Parenting is a journey like no other. If it were to be compared, it would not be a songbird that sings a single note at a time. Rather, it would be more like a Tuvan throat singer who is able to vocalise songs that have one low, constant note with different higher notes being added continuously to make up the harmony. Each song has no strict beginning, middle or end but ebbs and flows continuously, with the singer striking notes of both unbelievable joy alongside tones of deep sadness. A new melody is created each time.

If parenting is this kaleidoscopic soundscape that is neither one thing nor another, how then does one distil a lesson in how to parent or write about it in any meaningful way? Certainly, any parenting advice that sticks to predictable rhythms is advice not worth taking. Little in my experience of parenting allows for such rigidly imposed guidelines.

  DOI: 10.4324/9781003385042-26

There is one tool at the heart of my psychoanalytic training, however, that stands out for me in its ability to grasp the opposing and sometimes paradoxical tonalities of the parenting song and that can guide us in our task at hand. It is the tool of "listening with the Third Ear", a phrase introduced by the psychoanalyst, Theodore Reik, one of Freud's first students in Vienna who went on to be an influential practitioner and thinker.

Reik explains that while knowledge and experience are important in understanding each individual patient, it is the analyst's ability to "hear" deeper layers of meaning – that which has not been explicitly stated – that creates a unique analytic relationship. In simple terms, the analyst is able to receive and perceive the unsaid emotional communications conveyed by the speaker, rather than simply understanding the words themselves. To listen with a "Third Ear" requires a kind of sixth sense that allows the patient to be experienced, felt and intuited. It requires the analyst to have the confidence to allow the unsaid to bubble up and be heard. It requires these invisible sonic narratives to be acknowledged and held.

I want to offer the idea of the "Third Ear" as a way of approaching the parenting song. Whilst our first two ears *hear*, our third parenting ear *really listens*. It requires us to use all of our senses, and most especially our deepest internal responses, to interpret our child's messages from the time that they enter the world.

The practice of "listening with a Third Ear" asks for a parent's passionate curiosity. It asks that we go beyond the hustle and bustle of parenting – the planning, the feeding, the doing, the running – so that we can listen to that which is less obvious. It requests us to watch out for the subtle signs, given and received by our child, both consciously and unconsciously.

First and foremost, it requires that as parents, we create the space to listen to our own thoughts and reflections. This is not always an easy task. We often blur the lines or resist difficult issues to keep our vulnerabilities at bay. We may need to expand our listening assembly and get help from a partner, friend or therapist. It is sometimes this greater council that allows us to overcome our unwillingness to hear – especially in relation to our children. By finding the means to listen properly to our own internal voices and the mosaic of echoes from our childhoods, we will be better placed to take on board that which may seem disturbing.

I offer this parenting gift as one who really wishes I had tuned in with my "Third Ear", particularly in the situation that I describe below. Two caveats. Even though my daughter's challenge was mostly a physical one, her story stands as a powerful metaphor for how some people are receptive to experiencing/feeling/listening to something deeper than others and how life-saving listening more deeply can be. The second caveat is that a good parent will always have angst and doubt about how they could have done it better and so my longing does not come accompanied by a sense of guilt but rather a sense of compassionate observation of a specific moment in my parenting journey.

My second-born was fussy from the moment she arrived in the world. She couldn't latch as she was placed on my breast. From the start she struggled to feed. We heard her cries of distress and tried to comfort her as best we could. We saw multiple paediatricians, all of whom reassured us that there was nothing wrong with our precious baby. They said her cries were of hunger and that we should think of supplementing the breastfeeding with bottles of formula. They, along with us, were failing to listen with the "Third Ear".

By six months old, my daughter's cries had become more intense. Again, neither my husband nor I, nor the doctors involved, thought that there was another reason to investigate the cause of her anguish. "She will grow out of it", we were told, and in our vulnerability, we held onto these words.

One day, an astute nurse paid us a home visit and she heard our daughter differently. "This baby is really struggling", she said. "She needs to be investigated urgently." Under her instruction, and with a fast-beating heart, I called the specialist paediatrician that she recommended. Within the hour, I had bundled our baby daughter into a car and driven her to the appointment.

This doctor took out his stethoscope and heard something that all others had failed to hear. There it was. A murmur, an abnormal sound indicating that her blood was flowing turbulently through the vessels in her heart. He was ashen-faced when he described the problem.

"There is something terribly wrong with our daughter!" I cried into the phone to my husband on the other end. He was not yet ready to hear this news and assured me that all would be fine. He raced over to the hospital to meet me, nonetheless.

After a series of exploratory tests, we discovered that my daughter was born with a very rare and serious congenital heart condition. She had multiple life-threatening defects in her heart. The crisis was now so obvious that we were forced to listen with new ears even if we didn't want to hear what was being said. Our baby's life was in danger, and she required complex open-heart surgery.

There is much to say about the weeks that followed. Our family had lost our gravitational centre, but my husband and I pulled together rather than tumbling into the vortex that had opened before us. We drank in the love that came our way. One of the hardest moments was leaving behind her three-and-half-year-old brother with my parents whilst we flew to a hospital out of town that was able to treat her rare condition.

A long story followed but, for this purpose, it suffices to say that my baby survived the gruelling six hours of open-heart surgery. Today, she is a thriving 24-year-old who works as a health economist modelling the societal impact of genetic counselling for newborns.

More relevant to the task at hand is to extract the very ordinary lessons from this extraordinary event that very few families will ever have to endure. When a life is endangered, the senses are honed, and internal capacities are enriched. Through the ordeal, we discovered our "Third Ear" and started to listen beyond our daughter's strange heartbeat. This more vigilant ear found the strength to listen to the cadences of our own deep anguish and intense fears as well as to take in the words of reassurance and optimism. We came to differentiate between our daughter's cries of distress from those of exhaustion, hunger and the special cry that she reserved for when a nurse entered the room. We listened carefully to her timid and faint pulse and poured our energy into amplifying her life force. By listening to the whole range of settling and unsettling sounds, we were able to believe in our little girl's capacity to take life into her and flourish.

We still ponder over the nurse's special gifts that allowed her to hear what we had all failed to do. Over time, however, we came to realise that the doctors who were initially deaf to the nature of our daughter's cries and the astute nurse who really heard the anguish, were both mirror parts of ourselves. They were our own internal protagonists that initially refused to let in the painful situation and then later learned to accept it.

While we became so acutely attuned into our daughter, our son's anguish was more difficult to listen to on our return home. On the surface, he had been looked after superbly by his grandparents and our friends who had rallied round to help. He repeatedly told us of all the amazing outings he had gone on, all the exciting activities that he had done with his beloved grandfather and the many gifts that he had received. We were so relieved that he had been held and contained in this way.

But had we listened more carefully, we might have been able to receive his own small voice of terrible distress. It is entirely likely that my son had thought that his sister would die although it was of course impossible for him to express this at the time. And in his ordinary childish fantasies, it is also likely that he had perceived himself as the cause of all his sister's troubles. We failed to catch these inner murmurs and instead chose to hear only what lay glittering on the surface. We were so overwhelmed with the business of a sick child that it was difficult to make space for our son's anxieties that were likely to have been bubbling away during this painful time. To this day, I regret our deafness to these inaudible narratives. I wish I had had more capacity to encourage my son to express his anger and fear. I wish I had been more attuned to his difficult feelings. I wish I had named, described and contained these so that they did not proliferate in the dark.

Although my little boy prevailed and is today a successful young man about to marry, I believe his own life pathways and those of our family would have been eased if we had listened to him more carefully. Even in the writing of this, I observe how my daughter's more dramatic narrative takes up more space on the page.

This story aptly demonstrates how difficult and scary it is as parents to always listen with curiosity and openness. There are so many different reasons that we don't want to recognise our own pain and that of our child. Some are of our own making and others are not. We long to hear that all is OK, that it was a good day at school, that the world feels safe and good. But without really being able to absorb the full range of our children's emotions, there can be no opportunity for repair. We can only repair when we listen to that which we don't want to hear – both in ourselves and in our children. We must seek to reduce the internal kangaroo court. We must seek to be kind and find compassion, inside at first and then in the parental relationship.

Having a child will undoubtedly challenge your sense of internal and external control. The only coordinates you need to cling onto are those that allow you to listen with curiosity to the inevitable challenges that lie ahead. Each of us has a "Third Ear" – a tool that casts light in dark places, that encompasses these nuances and adds insight to the breadth and depth of the parenting task at hand. Sometimes it is a low hum we listen for. Sometimes it is a more obvious cry. Sometimes listening requires deep excavation. Sometimes it is an easier task. Each is its own unique parenting song.

The job of both hearing and then of repairing is ongoing, requiring us to repeatedly tune in and be ready to make acts of reparation. By the time our children grow up, they are a patchwork quilt of all our efforts of listening and failing to do so. The parenting song turns into a jazz solo with all its own unpredictable trills and resonances.

Let me end by saying that the anguish of knowing that one's daughter has a life-threatening condition is not within the norm of parenting. Few, if any, of the readers of this book will have to confront such an extreme situation. But my journey has provided insights into the psychology and mental life of the baby that are as varied as parenting itself. This letter is an invitation to you, dear Parent, to attune yourself to the silenced cadences within you and in your child, so that new Tuvan tunes can be heard, and new stories can be told.

With much gratitude and love for the wonders of the parenting journey, Lauren Segal

Mother of two | South African Psychoanalytical Association | London, England

25

∧∧∧∧

Michael J. Diamond

Dear Parent,

I am pleased to share some of what I have learned as a parent and recent grandparent along with the many insights I have acquired as a psychoanalyst, both in learning from my patients and as a writer and researcher in the areas of fathering and gender. A number of the contributors to this volume have commented on important understandings that I will not take up, as for example, Heribert Blass's far-reaching discussion of fatherhood. Instead, I will focus on one key idea that pertains to parenting by both mothers and fathers throughout their life span. Though a rather subtle notion, it speaks to the inevitable challenges every parent encounters as their children navigate development from infancy onward. So, I'll get right to the point.

Children are greatly impacted by what their parents *carry within themselves.* This typically manifests both in external

 DOI: 10.4324/9781003385042-27

action and more subtly through unconscious communication that the parent may be quite unaware of. In the latter case, the communication may even be transmitted across generations arising from long ago. I will try to make my emphasis clearer in its application to the everyday realities of parenting through straightforward examples.

As a reader of this book, I assume that you take parenting very seriously and care about doing it well. You are undoubtedly willing to examine yourself enough to consider what psychoanalysts have to say about this most important parenting function – namely, that what goes on inside the heart and mind of every mother and father will play an inordinate role in impacting the child's own internal world and subsequent behavioural patterns and life choices. Consequently, a parent's *ability to self-reflect* in order to more effectively foster their child's growth, both before and oftentimes only after reacting, is an especially important quality to cultivate. As a learnable skill or "muscle" for good parenting, it requires strengthening and maintenance throughout mothering and fathering's many joys, disappointments and challenges.

Operating like a "muscle" that tends to get stronger with experiences, it is often facilitated by input from others, including one's partner, other seasoned parents, and perhaps one's own therapist or analyst. Moreover, in becoming more practised in using such reflective skills that are addressed towards understanding what might be going on emotionally for one's child as well as for oneself, particularly in more difficult interactive situations, the "muscle" itself can begin to operate more spontaneously. For instance, I recall feeling very upset when our child's preschool teacher called to report that our little girl hit another child on the playground. I was extremely disappointed and, while struggling with my impulses to discharge my uncomfortable feelings, I imagined angrily berating our child for being "very bad". Fortunately, before doing so, my wife and I were able to think about what may have been going on in her emotional life that led to the unwanted behaviour. We realised that this was the week her mother went back to work and wouldn't be able to pick her up from preschool. By thinking rather than just reacting, I was able to recognise our girl's likely feelings of being upset that "mommy went back to work this week". This enabled me to help our little girl learn that while there are consequences for hitting others, there are better ways to deal with "angry feelings (because mommy can't pick you up today)" other than by physically lashing out at others.

In order to strengthen this key facet of the parenting role, a parent needs to remain *curious* about what may be going on both in the child's inner emotional life and in one's own mind. Additionally, a degree of *humility* is necessary to accept that there is meaning to be found in the child's as well as the parent's so-called "transgressions" – even though its meaning may be unknown and remain so for some time. In the previous example, assuming my own initial behaviour was to angrily yell while berating the "very bad" child rather than trying to understand what led to the problematic conduct and subsequently intervene more constructively, it might be best to apologise for yelling and name-calling. Being thoughtful in this way before discussing the reasons for not hitting others (unless perhaps defending oneself), while curiously wondering what feelings might have preceded striking another, render it more likely for the child to listen to and learn from the experience. Nonetheless, it remains necessary to set limits and uphold consequences in order to curtail problematic behaviour.

It is important to realise, however, that within each of us, there are at least two major obstacles that interfere with creating the needed space to think or reflect in beneficial ways. Firstly, the most insidious hurdle concerns many parents' *"perfectionistic ideals"* about parenting. Many otherwise dedicated and involved parents find themselves searching for the secret to "correct" parenting – frequently by making childrearing into a pressured, consuming project to find more specific "how to" recommendations. Because every child is unique, and each parent–child dynamic remains distinctive – even within the same family – precise childrearing is rarely predictable in advance. This puts the onus back on a parent's developing trust in oneself, expedited by coming to know one's child for the unique human being they are. Being what most psychoanalysts consider as a "good enough" mother or father, means accepting one's personal limitations and finding ways of tolerating and repairing misunderstandings or failures in raising the child. Absences, deficits and unwelcomed intrusions and actions are inevitable and, moreover, are necessary for children to learn from in order to develop a healthy sense of self. In this respect, the "less than perfect" yet sufficiently self-reflective parent can become the child's model for learning from frustrating experiences.

Parenting fundamentally entails experiencing a wide range of emotional experiences, many of which may not come to conscious awareness. To name a few, consider the feelings of joy and frustration, pride and envy, satisfaction and disappointment, excitement and exhaustion, affection and resentment, and love and hate. Some of these feelings are welcomed while others collide with our fantasies and ideals of acceptability. In terms of the latter, it behoves the parent to at least partially recognise, tolerate and manage these more challenging emotions rather than crudely inflicting them onto their child, partner, or in berating oneself.

The second major impediment to creating the necessary reflective space is the excessive *need for the child to reflect the parent's success* (typically in specific ways). This tends to be particularly detrimental for the child's development. Whereas virtually every parent desires the child to be healthy, happy and successful, this wish can become too highly conflated with the parent's need to be viewed as "successful" or even "perfect". When the parent's self-worth or, in today's jargon, "narcissism", is dependent on the child's success, a great burden is unconsciously placed on the child, who is subtly pressured to "take care of" what the parent has not achieved.

Being less likely to be seen and valued as a separate, unique individual, the child's inner world is left populated by an unconscious demand – operating somewhat like a "ghost" – to be other than who s/he is. For virtually every parent, it can be difficult to see your child doing things differently than how you wish for them to do it. For instance, say your little girl wants to play with trucks and monster games, refuses to wear dresses and prefers being a *tomboy*, while you, as her mother, desperately want her to behave in a more "feminine" manner like you. It may even feel shameful as if she is making you look bad, which creates a predicament for you so that you insist she wear dresses. This might result in an angry power struggle between the two of you. Yet there is more to the tussle than meets the eye in that demanding she *match* you on the outside may reflect your effort to control the *mismatched* feelings stirred up inside you. In this case, you may need to be a bit of a detective in order to understand and manage what is driving your own "need". You might even remember how, as a little girl yourself, you felt incredibly angry about having to please your own mother in certain ways and that sort of anger comes alive in a disguised form with your daughter. This understanding might be far more important for you to attain rather than arm wrestling over who wears what sort of clothing.

Similarly, related quandaries might surface for you as a sports-loving father with a disinterested and unathletic little boy who refuses to play team sports and prefers drawing and arranging flowers to your dismay. Likewise, it can be especially unsettling for a parent with a young child who feels they are in the wrong body and wishes to be treated as cross-gendered or non-binary. The same sort of conflictual feelings might also emerge for a highly educated parent of a teenage child who has no academic interests nor desire to attend college. These are understandable dilemmas for most parents, and it is not uncommon to need a little help in coming to see your child for who they are, rather than for who you want them to be.

It is important to add that the ability to open an internal space when necessary (in order to reflect upon one's child and oneself) is never completely fixed. Oscillating at various times throughout life, a parent's ability to access this reflective skill is more difficult when flooded with one's own intense emotions or traumatised by life events. When such understanding is less obtainable, patience and sufficient self-compassion is vital. Failing to attune sufficiently at times is inevitable and the ability to remain engaged, accepting of limitations, and yet desiring to understand who your child is at any given moment is a life-long attainable challenge. Herein lies the painful realisation that you and your child are actually separate beings; and if we want change in life, we can't find it in them, rather we have to find it deep inside ourselves.

In closing, I wish you a most fulfilling journey in what is likely to be the most important and perhaps treasured "role" you will ever assume. Your children are fortunate to have a parent like yourself who takes seriously the responsibilities along with the joys and pains of being their parent. I hope you remain curious, caring and sufficiently tolerant of the inherent tensions as well as mostly aware of the life-long pleasures throughout the challenges of involved and maturing parenthood.

With my very best wishes,

Michael J. Diamond

Father of two children, grandfather of three | Los Angeles Institute and Society for Psychoanalytic Studies | Los Angeles, USA

26

Corinne Masur

Dear all,

I have decided to tell you something very difficult, and perhaps in the telling I can further work through what happened.

When my son was three years old, I abandoned him. This is the most painful thing I can tell you about myself as a mother.

One Sunday morning when my son was three, he was sitting on me, watching *Teletubbies* on Public TV. I was sleeping – and this was a good situation for both of us. He liked to watch TV, which we rarely let him do, and I liked to sleep, which I did not get to do often enough.

When I woke up, having successfully slept in until 9 am, I immediately felt unwell – but really, extremely unwell. I told my son to go and get his father which, remarkably, he did. And when my husband came in, I told him that I felt sick. Being a physician, he started to do his doctor thing; taking my pulse,

DOI: 10.4324/9781003385042-28

listening to my heart, etc. He found nothing wrong – but I knew better.

Something was very wrong.

My father had died of a heart attack when I was 14. It was sudden and complete. He was in his bedroom, having just gotten up from an afternoon nap. No one knew what had happened until my mother went upstairs to change her clothes for a dinner party she and my father were giving that night.

Since that day I had been terrified of having a heart attack myself. At the age of 16, two years after my father's death, I changed my diet, eating what I considered to be health foods, baking wholegrain bread and making homemade granola. Throughout my adulthood, I continued to eat this way, to exercise and to do all the things purported to help avoid health crises. But at 46, there I was, on the floor of my bedroom, crawling towards the bathroom, knowing something was terribly wrong. And while I didn't put the words "heart attack" to what was happening, I did have the impending sense of doom that is often associated with the experience of having an myocardial infarction.

And when the paramedics came and performed an EKG right there in my bedroom, they did use the words "heart attack".

I don't know what my son understood about what was going on in the bedroom that day. He has never said. But I am quite sure he saw it all. And I don't know how he felt about it. I don't know how he felt about being dropped off at the neighbour's house as my husband rushed to follow the ambulance to the hospital. I don't know how he felt about going back to his grandmother's house later that day. And I don't know how he felt about not having me at home for the next ten days.

I know he must have felt confused. I know he must have felt anxious. And I know that he certainly missed me – but what effect did my sudden departure have on him? And what was it like to be without me for ten days and nights?

Grief and loss are topics I have thought a great deal about after having lost my father at 14 and after treating many children who have lost a parent – so I know that my son suffered. He must have wanted me to come back. He must have wanted to go through the same daily rituals as always. He must have wanted to be in my arms.

But I was gone.

In the ensuing 20-plus years, I have tried to ask him, from time to time, about how he felt during those days – but he has never been able to tell me. I remember once examining stones with him in the driveway when he was about four. I asked him what he remembered from when I went away for all those days. Of course, he just shrugged and said, "I don't know".

Was that a defensive manoeuvre on his part? Not remembering when his mommy left and didn't come back? Was he protecting me by not telling me? Or did he really, really not remember much?

A little while after experiencing the first symptoms of my heart attack, I went into a malignant heart rhythm and essentially died. Fortunately for me, I was in the emergency room at the time and they brought me back. And then they flew me by helicopter to the nearest university hospital where I received excellent care.

I was very lucky to survive.

But since then, I have been haunted by the fact that I left my son. I have not been able to escape the thought that I might never have come back from that sudden ambulance ride. I have wondered what effect my (sudden) leaving had on him and I still wonder what scars might exist on his psyche as a result.

You will say, "well, you didn't *mean* to abandon him!" And that is true. But to a three-year-old, it is still the same. He needed me and I was gone.

When I had this heart attack, I had never been away from my son for even one overnight. Or maybe there had been one night. But there certainly had not been two. I had seen it as my job as a mother to be there, to be consistent, to put aside my own pleasure – at least for a few years. I had waited a long time to be a mother and I wanted to do my best to provide a secure base for my son.

But that heart attack robbed me of the control I thought I had. I left my son and couldn't come back for what must have seemed like an eternity to him. I abandoned him – and yes, I know I didn't mean to – but nonetheless, I did, and he must have yearned for me during that time. After all, there are times when you are three when all you want is your mommy.

I learned, at that time, that as a person and as a parent, there is only so much control I can exert. I also experienced something I already knew, which is that children suffer pain, and that is a part of being human and not something we can necessarily protect them from.

On the other hand, from the time he was 14 until he was 22 my son did volunteer work at an ambulance company. He became an EMT and took pride in this role.

Did this have something to do with what happened when he was three? Did he try to master his experience of helplessness as a little boy watching his mother being taken away by ambulance by becoming an ambulance attendant himself? Did he turn the helpless passive feelings into an active role by doing this – and did it make him feel better? Did he develop a saviour complex, feeling that he has to save people – or specifically, women – in distress as a result of his experience as a child?

These questions run through my mind now and then – unsolved mysteries of what effect my leaving my son at age three had on him.

And these thoughts are a reminder to me that we all fail in one way or another as parents. We all abandon our children in ways both subtle and obvious. Whether intentional or unintentional, we are not always there. Illness, sadness, issues in our marriages and partnerships, problems with work and so many other things get in the way.

At the same time, we know that our presence, our availability, our interest and our love are crucial for our children's development. They need these things for their sense of themselves as loveable beings and for their future capacity for stability and attachment.

So, again, how do we reckon with this?

I want to end this letter on a positive note. I want to say, there is growth in loss! My son became an EMT! Look at him! But I cannot do only that – because while there is growth in loss for some people, there is also loss in loss. What my son lost in those ten days of my absence could have been his trust in me. Or it could have been his trust in relationships. Or it could even have been his sense of himself as loveable.

And I will never know. I will never know exactly what effect it had on my son when I abandoned him for those ten days, or for that matter, what effect it had on him that I was a somewhat diminished mommy when I came back.

I could not control everything that my son experienced as a little boy, including my sudden absence. And I cannot know what effect this had on him.

These gaps between what we can control and what we cannot, what we can know and what we cannot – these are parts of being a parent. However, these are not necessarily the parts of parenthood that we anticipate.

Not only will we fail at times, but we also have to live with the fact that we cannot know what effect these failures have on our children.

And this is excruciatingly hard.

Corinne Masur

Mother of two | Psychoanalytic Center of Philadelphia (PCOP) | Chester Springs, Pennsylvania, USA

27

Gaetano Pellegrini

Dear Parent,

One of the most important discoveries I was able to make as a parent was anticipated before the birth of my daughter. I was attending the last year of a course for psychoanalytic training. In Italy, spring had just begun, and I was with my colleagues in a beautiful room with a wooden ceiling and large French doors overlooking the garden. We were there to attend a seminar on the psychoanalysis of children.

Our lecturer alternated theoretical teachings with some clinical examples and sometimes asked us questions, to invite us to think more personally about the topics she was proposing. Some of us had children and brought reflections or episodes from their own experience as parents. I had recently learned that I was going to be a father. So I was in a somewhat peculiar condition: I was very involved in the subject matter but did

DOI: 10.4324/9781003385042-29

not have the background of experience that would allow me to see it from the inside as well. I stood in relation to parenthood as if in front of those large windows: I could see the meadow light up in the bright green sunshine, but I could only guess its softness or imagine the somewhat wild scent of sprouting vegetation. The anticipation enveloped me in an emotion so vibrant and intimate that it altered my own senses: my eyes would sometimes glaze over with emotion, and in my throat, I had the feeling of something big asking to come out. And so, when it was my turn to speak, I could only add that I was very excited about this anticipation but still had no first-hand material to bring into reflection. My colleagues really understood this, and I still remember their warmth as one of the best experiences of my training years.

Then, once the seminar was over, the large windows opened, and we went out into the garden. After a winter spent in the fogs of the Po Valley, on the routes between Bologna and Padua, that mild sun warmed our skin like a blessing. The atmosphere was cheerful, our voices mingled in the air as if they belonged naturally to it. There is this thing about new life: the inside and outside combine harmoniously and seem to have known each other forever.

Also among us was the lecturer, who liked to stop and chat with us. One day, she asked me how I was feeling about what was coming. She reassured me, I thought providentially, since I was feeling a bit anxious, that I would be a good father. Then she bent down and picked up a small stone from the ground. She said, "You see, in the eyes of a child, even a pebble is a world to be discovered. Everything they encounter becomes a revelation, a new finding: what may seem insignificant to us, to them is an inexhaustible treasure trove of wonders and possibilities." I remained touched and grateful for those words.

It was not the first time I had paused to look for meaning in the little things and to explore the nuances of my feelings. But so far, I had related all this more to a general sense of existence. Now that thought was taking shape in a specific life, giving body and destiny to what we call a "person" at some point.

A few months passed and I was finally able to experience it. Not only that, but I also made another significant discovery: our good fortune, as parents, is that we can – through our children – return to those past experiences, a second time. As if by magic, in that enchanted moment that will be playtime, a pebble will stop being a pebble for us as well. If we are lucky, as parents we can relive the milestones of our childhoods, from the most minute to the most significant. Sometimes, especially if those experiences were painful, we are given a second chance to reprocess those memories, preserving them in us in a richer, fuller and more satisfying way.

This is real magic, and like all magic it passes through the mysterious territories of the unconscious. It is something – you must know, dear Parent – that is repeated even within that entirely unique encounter that is the psychoanalytic clinic. In that "wunderkammer" with walls papered with dreams, a subtle wind blows that animates objects. It is like a spotlight that shifts around, illuminating what we have already experienced in our past. We analysts call it transference, where our original impressions of those we first loved and interacted with are "transferred" onto our present relationships, bringing those early dynamics to life and giving us another chance to work things out. Revisiting out past relationships in a very real way, even when they seem to have died out. We have learned though, not without toil, that managing this process is not easy, and we have to navigate the sometimes troubled waters of our past.

But beyond suffering, which humanly accompanies us all, it is the possibility of reliving in the present our most distant memories that I want to convey to you with this letter. As we grow older, we discover the value of our memories. And that it is not just a figure of speech to be appreciated as the years advance. Closing one's eyes and going back to certain moments, no matter if happy but full of meaning, is what is most precious to a human being when one is alone. Here, what I would like to say to you is that in being close to your daughter or son, when you are there with your head hunched over their toys, your knees bent to look closer, in that moment you might be lucky enough to relive that personal, intimate, memory of yours, through the life and experience, the presence of your child.

You have to be careful though. I'm telling you this because as with the transference, the magic stone here contains pitfalls: you have to be careful not to fall. You have to learn to keep that light balance that allows you to be close, see yourself through them, without getting confused with them. Because in reality they are a whole other person and − if it is very likely that they are experiencing (unconsciously) part of your sensations − they will in turn be producing others, entirely new, entirely their own.

I should also tell you about the deep paths that follow in us the "pebbles" we pick up in life. Perhaps I should explain to you the many different ways in which we unconsciously get in touch with the world. I should tell you a few words at least about that prism that reflects a secret light and which we call "identification". I was asked, however, to avoid psychoanalytic jargon in this letter, and that seems fair. And then it's maybe even better to leave some questions open, who knows, someday (maybe it has already happened) you will also have the pleasure of playing in the garden of psychoanalysis.

I wish you exciting explorations.

Gaetano Pellegrini
Father of a little girl | Italian Psychoanalytic Society (SPI) | Bologna, Italy

28

Fred Busch

Dear Parent,

I've found being a parent is one of the most rewarding experiences in life, and also one of the most difficult. It was a joyous experience when my first child was born. However, I still remember the fear I felt when we brought him home. What do I do now, I wondered? I knew I wanted to be closer to my children than my own father, who was typical of the time. I knew he loved me, and was proud of me as I got older, but he had little time or inclination to involve himself in my upbringing. Thus, I had very few ideas on what it meant to be a father. I was a child psychologist when my first child was born, and this gave me some ideas about development, but not how to further development by *being* a father. Eventually I figured out some basic ideas on what it means to be a father, and I will share these with you later. I guess I did a pretty good job,

 DOI: 10.4324/9781003385042-30

as reflected in my two sons as fathers, and how involved they are in their own children's lives.

What I'll be writing to you about is based on my experience of raising two sons (with children of their own now), my years of observing children and mothers in nursery school and toddler groups, and in my counselling and treatment of children and parents. While I will point to some problems we can cause our children by inattention and neglect, the wonderful thing about children is that they are resilient, and if we recognise a problem we're causing and can reverse it, children will forgive us.

The best advice I can give you is to pay as much attention as you can to your babies and young children, but don't smother them. This is a time when infants and young children build basic trust in the world, and will end up feeling that strong emotions can either be managed, or not. This happens in the thousands of interactions with parents where the child's intense emotions can be calmed by a soothing parent, and eventually internalised so the child can soothe himself. I have a clear memory of this with one of my sons when he was playing with a friend and fell, lightly scaping his knee. He then got up, rubbed his knee a bit, and continued to play. Before this time any fall would lead to his crying and needing his "blankie"[1] to calm down.

---

1 I did research on "blankies" or transitional objects as they are called in mental health circles in the 1970s. Why are they called transitional objects? It is because they serve as a transition from the primary caretaker to more independent functioning. That is, a blanket becomes imbued with the primary caretaker's safety and calming function so that when upset the child depends on the blanket rather than the necessity of the primary caretaker's presence. At a certain time, the child goes from needing the blanket to self-soothing as described above. In my research I was struck by the anxiety parents felt over the child's dependence on their blanket. However, I found that children give up their blankie on their own when they can begin to self-soothe. Some parents are anxious for the child to give up his blanket, and hide it away once he stops using it so frequently. However, my research showed that the most successful endings are when the parent put away the blanket in consultation with the child, so that he always knows where to find it when he needs it. Eventually it is forgotten.

The toddler stage can be confusing for parents as the child shows signs of still desperately needing parents, while also starting to show signs of the wish to separate. This can be seen when in an open space the toddler will take off in one direction or another, but always stop and look back to make sure a parent is still there. It is a time when toddlers take their first steps. Their awkward gait and tendency to dash off towards whatever captures their attention, like a passing car on the street, understandably leads to parents holding them tightly in crowded areas. However, there is another kind of holding on to a toddler or child that can potentially interfere with development. For example, I saw the following interaction in a park near my home.[2] On this particular day I noticed a mother with her three boys, who looked like they were age seven, five and four. As the two older boys ran ahead, the youngest clearly wanted to follow his brothers, but his mother tightly held his hand. It seemed like this was more for the mother's need than the child's. This is a common problem for all parents as children grow more independent, we want to hold on to them for a little longer. I remember when my wife and I drove my first son to college. While he started living in his dorm, we had booked a hotel for four days. There were many activities for parents the day we arrived, but on the second day, it looked like we were the only parents still around. We decided to leave that day and explained why to our son. He was happily ensconced in activities for incoming freshmen and seemed relieved that we were leaving. Our second son drove *himself* to college.

---

2 In public spaces I often watch children interact with other children or a parent. It provides interesting information on how children negotiate interactions with others, and how parents may help or interfere in the process.

One of the most difficult times for parents is what used to be called "the terrible twos". This is when a child starts to say "no" to almost everything, and there can be battles over going to sleep, coming to the table for dinner, getting dressed so a parent can run errands, etc. This can become very frustrating for parents, and one can easily become irritated with this recalcitrant child. It is when we, as parents, are at our most challenged to not get into a power struggle with our toddler. We often justify punitive measures by citing such things as "one has to show the child he has to obey rules, and he can't do whatever he wants". It can help if parents know this "no" stage is an important part of a child's beginning separation from parents. It is the child's first *active* attempt to become a separate person from the parents. Stifling the child's "no" with punishment will only prolong this period. However, children do have to eventually eat, and go to bed at a reasonable hour. The only advice I can give is if parents approach this period with the knowledge that this is a necessary step for children to go through, it can lead to some empathy with what the child is doing, and not taking it as a challenge to one's authority as a parent. Your child is testing out being an independent person and they are frightened about that. This is often repeated during adolescence.

Unfortunately, there are no *do-overs* in parenting, but there is one thing I would try to be much better at. Let me start by saying that I think one of the most important parts of raising children is that the parents generally *care about and respect each other*. When parents are in conflict children know it, and generally feel they have to take sides. This is especially true when children are actively brought into the conflict by one parent confiding in the child the many ways he/she feels not well treated by the other parent. It often leads to the child losing respect for the other parent, which has a profound effect on future relations. When I treated children, I found this to be typical of parents who brought their children to see me. Not always, but enough so that it became a familiar pattern.

From my clinical practice I've learned that what is ubiquitous across patients is a need to be seen. I don't mean seen in just a visual sense, but a need to be valued, considered and appreciated as a separate human being. If this doesn't occur there are usually what seem like two opposite results but are two sides of the same coin. On one side there is an insatiable need to be recognised, and on the other deep feelings of "something's wrong with me", and an inordinate amount of self-criticism. This is because children are developmentally egocentric so that if a parent is preoccupied, or very busy, or the myriad of things that lead us to focus on issues other than our children, the child is incapable of thinking, "Dad is worried about work" or "Mom is on a deadline to complete her book", etc. Instead, the child feels there is something wrong with him/her. For example, I had a patient who spoke in a booming voice. It was some time into treatment that it became clear he was a *replacement child* . . . i.e., he had an older sister who died around age four, and his parents quickly had another child to replace the one they lost (my patient). However, from what we could reconstruct, it seemed like both parents remained depressed and withdrawn for many years. Thus, we could eventually understand that his loud voice was what he concluded he needed to do in order to reach someone and have an effect upon them.

Many people wonder, if a parent is a psychoanalyst, are we analysing our children all the time? While I tried to use my knowledge as a psychoanalyst to help me understand my children, and to help them understand themselves, directly interpreting something like one would with a patient was a rare occurrence. However, there were times when I used my knowledge as a psychoanalyst to help my sons understand something that was troubling them. One incident stands out.

One evening, when my son was six years old, while having dinner with friends I received a phone call from my son's babysitter, saying he had scary dream, and she couldn't calm him down. I came home immediately and found my son anxious and scared. As we talked, he told me that he had a dream where his room was spinning around very fast, and even when he woke up the room continued spinning. As a psychoanalyst I knew that dreams were usually stimulated by something that happened the day of the dream. So, I told him this, and he immediately remembered that he and some friends were playing in the school playground at lunch time. He was sitting on a piece of equipment that is round, with a wooden bench to sit on that can be pushed around at various speeds. His friend, Jason, started pushing him around and that was OK, but then some older boys came over and started pushing him around very fast, and he was afraid he would fall off. I then wondered if he thought this might have something to do with this frightening spinning feeling from his dream. He visibly relaxed and had a big smile on his face. For several months after that, when I'd go to wake him up in the morning, we spent some time trying to figure out what happened the previous day that stimulated his dreams.[3]

3 As he got older, he remained the more psychologically minded of my two sons, and he received an advance degree which led to him being a therapist in training, but he chose to pursue another component of the field, which involved helping indigent people.

To conclude, I have found if parents have good intentions, and pay enough attention to their child, the child will generally do fine. Further, if the child feels loved, he/she will forgive our mistakes as parents. We cannot strive to be perfect parents, and we need to also forgive ourselves when we are not at our best. Being a "good-enough" parent is the best we can hope for.

I send you warm wishes in this complicated task of raising a child.

Sincerely,

Fred Busch

Father of two men, and grandfather to three children | Boston Psychoanalytic Society and Institute | Boston, USA

29

∧∧∧∧

Cecilia Caruana

Dear Parent,

Money-phone-cigarettes-and-keys

Many years ago, and for the longest time, whenever I left my house, I would mentally repeat this list at the door to make sure I had everything on me. Even today, by force of habit, it still comes to mind; and habit is, after all, nothing else but internal pressure to not stop being that which we already are. An inertia that leans towards keeping things predictable, which goes up in smoke when a baby arrives.

When my son was born, I had already turned 40, an age in which I had had time to think about many things and do many others. I felt prepared and excited, like most new mothers at

DOI: 10.4324/9781003385042-31

that age. Sometime later, when my child is close to being two years old, I am writing this letter to you.

The arrival of a baby makes you automatically their mother, and you start to be present in their growth and development with a sort of bewilderment, delighted that you have something to do with what is happening. It seems that it can't be true that you are contributing to something so beautiful. That feeling is an overwhelming one, that takes over everything, and it is because you don't give life once and for ever; you are continuously giving it while you are actively responsible for your child to move forward with as much happiness as possible. If you are lucky enough that the baby's adaptation is good, you're going to have a source of joy and love at home that you didn't have before their arrival; that you sensed before but did not know until the baby arrived. Well, this is the wish anyway!

Careful what you wish for, lest it comes true

I like this saying, because it distils a feeling that also accompanies me since my baby's arrival: he has made me into a qualified housewife. I may be a little naive, but the truth is that I hadn't considered this. If growing up and getting older means making sacrifices, having a child is both the greatest gift and the greatest sacrifice. This paradox is a common idea that you've heard a thousand times before becoming a mother, but the truth is, that this experience breaks through like a shock wave that begins with childbirth and grows as the months go by.

The "problem" is that the arrival of your child does not erase anything that has happened before. Your new identity as a mother does not eliminate the child or the young adult you once were, it simply crushes it. Now there is no space left for those younger yous, and the reality that your new identity demands from you takes over, forcefully. It is at this moment when you realise that you coexist with several versions of yourself and that they all strive for fulfilment, but only one of the versions will be consummated. That is, only one of the versions of yourself, the one resulting from this tension, will materialise.

This competition of sorts starts slowly, but firmly. I remember (with great affection) our walks under the winter sun, when my baby was only weeks old. Those days, time would stand still, my son and I in a state of happiness, like an infatuation. In time, you realise how life continues, but your son is still there, he doesn't leave, and he still needs you as he did on the first day of his life. Meanwhile you start to rebel against that bubble because you also want to reconnect with *your* world, with your old and loyal interests that are waiting for you somewhere else.

It's like one of those nightmares in which you run and run but never get anywhere; you find yourself spending a lot of time making endless shopping lists or noting what to take for the weekend, looking for the right clothes to wear in summer, fall, spring and winter. Analysing the processes of defrosting baby food or the different formula milks. Looking for beaches with easy access, buying baby-friendly sunscreens. Returning home when you were already out because you've left your pacifier behind. Wasting time doing nothing. Looking for a suitable car seat for your car and for the grandparents' car. Looking for a stroller sack that is warm in the winter and cool in the summer. Arguing with your partner about all these issues when the night comes. You become a modern Sisyphus – the exhausted Greek king – always ready to push your rock up a mountain for all eternity.

When parents with young children get together, if you pay attention, you'll hear conversations oscillate between talking exclusively about: their kids' accomplishments . . . and escaping. They spend their time fantasising about holiday and travel plans that rarely come to fruition. And it is because they long to be what they once were: young and eager to discover and once again let themselves be carried along by life as light as a leaf. They long for all those first times; their sexual awakenings, nights spent on the beach with their friends, parties on terraces, sunrises, and exploring faraway countries. All of those impressions and feelings are stored away, they live with you and accompany you like recent dreams: with the impression that they belong to you, but really they no longer inhabit you on the sensory plane. You find yourself with no conversation topics, without being able to follow the daily news. You feel outside; more specifically, outside of what you once were. No books, no series, no movies. The world narrows, and you feel that you've lost your place.

Facing such a panorama, one day I decided to immerse myself completely in this journey and let myself go. To dive into maternity and let myself go. A sweet death for the woman I once was. I no longer pretend to be myself anymore, I surrender. From now on I will be X's mother. X's mom. That's what they call me in her nursery "X's mommy has arrived". That's what his father calls me when X is around: "Mommy-mommy . . . MOMMY". It is a clear and defined identity. There is nothing to build. There is no job market fighting for that identity, there is no better mother of X than you, you are the number one. Well, you're the *only* one.

I know of many a woman who has journeyed past that point of no return. But rest assured, dear Parent, that this tug-of-war identity struggle resolves eventually. I don't really know how, to tell you the truth. In the best of cases, with the help of a psychoanalyst. It feels so good to have a space to reclaim, in the company of an adult, that child that you also still are! A space where you can lie down, let yourself go, let your mind and your attention rest. Be taken care of too. And at the same time, a space to have time to think a little about yourself, about the direction your life is taking.

You are not alone; humanity walks with you

The arrival of a child stirs up feelings. When I was a child, I saw my mother as an exceptional being who was not only the most beautiful of all, but was also able to give me all the confidence and security I needed. I assumed that she was perfect, just as I also felt the world around me was perfect, and I did not think that behind that facade hid the deep sacrifice of parents. I had never even considered that my grandparents had once been children, and then young adults. Well, there you go: I've never been more aware of the cycle of life as I am now.

I was reminded of certain strange feelings (typical of puberty) during the first days of having a baby at home. You see yourself in the mirror and you recognise yourself, but you are not the same, something has shifted and feels strange. These changes to your factual reality go at a much higher speed than your mind, which normally needs more time to assimilate. I remember having catastrophic dreams when my son was born, which had never happened to me before. It is possible that they were related to the effort my mind was making to adapt to all the newness, and to the fears one carries with all change.

Suddenly, something has moved and now you find yourself in a different place. More specifically, you are now behind the scenes, watching and orchestrating the production of a son's film, while you are simultaneously getting to understand how yours was made. It is now when you realise what it took to raise you: that mix of love and sacrifice of others that enabled your development. Any parent knows that there is no greater fallacy that the myth of the man who made himself. It is the birth of a child that connects you to your ancestors, and you turn to look at them with different eyes, not so much with childish idealisation, but rather full of admiration.

You see yourself working hard to make your child's world as great or better than yours, your entire life goes into it and, honestly, there is nothing better to be doing. While at the same time, you struggle to keep hold of the identities that have shaped you: the professional, the friend, the girlfriend, etc.

The Ying and Yang of maternity

This new life tension is a kind of wake-up call which obliges you to open up in your mind. It forces you to think, you have to make small and big decisions on the go. Because the truth is that no matter how you had imagined how your life would be, it won't be the same with children. To begin with, it's impossible to predict what kind of child you're going to have: what their character will be like, their demands, etc. But you also don't know yourself as a mother until you became one, not to mention the family dynamics that begin to emerge.

So, you go out to the field again. Life has prepared a match which you are stuck playing. You are taken completely by surprise by the arrival of your child, and, at the same time, you are in the eye of the hurricane, constantly thinking about yourself and your new family. And in this, paradoxically, there is something rejuvenating: the mental gymnastics that take over while you change a diaper, or you pick up for the fifth time during an afternoon of play.

Your children make you evolve. They force you and your partner to stop being those old farts that got together one day to become a duo that had to love each other and understand each other in order to take care of a child. This is another gift that a child brings: the need to improve your environment though making yourself better. Leave deep-rooted obsessions to clear your mind and take up other habits.

It is true that the couple space suffers too, the previous pre-kids one. But a new space appears where both of you are now in charge. Two minds captaining a ship, forced to agree, but now together and able to share the deep satisfactions that watching your child grow brings. With some luck, on that ship a man will grow, who will set sail in later years to keep on conquering other lands. And I wish with all my heart that someday he too will leave home carefree, but easily remembering to take money-phone-cigarettes-and-keys.

With love,

Cecilia Caruana

Mother of one | Psychoanalytical

Association of Madrid (APM) | Ibiza, Spain

30

Eike Hinze

Dear Parent,
A little boy paints a picture of his family. A huge eagle is spreading its wings next to the words "My father". Deep below, at the bottom of the drawing, the rest of the family is gathered together: the mother is a little pig, the older brother is a penguin and the boy himself is depicted as a little kitten. You may have a lot of ideas about the family dynamics and how this little boy has dealt with them internally. However, I would like to limit myself to just one aspect: the idealisation of the father. As a father, you will not often experience such admiration in the course of your life. It is important to accept it. However, this is not always as easy as it seems. As a father, you don't feel as wonderful and great as your own children sometimes want to see you, and you are inclined to reject their idealisation. However, little children occasionally need to see

 DOI: 10.4324/9781003385042-32

their parents bigger, more powerful and more wonderful than they really are. This is the precondition to also see themselves as big, powerful and wonderful. Only this will allow them to experience themselves realistically and self-confidently later on. As a father of two sons and grandfather of four grandchildren, I know of course that life with children does not only consist of moments like these. Children need to be allowed to devalue their parents and express their ambivalence between love and hate. I remember another picture which my little son once drew on the wall of our bicycle cellar, depicting me as a monster and describing me as a witch with buffalo horns. I no longer know what made him so angry at the time, but I'm sure he must have had a good reason. It is important to teach your own children that relationships always contain a certain amount of ambivalence, and that these mixed feelings do not stand in the way of a loving bond.

I clearly remember an incident that happened when my children were still in elementary school. I had built a tree house in the garden and one of my sons tried to abseil down from it. The rope slipped through his hands, and he landed clumsily on the ground. At first, I just thought how funny the situation was and burst out laughing. It was only afterwards that I realised that he had actually hurt both his hands very painfully. I was ashamed and felt guilty for having treated him so cruelly and with so little empathy. I had to endure the anger of my family, and my son blamed me for my behaviour for quite some time. In the meantime, it has become a running joke in the family when it comes to making fun of their father.

Not all examples of parents being guilty are as harmless as this episode. We shape our children in many ways and are responsible for their future paths in life. We are happy when our children become successful and content with their lives. However, some developments can also make us wonder whether we did something wrong and passed on problematic issues. I personally grew up during the war and in the post-war period. Very early on I developed the attitude that I shouldn't cause my parents any unnecessary worries since they were already having such a hard time surviving and providing for the family. That was certainly one of the reasons why I became a good pupil and never had any difficulties at school. My sons, too, were good pupils and never burdened their parents with school problems. That certainly was a reason to be happy. My wife and I were content that we had provided them with a secure home and had passed on good intelligence. Over the years, however, other thoughts crept in: had I perhaps unconsciously imposed an overly high and potentially oppressive performance ethos? I know how happy I am when I discover other traits in them that seem to relativise this influence. Having your own children teaches you how to deal with your own feelings of guilt. You might brood over all the things you possibly did wrong as a parent, but on the other hand you could also try to absolve yourself of all responsibility and project all misfortune onto others – "It's not my fault, it's the fault of others, especially when it comes to my children!". You could also find a middle ground and develop an appropriate sense of responsibility. Children are good teachers in this respect.

The relationship between parents and children is not a one-way street. It's not just the children who receive something from their parents for their development and their paths in life. They give their parents so much in return. I'm not trying to gloss over all the burdens that you as parents know so well. I remember the time when our children were very small and sometimes brought us parents to the brink of despair. Back then

I said: "Children are only bearable if they are your own. There must at least be the narcissistic satisfaction of having brought something of our own into the world." On the other hand, children delight us early on with their enthusiasm and creativity. They take us back to our own childhoods. But we don't just come across pleasant and beautiful things. We also encounter the horrors of our own childhood; but we have the opportunity to do something different with our own children. We will certainly never be ideal parents. But we can seek to break new ground and not repeat the mistakes of our parents. You, i.e., the parents of your generation, have the unique opportunity today to step out of the limitations that have shaped generations before us. You can use your inner and outer freedom to offer your children opportunities that do justice to their inherent developmental potential. Children of previous generations were often seen as little creatures whose wildness and uncivilised nature had to be tamed. They had to be educated. Today, we can guide their development, not forgetting that certain boundaries also need to be set. Over the years I have become convinced that children also have a good inherent sense of boundaries. One of my sons once told me at lunch that he had broken the Mercedes star off a car. I strongly criticised him, stressing that this was not right. I think I was overplaying my parental authority at that time. My son clearly *already* knew that he had misbehaved.

When you are with children, you don't have to dictate what you want to do together. If you follow the children's spontaneous ideas, a very creative way of being together and playing enfolds. We adults can learn a lot from this spontaneity. When the children get older, they reach puberty, develop their own interests and peculiarities. They also worry us. Time and again, we are thrown back to our own childhood and youth and also see our own unresolved problems, in them. However, we can draw on our wealth of experience and support our children. There comes a time when our kids start to become better than us, to overtake us. It wasn't long before my sons could play the piano better than me and were better at tennis, table tennis and skiing. This was not just because they were younger and more talented, but because they had development opportunities that I didn't have as a child. Sometimes you may also envy your children. Again, this results in an impetus for development – this time not for the children, but for the parents. I have had to come to terms with imperfections in my own life and allow my children to overtake me. This is a developmental task for us parents. We must allow our children to go their own ways and not try to project our achieved or failed life goals onto them. I was deeply offended when, as a young man, I was not called up for military service because I was too short-sighted. I reluctantly realised that I had fantasised that my sons would make up for it. However, they both refused to do military service, both for reasons that I believe were fully justified and in keeping with their respective personalities. It is not our children's duty to repair or supplement our life plans. On the other hand, it may be difficult to discover characteristics or personality traits in my children that I reject in myself. The temptation then arises to fight them in the child instead of confronting oneself with these issues.

I realise how I have imperceptibly moved from the development of the children to my own, namely that of the parents. The fascinating thing about having children is that it gives you the opportunity to develop together. Returning to where I first began with the child's painting of the eagle: a huge part of the parental struggle is that our children see what they need to see in us and we in turn see what we need to see in them.

The challenge for us, dear Parent, is therefore to meet that "hand drawn eagle" and face up to the realities of who we truly are. When the time finally comes for the children to leave home, hopefully both children and parents will look back on a shared development. Without my children, I would certainly have become someone different than the person I am now. I would be much poorer emotionally. I mentioned how my sons very quickly overtook me in skiing; I think back to my 60th birthday, when I went up the T-bar lift and suddenly my sons and their friends were waiting for me in the snow and gave me a wonderfully unexpected birthday serenade.

There is a saying in German: "Little children, little worries. Big children, big worries." I think that's too pessimistic. Of course, we share worries with them. But that is not all. We also share part of our lives with them, and in turn they give us a feeling of fullness and satisfaction.

Warm wishes,
Eike Hinze
**Father of two and grandfather of four |
Karl-Abraham-Institute | Berlin, Germany**

31

∧∧∧∧

Claudia Sheftel-Luiz

Dear Parent,

I was as idealistic and excited about parenting as any new mother and had prepared for it more than most. To begin with, I had chosen psychoanalysis as my field precisely because it would not only afford me flexible hours, but also because I would learn so much about secure attachment, child development, and anything I'd need to make sure my kids would turn out well-adjusted and happy. I was determined for them to feel loved, respected, and that we would *all* be happy. I chuckle at that simplistic fantasy now.

Soon after my eldest was born it hit me that I would be off-grid from the plan above. It hit me like a ton of bricks that this was going to be a 24/7 proposition I could never turn back on or take a vacation from. The sheer enormity of it all made me feel helpless and small. It was the forever-ness of the whole

 DOI: 10.4324/9781003385042-33

experience – the weight of responsibility, the enormity of the task, and worst of all, the feeling that, perhaps, I wasn't up to it.

What I didn't know then (that I know now) is that for some new mothers, challenging energies that you could never have imagined (much less prepared for) can come upon you like a tidal wave.

Mine and my baby's babyhoods

My own mother had told me something about my own infancy. I was born in the late 1950s in a hospital in Rome where penicillin had just been introduced and, therefore, hygiene had become less valued. I arrived home with terrible boils covering almost my entire body, infected and in pain. My mother, a complex trauma victim still in her twenties, had not been able to feed me properly in the midst of her own overwhelm. With our primary care doctor away, it was many days before she took me back to the hospital, jaundiced, malnourished and severely infected.

But, of course, I had never remembered any of that. Until my first daughter was born. Then, my body remembered. She was a perfect baby, with a non-eventful birth. But the anxiety I experienced, and debilitating worry that she was sick, that she wasn't well, that something bad was happening to her, was epic. Not surprisingly, my milk dried up, and even with a lactation consultant and pumps and a rigorous system involving feeding tubes and hydration and God knows what else, I felt like I was barely keeping her alive.

I became hyper-vigilant against anything being less than perfect for my daughter. Weeping uncontrollably one day, because I had missed a window of opportunity to stimulate her in an "alert phase" by playing her Mozart and introducing her to a spice blend meant to augment her intellectually, her frustrated father took the book that was guiding me and threw it across the room. He'd had enough, as neither of us could grasp the severity of my anxiety and terror that things could fall apart.

Coming to terms with the reality of feeling overwhelmed

Dear Parent, it is so good to know and be prepared for the possibility that we may enter into states that nothing and nobody can prepare us for, that infuse our children with feelings we ourselves don't understand and cannot wrap our minds around. These are like emotional "ghosts" from our past, and from generations past. We need to talk about this more.

Fortunately for me as a psychoanalyst still in training, I was required to be in my own therapy. I was encouraged to bring all of my pain, my fears, my grief and how lonely I felt, into treatment. And there was no shadow of a doubt for me that I had more "work" to do emotionally. It was a painful awakening, but an important one in retrospect.

It actually took me a while to figure out that my children would suffer at the hands of my internal malaise. I thought that if I did a good enough job taking care of them physically, that maybe it would be enough. It wasn't. I will never forget the first time I was hit with the idea that the ghosts from my past could be hurting my children when a trusted advisor misguidedly suggested that they would not be spared future anxiety, due to my own. I almost felt like I might have to be hospitalised for a nervous breakdown – it was the worst feeling I had ever had.

When it comes to our children, I can think of nothing more unthinkable than believing we could be hurting them or making them unwell. It was unthinkable to me – unforgivable. I felt, perhaps, that I did not deserve to live. All we want is for our children to be happy, and to believe that we can do it well.

I briefly went on a course of anti-anxiety medication to make it through about a week of feeling inexcusably flawed before coming to terms with the reality of my life. I felt disturbed, dysregulated by anger, plagued by irrational fears, and ashamed by the degree of emotionality that seemed only to be getting worse.

I felt small, and so, so helpless.

My determination to parent my children prevailed though. The reality of things hurts so much, sometimes. But it can also set you free, as I hope to convey by the end of this letter to you. It was depressing to see all these negative things about myself and my daughters, and it did not make me a joyous, fun mother.

Cut to the present, 25 years later, seeing how resilient, courageous, connected, healthy and successful both my daughters are. How did this happen? How could this be? Despite the painful realities, despite the ghosts and my debilitated state, my children have done extremely well in every way I had wanted and hoped. And I believe I now understand why, which is what I want to share with you now, dear Parent.

What I did right, despite the "ghosts"

I did not, at any cost, want my children to have the same experience as many of my analytic patients, who had to search for narratives for their own disorders. We typically internalise free-floating disturbances, blaming ourselves, or simply having ineffective language – like "depression" or "anxiety" for those horrible "ghosts".

What happens is that most children, when they see their parents dysregulated or agitated, make up stories about it. They think: "I'm not good enough, Mom or Dad don't like me", and develop feelings of worthlessness or of being unloved. Or they think, "I have to make things easier and take a backseat emotionally", and they become parentified. Without hearing the real story, children have to make one up, and typically, it's neither a good story nor the right one.

The theory explains it: children don't separate from their parents until well into their twenties. Before then, their parent's thoughts and feelings serve as "auxiliary egos". This means that where a child's brain is not developed, they are guided by a sense of the parent inside themselves, which they are attached to, called an "internalised object". Internalised objects protect and guide children, and it is not for lack of love that everything can get internalised, even the disturbed aspects of family life.

This brain psychology explains how the "ghosts" carry nameless, story-less, unexplainable energies children feel and parents try to make sense of with narratives that are often too much for children to understand or bear – narratives that carry feelings too big for children to manage, about rage, grief or despair. Without a good, emotionally digestible working narrative, children exposed to even mild underlying levels of depression and anxiety ultimately carry a silent frustration and despair about the disorders that visit them chronically and perpetually, sometimes for life.

I didn't want that to happen to my kids.

So, I swallowed my pride and shielded them from defensive narratives that would justify or condone my excessive emotional reactions. I was able to stop myself from launching into defensive diatribes about why I was upset. That would have been too much for them – I knew that my agitation was none of their business, and that it shouldn't be, and I felt bad enough they had to witness and experience me upset. Here is what I told them, simply, after uncontrollable fits of agitation or disturbance, in calm moments later: "When you see me like that, it is not how things should be. I am so sorry. I am working on not being that way."

Sometimes I could tell them this right after I'd had an emotional fit or a bout with depression, sometimes I'd say it to them if I sensed they needed to hear it, but always in a calm moment, without going into much more than that.

My children were also able to tell me eventually that I had upset them, which was very hard to bear, but which I welcomed, knowing, as I hope you will too now, that it is so healthy for their mental well-being to have their own experience deeply heard.

There is a fine line between wanting our children to become like loving parents to us, soothing us, comforting us and forgiving us, versus providing them with an honest narrative about our disturbances, to protect them. It's a place you have to find inside yourself that knows the difference. This is a place of sacrifice; a parenting where you know you are the mother or father; where you can feel within that you are telling them about yourself for them, just as you would give them a healthy meal, or find a good school, or tend to a bloody knee. It's done in an atmosphere of protection and comforting calm even when it's hard inside.

It's OK to be imperfect. And admit it

I worried that my lack of consistent pride in myself, and my admitting instead that I could be a basket case sometimes, would ruin my children. What kind of role model was I? But as it turned out, my children appreciated that their own experience of me, when I was not at my best, was something I could hear and bear. In the end, this made me a better role model; one who was not afraid to get to know herself and hear them.

These simple words, dear Parent, "I am not well, I am still growing", when it comes to painful states inside yourself, protect children from living in the un-truths that lead to making up stories. Made-up stories lead to crazy stuff. Anxiety, alienation, relationship problems, dissociated states, self-doubt and worse.

My children suffered at my hands, but they were told, and always knew, "this is not as it should be". As they grew into young women, my narrative freed them up to develop their own narratives about themselves and me. Those narratives were finally expressed to me as they grew older. This is when, as they separated, they could finally tell me, "It hurt me so much when I lost you to your dysregulation. You were not available to me emotionally. Why did you leave me?" These are difficult conversations. But they do make children feel whole and never alone.

All feelings are welcome

My children never could be free of pain, the way I had wanted them to be. Each of them had unhappy moments, replete with conflict, failure, worry and disappointment, because this is real life. I could not protect them from challenges, but I could help them process things. I got help with it, and dear Parent, I hope you will too.

Now, a quarter century after first re-living my own birth and infancy, my children are successful. They both love what they're doing with their lives, and they enjoy loving and feeling loved by a large variety of people. I can rest, now. I have done my job. They have their own lives, and they are stable, loving and forgiving. Whatever pride I had to relinquish to make sure they wouldn't internalise or take responsibility for my unre-solved issues, was worth it. Because they sure are making me proud, now.

Imperfectly yours,
Claudia Sheftel-Luiz
Proud mother of two wonderful young women | National Association for the Advancement of Psychoanalysis (NAAP) | New York, USA

32

Susan Mailer

Dear Parent,

When I was in my early twenties, I was immersed in the feminist wave of the 1970s. Many books were published during that time centring on our bodies, the most popular was *Our Bodies Ourselves*. It was the "go to" book for many of us who wanted information about the changes in our bodies from our early teens to childbirth and beyond. It included themes like methods of birth control, menstruation and, of course, childbirth. That book and several others helped us develop the conviction that we were in charge of our lives, we had agency and the power to choose.

Years later, when I was thinking of getting pregnant, I had a very clear idea of how I wanted to give birth. My expectations around the process were enormous and I felt it would happen just as I imagined it. I decided, as many of my friends, I would go the route of natural childbirth. I read about giving

 DOI: 10.4324/9781003385042-34

birth in the water, also about the many ways my partner could participate, and the breathing exercises that would help the process. I was convinced of the beauty of the experience and how it would help my baby arrive well prepared into the world. Natural childbirth was the way to circle around the medical establishment and do without all the foreign substances that, I thought, would impede my baby's clean and safe arrival. I reflected on how for centuries women had had babies in the wild, or at home, with the help of a midwife. The medical establishment had taken away our power to give birth in a more natural manner. At least this is what I thought at the time.

When the time came, I was not living in the United States but in Chile and I soon discovered that this business of natural childbirth was not something that was done by mainstream obstetricians. I did find one who was willing to listen to me and together we planned the birthing process. We agreed on the basics; he would respect my wish for no anaesthesia and would lower the lights when the baby was about to come out. He would lay the baby on my chest, near my breast, before cutting the umbilical cord and would wait a few minutes before adding burning drops to her eyes to prevent infections.

During the last month of my pregnancy, I found out my daughter was in podalic position, that is, feet first. As the days went by, I began losing hope she would turn around, and asked my doctor what could be done. He was categorical. "If the baby is podalic we will do a C-section. There is no way I will permit a normal birth if she doesn't change her position." I was appalled, discouraged, angry, furious, and considered changing doctors. At the time there was no such thing as Google or Chat GPT, so I turned to books and consulted other doctors. All had very little doubt it would be very dangerous for the baby.

Yet I insisted, after all my father had been born podalic and there seemed to be nothing wrong with him. When I turned to my grandmother for reassurance, she reminded me of how my father's birth had been the single most painful experience in her life. But despite all the warnings I couldn't relinquish my ideal version of childbirth and stubbornly stuck to the plan. Somehow it would happen as I wanted.

My obstetrician eventually understood he had to be very firm with me. He was empathic and kind but left no room for doubt. "I know you've invested a great deal in having your baby with no anesthesia and in the most natural way possible in a hospital, but you've got to understand that giving birth to her in this way is putting you and the baby at risk." And then he added a phrase that has stuck with me for the rest of my life. He said, "There is much more to being a mother than childbirth."

It turned out the doctor was right. Once I realised there was no way out of the C-section and prepared myself for the operation, I was able to receive my healthy baby with more love than frustration. Slowly I grasped there were many things that escaped my control, and one of them was how my baby had chosen to be born. I am not saying she had decided to stay in that position and be born through a C-section. Rather I do believe that there were other factors involved, of which we knew very little, and could only conjecture, such as the size of her umbilical cord, or the form of my uterus, or perhaps her own preferred position in utero. Another question I grappled with was whether underneath all the bravado, I was unconsciously scared of feeling pain, or of having my genitals undergo some kind of transformation that would deform them. Eventually I was able to live comfortably with these unanswered questions and settle into the long journey of taking care of my child. It was the beginning of my understanding that she was an individual separate from me and my own desires. In years to come, while she was growing up, this comprehension, that she would be her own person, and not the one I had envisioned in my fantasies, only grew stronger and helped me realise I could only show her a way and she would be the one to choose which path to take.

Many years later, when my daughter was pregnant for the first time, I saw her go through a very similar process. She was determined to have natural childbirth and considered (and thankfully discarded) having a home birth. But, to her surprise, the baby never turned around and just as she had insisted 30 years before to not budge, her baby was also determined to stay in the same position. And the doctor's attitude (a woman this time) was the same as my obstetrician's. Perhaps the biggest difference between my experience and my daughter's was that I had the wisdom learned from her birth. I knew how disappointed she was. I understood she was unreasonably angry at her baby and felt guilty because of it, and at the same time could not let go of her resentment completely. I knew she thought she had failed at something that was all-encompassing and important, and unlike her friends who were having babies "the natural way" there was something amiss in her because she had not been able to do so. I listened to her and felt with her. I remembered my own frustration with her birth and how grateful I ultimately was that she turned out to be a healthy and vigorous human being.

Pregnancy brings with it insecurities that are difficult to handle, starting with the question "Will I be able to get pregnant?" and going on to "Will my baby be healthy?" The experience of having a growing being inside one is powerful and beautiful. We remember moments of our own childhood and may even evoke some of our earliest moments of life, all this through the world of sensations. At the same time pregnancy conjures up new fears, such as "Will I be able to handle this responsibility?" or "How will my life change?" Or "Will my body ever be the same?" In the middle of this maelstrom of self-doubt perhaps the one aspect of having a child a woman thinks she can control is the birth itself. Imagining the perfect ambiance, with an unobstructed medical procedure, helps us lay our fears aside and convince ourselves we can choose how to bring our child into the world.

The pain of not getting what you want, especially when it hinges on such important issues as your womanhood, or the belief that you are in charge of your pregnancy and can and will make your own decisions, is enormous. The frustration and self-doubt of not reaching that longed for goal of "perfect childbirth" is a profound wound. But I think it also provides an opportunity to fully understand that you are never totally in control. Ever. Accepting that the ideal situations you have built up in your mind about childbirth and motherhood have not turned out to be what you thought poses a considerable challenge, but it also enables you to make mistakes and not be perfect, without punishing yourself over it. I believe it helps you become a good enough mother, one who can open a space between her desires and her children's, and in that way help them on the road to becoming independent human beings.

I sometimes think of my obstetrician, who had the wisdom accrued from helping many mothers through the process of childbirth. The way he said "There is more to being a mother than childbirth" carried with it the conviction of experience and the knowledge that, eventually, I would fully understand what he meant.

With kind regards,
Susan Mailer
Mother of three children | Psychoanalytic Association of Santiago | Santiago, Chile

33

Giovanni Foresti

Dear Parents,
Are guilty feelings good or bad? This is the difficult question that I want to address with you today.

My wife and I are a long-lasting couple sharing more than 40 years of life together. We have two (now adult) daughters. I have decided to focus this letter on one of their common peeves. They often remark that we never fight, that we always agree on everything. Their view has always been that my wife and I are a tight unit, sturdy as a wall that cannot be shifted. The strange thing is that this is certainly not true. We always argue about everything. But there *is* something we have in common; the idea that guilty feelings are inevitable and that understanding their origins requires time and a certain cadence. Forgiveness is the desirable outcome, obviously, but there is a process to get there – a relational process (no one can forgive

 DOI: 10.4324/9781003385042-35

her/himself alone) that needs strength, a certain amount of pain and time to understand.

My wife was (and still is) a feminist and had decided to study medicine to become a gynaecologist. She considered herself to be a female doctor taking care of women's distresses. Her professional life evolved differently and, torn between her love of dance and her desire to be a doctor, she chose to have an analysis in order to address what felt deeply distressing within her own inner life. I, too, have had my own analysis – a requirement of analytic training, but also a personal necessity (but more on that later). Now a couple, post-analysis, our relationship has, and continues to be, a rodeo. She says I was an awful fiancé, but with the passing of time I've become a decent husband and a good enough father. At home, I am never "professional": I spare my patience for patients because, unfortunately, it's in limited supply. What our daughters perceive as a "tight unit" is the habit to respect the spontaneous feelings of the other and to step aside, ahead or backward according to whatever we are feeling in that moment. We know that we need the cooperation of the other partner to get out of the mess. Nothing *is* right per se. Everything has to be made acceptable and *perceived* as probably right.

An example typical of our family life? An undesirable feature of our home is bad cooking. My wife works in a hospital all day long and comes back exhausted (but actually, she isn't a better cook when relaxed and energetic; simply, she never learned how).

"Eat the soup. No grimaces", she said to my younger daughter.

"After all it's not worse than any of the other dishes", I often add. Remembering that at the beginning of our life together she had never cooked. And that her mother was not better at it either. She is now a master chef in comparison to our unfortunate old days.

"Smile, smile, you ungrateful people. Why do you all come home late? Try to prepare something good to eat, instead of mocking me."

"Really, I like this soup Wife. It's good. It's above our family standards. You were probably *distracted*" (the daughters comment on good dishes by saying: the food is good; mother was probably distracted).

"Do you want me to feel guilty? I was convinced that our family was grounded on good food, and you all keep blaming my cooking."

"You're right as always, Darlin'. This seemingly awful soup has been purposefully done as such to remind us of the progress you've made. But, respectfully, it isn't as terrible as it could have been. You spared us all the real extent of the improvement."

"Spare us the remake of the Addams Family, Gomez. Leave the soup if it is really that bad."

"Thank you Morticia."

If you see this little story as futile, it's because you underestimate the Italian religion of food (and my wife's hostility for traditional female *corvées*). The jokes are a way of dealing with disagreements and reflect tolerance for our differences and the ability to shift from one point of view to another. In analysis, having so often experienced and suffered the cycle of guilty feelings (denial-shame-pain-recognition-repentance-reparation), we now feel relatively equipped to face ordinary family misunderstandings and the (luckily infrequent) extraordinary big fights.

But I do wonder about the fights that happen inside our-selves, and how sometimes this spills out between us, affecting the family dynamic. Let me now add something I do think rel-evant on this point. We are living in difficult times: uncertainty and confusion have never been so widespread and so disturb-ing. Even in the past, people often felt confused and unsure what to do. But in the twentieth century, people believed in sets of values that shaped how they saw the future based on the well-established horizons of a small number of beliefs. Ideologies, the Great Tales that gave us meaning in life, divided cultures and human groups from each other. But they also brought together generations through shared beliefs that made conversations easier (though they got too harsh at times) and helped people grow mentally (though they were sometimes too rigid, too fanatical or too one-sided). Religions were a little hard to see because of the myth of progress, which was mostly seen as progress in science and technology, but they were still there, and their stories made sense. People's need for hope was rooted in the idea of progress. People, whether they were religious or not, were not desperate and could depend on something like faith.

In one of his masterpieces, *The Road*, Cormac McCarthy describes a post-apocalyptic world. The main characters are a father and his son and the book tells the story of a couple who struggle to survive in a world where civilisation has been destroyed by a catastrophe of some sort. Why did such a story become a world success and was immediately awarded with a Pulitzer Prize? Apart from the quality of the writing and the fame of the author, we can see the huge impact of the story as an example of the themes mentioned at the beginning of this letter. We are all worried about the future of our present and a furiously consuming world. If we are old enough, we know that we will likely escape the catastrophe we feel hanging over our heads. But we are worried for our children. And we feel desperately guilty too. It may be that we don't realise these feelings because, as the psychoanalysts show their patients, these guilty feeling are often partly conscious and, for an even larger part, unconscious, and are therefore unavailable to us in a "knowing" way.

As with everyone else, you don't get much help from neo-liberal policies, postmodern ideas, post-welfare institutions, secularised churches, or markets, businesses, or people who are addicted to money of all kinds (liquid Gods). It's probably the first time in human history that parents have problems in having faith in the future and in "progress". Few human beings have been experiencing for a long time and so deeply the feelings related to the social evidence of belonging to generations that have been too greedy. We all know – somewhere, deep in ourselves – that we are leaving our children a world which is worse than the one we came into. It's difficult to face the guilty feelings of our girls and boys, if we ourselves feel overwhelmed by the guilt of bringing them here in the first place. The question we are dealing with was summarised, at the beginning of this letter, with a few simple words: are guilty feelings good things or bad? Are these subjective experiences rooted in emotions that support psychic growth, or are they something that simply mortify the ones who feel them? All of us easily intuit that the answer is: both.

The hypothesis I thought useful to discuss with you regarding the importance of experiencing guilt, is to face its emotional consequences with fear and seriousness but also with hope and patience. The origins of what I've here tried to write is the outcome of the long work with the woman who accepted, almost 40 years ago, to be my analyst. She had spent a large part of her professional life thinking about adolescence and working in a jail for young people in Milan, Italy. This place is named after Cesare Beccaria: the eighteenth-century philosopher who wrote *Dei delitti e delle pene* (On Crimes and Punishments [1764]). My analyst (whose nickname was *Lady Homicide* because of her expertise and experience in treating young murderers) has been very clear in her work on this theme and I'm sure that this is a major component of her legacy. The unconscious and conscious guilty feelings are very important emotional ingredients, when one tries to understand the hidden motivations of human behaviour. Back in 1916, Freud wrote a two-page text describing that children and adults alike may behave transgressively because of guilty feelings that are not the consequence, but rather the *cause* of their behaviour. They act as they were looking for a punishment that could stop their inner distress. We call it rightly a "sanction" because human beings have always recognised this.

If I think about the feelings related to "guilt", "repentance", "forgiveness", "atonement", "rehabilitation", "reparation" and so on, I do have in mind the images of a parental couple. It's because I can feel the pain parents have to suffer, when they face the responsibility of being parents, that I do what I do. I have doubts about the clinical efficacy of psychotherapies. Yet, I'm sure that one result is often attained: patients become better parents.

Without capacity for suffering, enduring and overcoming guilt, we cannot develop a responsible attitude towards it. What is a responsibility, after all, if not a building of the capacity to withstand and face the hard questions ourselves? Psychoanalysts have discovered that guilty feelings are often at the heart of suffering and these hidden feelings can seriously hamper emotional development. The tragic complexity and ambiguity of guilty feelings means that we often avoid thinking about them all together, assuming any efforts to be futile or to backfire. The specific social and cultural problems mentioned above may explain why our paralysing puzzlement has transformed guilty feelings into something to be absolutely banished – an ordinary human trouble with a very bad reputation. Even the astute Pope who guides the Catholic Church used to say: who am I to judge?

Yet, luckily, we do have something truly reliable to fall back on. Parents are not alone, by definition. They are a couple of linked but independent subjects and, therefore, they are a potentially effective working group. Together, they can be a powerful thinking ensemble that can balance what is difficult in our external worlds as well as what is challenging in our internal worlds. The upsurge of guilty feelings may be destructive and become an unbearable, ontological shame. The crucial ingredient in its recovery is forgiveness. This process must first be dealt with on a personal level, and then we will be equipped to help our children with it. A working couple, who really know themselves well, is a crucial ingredient in this endeavour.

None expressed the idea of the importance of balancing these opposite dimensions better than the political scientist Hannah Arendt (1958). "We all", she wrote simply, "depend on plurality, on the presence and acting of others, for no one can forgive himself and no one can feel bound by a promise made only to himself; forgiving and promising enacted in solitude or isolation remain without reality and can signify no more than a role played before oneself" (p.237).

Ciao!

Giovanni Foresti

Father of two | Italian Psychoanalytic Society (SPI) | Pavia and Milan

34

Ines Bayona

Dear Parents,
Gratefully, I accepted this privileged invitation, as it gave me the opportunity to share a topic that has been on my mind for years, feeling, listening and not listening in my clinical work: the VOICE in all its states. The voice of silence, the voice of pain, of suffering, the voice of joy, of tranquility and inner peace, the shouting voice, the voice of love for oneself and for others. That VOICE: interior and the voice for the other.

I know the invitation is to write to you, dear Parents, and so you will receive a letter, where I hope to trasmit to you through MY VOICE (with its tonality, intensity and meaning) what I have lived and considered to be "indispensable" for raising children: Namely to favour and encourage creating, and empathically developing ONE VOICE, that is uniquely one's own. THE VOICE that is HEARD equally in silence and in noise, and one that reaches the heart of whoever receives it, in

DOI: 10.4324/9781003385042-36

spite of the internal and external trappings of life. Both for the benefit of ourselves and others. Now that I mention "empathically", I remembered the work of a pioneering psychoanalyst, Sandor Ferenczi, and his book of clinical letters from 1932, titled "Without empathy there is no cure . . .".

I will share with you, then, what that inner VOICE is, within ourselves, as well as the VOICE towards the outside, towards others. The two are inseparable and you, we, must keep it in mind and transmit it, allow and encourage it in our children. I am sure that you will not regret it. As Socrates said in Phaedo 95e, "The voice, your voice, my voice: Desire to be transmitted heard and received by the other . . . I will tell you, if you want, my own experiences on the issue."

This memory, from some time ago, is a good way to start. I read a book that I vividly remember had a *major* impact on me, as a person and as a psychoanalyst, and it came back to me when I received this invitation: *The Man with the Beautiful Voice*, by Lillian B. Rubin; referring to the impact of the analyst's VOICE on each patient, in the analytical and in the therapeutic relationship. This book has helped me a lot in my clinical work, to transmit to my patients what I really think, what I should and can give back to them, through the voice of silence and the words, "with my own voice, with the voice that I feel and think they will be able to receive, comprehend and eventually understand", to be able to relieve and yes, why not say "heal" their psyche, their inner soul, that VOICE that can be HEARD and received. It is not just the technique of interpretation, or pointing out, or constructing; it is also the sound, the pause of the VOICE, that comes from the other side of the couch. In the case of you, parents, it is not just love and education, it is the way it is transmitted, with your own VOICE.

Now, this experience of the VOICE as an analyst, and in my case also as a mother of two children, is the VOICE that with each one's own style, dear Parents, you must develop in yourself in order to be able to transmit it to your children and others. This is my first message to you. First think about your own VOICE, the one I mentioned initially, the one that is inside, within and towards the interior and the VOICE that goes towards others, especially your children.

This sharing is not of clinical material, it is from what I observed in my clinical practice. I will share with you what a certain number of patients have expressed, or we have been able to discover and understand through their suffering, difficulties, bad life experiences, such as some traumatic situations like abuse. That they have mainly been unable to make their voices heard, or because their voices remain trapped in their throat, their bodies or because they do not even know what it means to be heard. I have been able to identify that, in general, they have a father or mother whose voice was not heard, who does not have their own voice. This clinical experience allowed me to understand that if a parent does not have that power in his/her voice, it is difficult for their children to have it, it is like there is no way of transmitting what we do not have internally, what we have not developed, cared for or even realised the importance of developing that care, and that personal voice.

This letter to you, Parents, goes with a second message and invitation. Think of yourselves not only as parents, but also as human beings, who must take care of and heal yourselves. When we think as human beings, and take responsibility for ourselves, by listening to our own inner voices, we can then think outwards, as parents, as a couple, as children, as friends, as colleagues, as bosses. In short, think from "otherness", think that, sometimes, the "other, in this case – that child" must come first, to contribute to the process of early development of their psyche. It is focusing, *that* voice on the child.

I like this phrase from the Spanish artist Antonio Gaudi: "To do things well, it is necessary: love, first; technique, second." This thought is key, to transmit that inner voice to our children, love is necessary, with love and for love, with empathy as I mentioned before. Education, discipline, the norm will follow, but everything with love and care.

As the entire experience as a psychoanalyst is built from theory, with our own history and especially from work with our patients, I share with you two experiences from my clinical work, which illustrate part of what I have wanted to convey in this letter. Both related to the psychological trauma of two patients caused in a great variety of situations by not having that inner voice that could have saved them from living situations of abuse, indifference, sexual abuse and (not only sexual) but emotional, work-related and economic hardships.

During clinical moments in the office, with a lot of pain, I listened to phrases, expressions like:

"I wanted to scream, but my voice couldn't come out."
"Why would I speak if I was not going to be heard?"
"I didn't want to say anything because I might make the other person feel bad, I was probably exaggerating."
"I had a lump in my throat from not being able to speak . . ."
"I walked away for months because I didn't know how to say what I felt."
"My parents' words echoed in my mind – shut up or I'll hit you!"

"How many times I screamed to be heard and still, I wasn't heard."

"My sick body spoke for me, screamed for me, and even then, I was not heard."

"I thought; if I speak, I'm going to be the one to blame, I'd better not speak!"

And so, many more expressions like these have cried and resonated in my office and in my mind.

Also, with a lot of pain, but from a different type of experience, I listened to another patient:

When I was a teenager, "silence" saved me, I think that not having a voice was my ally, I chose to go unnoticed, almost indifferent to others, in this way I avoided being mistreated as they mistreated others. I almost wanted to be invisible to avoid conflict. Today as an adult, where I have achieved a lot professionally and personally; I feel like it helped me, but at a very high cost of insecurity, fear, dislike of my body, and needing a lot of recognition. One purpose I have with my children is to have them speak, make themselves felt, allow them to express themselves with words and with their bodies.

Now, Parents, you may wonder what it is about the inner voice and transmitting it to our children. Starting from the fact that we as parents have already developed it and believe in our inner voice, we can transmit it in a conscious and, more than anything, unconscious way through the relationship we have built with our children or others.

What does that inner voice consist of for me, as a psycho-analyst and as a mother?

That inner voice should be:

- an emotional connection,
- in a healthy environment for an indefinite period,
- where loyalty should exist, with us and to that inner voice,
- also, it should allow the availability to listen to its resonance,
- a priority to feel heard and listen to others,
- where we should allow ourselves to doubt and inquire: pain, joy, sadness, anger, fear, uncertainty, conflict, suffering, guilt, desire, illusion, thought,
- to, finally, strengthen our self-love,
- to develop and build trust in others and in ourselves.

At the end of the day, it is to allow the ability to listen to its resonance, it is to feel heard by others and to empower the capacity to listen to others.

My final message to you, dear Parents, is: initially review what your inner "voice" is like, because it is what leads us to express that "outward voice" and transmit it to our children in a natural way, day after day, at every opportunity, being role models. Encourage your children to listen to themselves and allow that voice to come out.

Best regards on this amazing journey
that is "being a parent",
Ines Bayona
**Mother of two | Colombian Psychoanalytic
Society | Bogotá, Colombia**

35

^^^^

Mariano Ruperthuz Honorato

Dear Parent,

Becoming a parent is one of the most exciting, challenging and complex experiences I have ever had (and continue to have). I have two children: a 12-year-old girl, and a seven-year-old boy. During these years, I have witnessed – together with my wife – the phenomenon of human life. When a baby comes into the world, it gives birth to ideas and feelings, that pre-date its day of birth. This is surprising; if one thing distinguishes us as a species, it is the loving bonds we can build over time. Funeral rites involve special symbols and traditions that show how deeply we care for one another, starting from a young age. Similarly, being a parent is all about creating a welcoming space where a child's wishes and needs can thrive, providing both the physical necessities and emotional support they need.

Many of us believe in gods and protective beings because, deep down, we all feel quite helpless. We look to these influential figures for guidance and support, hoping they can offer us comfort and strength in life's challenges. This need for support might be why we feel drawn to worship and pray to deities, so we don't feel so alone or overwhelmed by what we face. Children are naturally vulnerable and depend heavily on adults, mainly because they are still developing their understanding of the world. This makes the role of caregivers extremely important. However, the way parents and caregivers behave is often influenced by their own emotional needs and past experiences, which can sometimes make their caregiving styles more about meeting their own needs rather than just the child's. Children awaken in each of their parents (and caregivers) strong feelings about their own childhoods. Ambivalences naturally lodged in each of us from our most remote past. Kindness, unconditional love and tenderness can be combined with feelings of disorientation, depression and even envy. For this reason, having deep contact with oneself, and knowing how being a parent directly mobilises these complex ideas, is incredibly useful.

The relevance of all this – and I say this as a historian – is that if there is one significant thing I have learned from my experience as a parent, it is that time is not behind us. We are immersed in an "earlier future", as several specialists have mentioned. What does this mean? Parents' past experiences and childhoods are present more than we would like. They are not buried in some ancient cellar. Even so, they are there to experience our first thoughts and feelings about having children. The existence of a braid of events that cross epochs, times, and spaces is astonishing. In my own analytical experience, I have learned how my children's lives are linked to people they did not (and will not) have the possibility of ever knowing personally. The genealogy of a birth has so many antecedents that it far outweighs a couple's desire (conscious or unconscious) to have a child. Knowing these ties might be frightening for many, but there is a real-life power for those who dare to make that personal journey. It allows for independence from old wills, desires and impositions that are not one's own and nested in the mind (and heart) of those who agree to become a parent.

Recognising that we are shaped by our past and that we depend on others both physically and emotionally has made parenting easier for me. Understanding that we owe a lot to our parents and accepting this without stress has allowed me to approach parenting more relaxed and personally. This has empowered me to find my own parenting style and be less anxious about not putting my own fears on my children. The childhood pains of parenting, with different magnitudes, durations and consequences, are also present when a child enters the world. At various times, we may fear that these experiences will explode destructively. It is not unreal or just a fantasy.

Not all parents have historically undergone a process of getting to really know themselves. So, the collective presence of others who help, support, teach and soothe is also essential to help the parent get used to this new suit of clothes. I wish we had more opportunities to get to know collective experiences of parenting support. Grandparents, grandmothers, aunts, uncles and friends, for example, are also sources of community support that I really value. I live in South America, with my extended family and, thanks to their presence, I was able to calm many of my fears. Seeing how other parents raise, care for and love their children has been an invaluable example for me. It has guided and inspired my own approach to parenting.

For many years, I worked in state institutions in my country before becoming a psychoanalyst in private practice, seeking to guarantee minimum care for many children at psychosocial risk. Over time, I realised how the original experience of the family places a significant mental weight on the child. Several of the children we treated had chronic histories of institution-alisation, rocky relationships with their parents, and vulnerable and threatening ties with them. Still, they always tried to return to their family of origin. Many lived in children's homes for years, receiving state education and care until they came of age. But they wanted to return to their families when they left these institutions. This was something I found professionally incomprehensible. However, learning from myself and several of my patients, I became aware of the specific weight of early experiences (real and fantasised) with our parents. The desire to have the opportunity to feel genuinely loved, valued and acknowledged as a child is a potent feeling and undying need.

The braid, therefore, is a symbol used to convey the knot-ting, links and intimate relationships involved in parenthood. They are threads that come from the past, mingle in the present and are projected into the future. The "family tree" exercise, where we map out our ancestors and descendants, is a popular way to visualise our connections with our family history. It shows how relationships are interlinked, shaping a crucial part of our life experience. Being a dad has been a constant learning process. My second child, for example, gave me a new oppor-tunity to become a more (and better) involved parent. Likewise, another point I find very sensitive is the couple's transforma-tion in how they love each other (tenderly and sexually) after a child is born. It is a time of adjustment as each parent assumes their unique caring role. This process may take time, and it's important for parents to remain calm and give themselves the space they need within the relationship. The couple alone now shares their time with the baby, and that care is essential.

As a man, that moment was one of the most unsettling for me: to be nobody for a few months and to help create the vital conditions for the fundamental care my wife was giving my children. "Being nobody" is an exaggeration, of course, because many things I did were beneficial. But the feelings of being "displaced", "forgotten" and "left out" were very real. I remember feeling the full force of my own childishness. Saying it out loud is still very difficult. Most people are pleased to be parents; the social environment powerfully reinforces this. However, it is not uncommon for silent envy, reproaches and insecurities towards the presence of the baby or the mother to creep in. To be attentive to these feelings is to feel first-hand how one's childishness is alive and well. This is one of the powerful Freudian discoveries: the difference between childhood and infancy. "Childhood" is a chronological stage of life. Depending on the social and cultural environment, it will legally last several years. On the other hand, "infancy" is a mode of functioning intimately dependent on our first years of life and conditions in our adult life. Unlike childhood, infancy never ends and lives inside us, even when we are adults.

All in all, the portrait of what "normally" should happen has variations that are to be expected. There may be less happiness, fear, anxiety and rivalry. The important thing is to have an internal line of self-communication to periodically test the pulse of our own chronicity. Having children brought me joy and also made me more conscious of life's limited duration. This awareness gave me the serenity needed to cope with my parents' passing and to come to terms with my own mortality. I remember that, on more than one occasion, I felt very conflicted about how to be a parent dealing with those feelings. Personal support, understanding the birth of life under these parameters, and a frank dialogue as a couple go a long way in helping us cope with this somewhat unavoidable situation.

In this way, dear Parent, I wanted to convey a vision of the passage of time and how it carries desires, wishes and ideals that are present, sometimes overtly and sometimes more silently, in the parenting journey. The braid of time ties in childhood experiences with ancestors – living and dead – who leave their legacy through both veins of the genealogy of father and mother. Today, we have several therapeutic resources to clarify this inheritance, with all the symbolic possibilities. Understanding it creates a greater independence from this legacy. This idea challenges the notion of being self-centred and disconnected from others. Instead, it shows that human life is about shared experiences, each of us living out our unique versions of these experiences.

Best regards,
Mariano Ruperthuz Honorato
Father of two | Chilean Society of Psychoanalysis – ICHPA and Psychoanalytic Association of Buenos Aires (APdeBA) | Santiago, Chile

36

Deborah Ashdown

Dear Parent,

When I began working as a newly qualified psychologist, my work with teens shaped the analyst I would one day become. My young patients taught me a great deal about the importance of asking unanswerable questions relating to our capacity for dwelling in a particular state of "being", that moves beyond the realm of our compulsive "doing". My own mind broadened as my young patients attempted to explore the hazy uneasiness of themselves in the world – an existential void, infused with overwhelm and confusion.

In a culture imbued with cultish productivity and a stream of dopamine-laced distractions, it is nothing less than a counter-cultural act of courage for a teen to enter therapy. It felt this way, as I anchored myself around the possibility of merely creating a space for my teen patients to become curious about

DOI: 10.4324/9781003385042-38

themselves, helping them to build a psychoanalytic mind. This would hopefully prepare their adult selves to regard therapy as a viable option and a worthwhile use of time to examine and reflect on their individual pursuit of life.

All this good intention dissipated when my children entered their teen years. Despite trying to refrain from being an intrusive parent, I am preoccupied with my teens. Their secretiveness, their need to separate from me, have admittedly left me more anxious than when they were babies. Surprisingly my experience of working with teens has helped, but nothing prepares one for the daunting task of helping your teen to find their own voice, choose friends wisely, face their own struggles, and set up their own boundaries.

Just as my own teen years became messy at times, I realise that I too need to let my teens make their own mess. This is hard, especially when experience brings insight and intuition about how things are likely to unfold from afar. I am surprised to find myself overthinking the lives of my teens. In many ways, I feel that living through the developmental years with your own children takes you back to your own fault lines. Yet, it is only in their finding their way out of the turmoil that they have created for themselves that they then begin to discover their individual selves.

My son who is now 16 years old, recently wrote a reflective essay. He has given me permission to share it with you, dear Parent. His words illustrate the delicate balance evident in how, at different stages of their lives, we allow a little more reality in, in such a way that it helps them to confront the fact that reality is not here to serve us, but has to be negotiated and reckoned with. In the teen years this "re-finding of reality" – as psychoanalysis calls it – becomes a pertinent way in which we help our children to build a robustness in the part of themselves that negotiates what is real and what is fantasy. At times, we may inadvertently protect them too much, and sometimes not enough, but on a whole this process is about being receptive and creating a space for exploration.

In my son's words

Before I begin this tale of torture, I must first give you some background. I was born to a mother, who since I entered this mortal coil, was a seeker of anything life enhancing. If she wasn't dragging us to artistic installations, we were off on road trips into the vast wilderness with back up water and petrol in case we got stranded in the desolate Karoo or Namib desert. Now, you have to understand I was born a cautious chap, and as I write this, I realise that the Gods must have had a really wicked sense of humour setting up this scene.

Let me take you to the start of the tale, which started with a trail: the Kranshoek Coastal Trail set deep in the rich coastal forest near Plettenberg Bay, on the Garden Route in South Africa. To say this trail is challenging is an understatement. It started with a hop, skip and a jump between logs scattered with fantastic fungi, with waterfalls in the background. Then we wound our way around the forest and down into a gorge. I remember this elated feeling as we spotted the coast. We stopped here for bite to eat as we took in the wild ocean. It was magical, but what followed made it hard to hold onto this magical feeling. This magic faded as we headed up the slopes to the plateau. The views were breathtaking, but I finally understood this term, as my breath wasn't returning as panic set in. It was extremely high, with a dismal deadly fall. My heart raced, and I froze and refused to move. My mother said we could do it, that I could do it, but could I?

With that one step, something incredible shifted in me. Our minds play silly tricks on us, we need to trust our survival instincts as they protect us from taking stupid risks. So, I trod carefully, and took a deep breath with each step. This tale of torture transformed into a tale of triumph. This experience shaped me, gave me strength and a belief in myself I didn't know I had.

When my son brought this essay to me to read, I was taken aback by how he had worked through this challenging experience. I do recall how angry he was with me at the time. I reflected that perhaps I should not have chosen such an advanced hike for my children but in reading this essay, it makes me realise that we endeavour to provide a space for our children to discover themselves anew.

If we constantly hover over them, their choices become blurred or compromised as they strive to separate from us. These separations happen in varying shapes and degrees at different times in the developmental life span; at 18 months, 24 months, at six to eight years old when our children begin formal schooling, and then again as teens. If you are too enmeshed with your child, there is no space for them to begin to think for themselves, nor find their own metaphors and meaning for what is unfolding.

The English paediatrician and psychoanalyst Donald Winnicott frequently refers to the "good-enough" mother in his writing, but he also emphasises the dangers and deprivations of too-good mothering. He shows how "a mother who fits in with a baby's desires too well is not a good mother" (1958, p.215). He continues: "The infant can actually come to gain from the experience of frustration, since incomplete adaptation to need makes objects real, that is to say hated as well as loved . . . exact adaptation resembles magic and the object that behaves perfectly becomes no better than an hallucination" (1958, p.238). The "too-good mother" interferes with an authentic interaction when they immediately presume or determine the nature of the issues that need resolution. In so doing, they stifle further invaluable interaction. If we are *too good*, Winnicott alerts us to two possible outcomes: the child either rejects the mother or remains in a state of arrested development, merged with her.

As parents we are landing pads for our children's experiences, a place to ground their feelings and gain a little more reality through our responses. If there is no landing pad, the child is left with a coiled mess of their own unprocessed raw feelings, mixed with those of their parents. This leaves them confused, afraid, unable to trust the other, or to feel they have a means of being experienced by the other. Instead of growing into an upright tree with solid roots and a secure sense of self, the child remains a vine, entwined around the ideas and identity of their parents. Children respond to this dilemma in varying ways, including withdrawing into their self, dissociation, or becoming overly omnipotent or bossy.

It seems like a Goldilocks metaphor helps to capture this, where one's approach can't be too hot, too cold, but just right . . . but just right is not perfect or "too good". It's vital for parents to make mistakes and create space for frustration, so that our children can begin to think for themselves and find form for whatever is going on inside of them. Providing our children with a screen at any age interferes with this process of feeling frustrated and bored, or lying fallow. "Lying fallow", a term coined by psychoanalyst Masud Khan, is useful as we think about what it means to help our children grow a mind – it is a transitional space, a mode of being that is an alerted quietude and receptive wakefulness; it is here that there exists a rich liminal space where a mind begins to shape itself.

French psychoanalyst Marilia Eisenstein takes this idea a bit further. She describes desire as inherently masochistic. In desire, the capacity for waiting becomes integral in creating a space for drive to emerge, a notion of force, that which propels us to seek the things we want. This is also what we want our children to find; the drive to live an emotional life of connectedness and passion. The words of French psychoanalyst Andre Green often hold me as I work with my patients and raise my teens. He poses a profound question which makes us stop and think about whether "we are living a life of quiet desperation, or one of passion?".

The concept of respecting frustration is not only true for children and teens, but also for parents. In 1949 Winnicott wrote: "Let me give some reasons why a mother hates her baby . . . the baby is ruthless, treats her as scum, an unpaid servant, a slave . . . he is suspicious, refuses her good food, and makes her doubt herself." Winnicott's words resonate as I contemplate the idea of how two minds shape and partially create each other. In my work with parents, mothers or fathers often express immense relief to have found a space where they can talk about their maternal or paternal ambivalence without judgement. They draw in the reassurance that they can justifiably feel frustrated and loving at the same time. In her insightful book, *Of Woman Born* (2021 [1976]), Adrienne Rich eloquently states: "My children cause me the most exquisite suffering of which I have any experience. It is the suffering of ambivalence: the murderous alternation between bitter resentment and raw-edged nerves, and blissful gratification and tenderness."

Now, dear Parent, this brings me to an uncomfortable thought. There is no clearer picture than that of a proud parent who watches their adult child graduate or enter the working world for the first time. They have separated and grown up, which is what they worked so hard to achieve, and what you wanted for your child. At this very time, however, these proud feelings can be complicated by unconscious resentment at feeling used, discarded, no longer needed, or simply just alone. This leaves me contemplating my intrusiveness mentioned earlier in this letter. Perhaps, as parents, there may be a compulsion beyond our conscious awareness to meddle in the daily arbitrary challenges of our teens and adult children, such as friendship issues, school, work, relationships and marriage. Could this interference be an attempt to solve the simpler more tangible problems because the bigger unconscious struggle in the parent – of ambivalence and separation – is way more difficult to handle, or too hidden?

These disquieting feelings and thoughts lead me back to Winnicott when he states: "I would rather be the child of a mother who has all the inner conflicts of the human being than be mothered by someone for whom all is easy and smooth, who knows all the answers, and is a stranger to doubt" (1955, p.58). Thus, as I continue to lean into being a mother to my son and daughter, I will persist in immersing myself in the complexity of this experience, steadily reflecting on my own responses and thoughts. Through this process, I will endeavour to create a wholesome space for my children to listen to their own thoughts and formulate their own responses.

Warmly,

Deborah Ashdown

Mother of two | South African Psychoanalytical Association | Johannesburg, South Africa

37

David R. Dietrich

Dear noble Parent,

This short contribution does not aspire to offer profound insights regarding parenting nor deep and esoteric knowledge derived from my decades of working as a psychoanalyst. Instead, I shall toss out a few thoughts that some of you may find useful. Looking back, I was not prepared to fall in love as limitlessly and as profoundly as I did when my children were born. Perhaps no parent is actually prepared for this awakening. I had, of course, read the wonderful book *The Magic Years* by the child psycho-analyst Selma Fraiberg who, for years, practised in Michigan and yet I did not realise the illimitable ways my world would change and how these experiences would somehow incubate and facilitate my capacities for love and compassion.

As I write this, I am mindful of the injunction given all contributors to this book to avoid using psychoanalytic

 DOI: 10.4324/9781003385042-39

jargon. Therefore, let me say this. From my very first cases that I treated as a psychoanalyst, I have been repeatedly struck by varying degrees and various kinds of self-criticisms, harsh and punitive self-talk, self-hatred and self-loathing in so many of my patients, young and old. In reference to this, Freud talked about the harsh and malignant "superego" as a construct of the human mind.

One man began his analysis with an enormous amount of self-hatred and self-loathing. He was an alcoholic and addicted to random sexual encounters, overeating, and an inability to be in love. Upon completion of his analysis, he was able to finally be in a loving relationship, forgive his parents for egregious abuse, forgive himself and work through the causes of his addictive drinking so that he maintained sobriety, and replace self-hatred with self-love and compassion. I have come to appreciate and recognise that virtually all of my patients have suffered from these manifestations within their minds and as these self-critical, overly harsh and self-hating patterns gradually become transformed into more benevolent, kind, self-accepting, self-compassionate and self-loving capacities, each individual discovered they had vast potential to be compassionate towards others and were then able to love others.

So, as the reader, you may ask, so what? Let me be more pithy. The psychoanalyst Hans Loewald wrote that when we (as ordinary individuals) see stone and we are asked what we see, our answer is that it is stone. However, when a sculptor is asked the same question, they answer very differently. The sculptor will say, I see this and that and it's very precious and beautiful and so on. The sculptor is able to see the hidden potentialities within the stone: what is there but also what hasn't yet been released or brought out by the sculptor. And the same is true for the psychoanalyst. The psychoanalyst is able to see the hidden potentialities within a person that have not yet been brought forth. From my analogy, I am suggesting that the new parent is like the stone and the patient. Within lie vast hidden potentialities. I am also suggesting the baby or the baby to be is also like the stone or patient. Again, vast potentialities are present. Likewise, I am also suggesting the parent is like the sculptor and the psychoanalyst, as is the baby. The baby helps to bring out these wonderful potentialities in the parent. And lest you think that I am speaking of some better than average parent or baby or psychoanalyst, I am not. Allow me to take a short cut. In the Hollywood movie, *The Last Samurai*, starring Tom Cruise and Ken Watanabe, Tom Cruise plays an alcoholic American army officer who serendipitously follows a path that leads to Japan. He is suffering greatly from having been ordered to kill innocent Native American families. He has enormous self-hatred. In the film, he is a prisoner of the Samurai but he very gradually begins to glimpse a potential way of life that offers freedom from his suffering, in a sense parallel to therapeutic benefits of psychoanalysis.

The leader of the Samurai tells the Tom Cruise character that the perfect cherry blossom is a rare thing, and you could spend your life looking for one and it would not be a wasted life. Later, when the Samurai leader is dying on the battlefield, he sees in his mind's eye countless cherry blossoms floating all around. With his last breath, he simply says, "Now I realise they are all perfect."

Of course, I am not Samurai nor a Hollywood actor, I am an ordinary psychoanalyst and parent. So, what am I pointing out? It is possible – potentially possible – for the patient in psychoanalysis to recognise this insight. It is possible for a parent to recognise this insight about themselves and their baby and child. It is possible for the child to recognise this as well. One way to think about this shift in outlook is to view it as a form of play similar to how the psychoanalyst Winnicott believed that the ability to play is necessary for the psychoanalyst and patient in the clinical situation. Obviously, it doesn't simply happen automatically. Psychological and emotional growth and transformation takes work.

So whether your child is conventionally beautiful or is born with so-called limitations or becomes ill, the metaphor I am using still applies. At one level, a patient or a baby or a parent may have a variety of issues and what we think of as imperfections. Yet we do not have to wait until we die to potentially realise (at one level) that our child is perfect. Like in the movie *The Last Samurai*, we have the capacity to become able to appreciate that our child is perfect and that (at one level) we also are.

While Freud was a genius, he was mistaken about certain things. I have come to realise that psychoanalysis is not an "impossible profession" as it has often come to be described in our field. And I would add that parenting is not an impossible endeavour either. I am very fortunate to be able to practice as an analyst and reduce the suffering of people. And because some of my patients are psychoanalysts-in-training and mental health professionals and parents or parents-to-be who also treat patients (some of whom are also parents) vast numbers of humans can actually be helped to reduce their suffering so they can become more benevolent and compassionate towards themselves, their children and others.

Donald Winnicott once said, "There is no such thing as a baby." What he meant was that the baby cannot exist without the mother who cares for it, referring to the intimate, mutually interdependent physical and psychic relationship of mother and child. I would like to alter his famous words to say that "there is no such thing as my parenting" (and this is my subjective and personal view. I do not suggest it applies to anyone else). What I mean by these words is to denote my children were parented by my wife (also a psychoanalyst) and by me. She is and was a wonderful mother. Our children were also (in some ways) "parented" by their grandparents. Parenting is a radically dynamic interdependent flow of activities like a river. And our children changed our parenting moment by moment because of who they were becoming and who they became. Our older child is a psychotherapist and our younger child is a defence attorney. Both are compassionate, strong and loving human beings who help other human beings. And as I finish writing these last sentences, it is with the awareness that parenting sometimes occurs within the contexts of invasions (such as Ukraine) or horrible attacks upon innocents in the Middle East and other terrible injustices against ethnic and spiritual peoples throughout the world.

Finally, I will close by bringing attention to the reality that there is no one size fits all in terms of parenting. Enjoy being a parent. Parenting a child is a lesson in transience and impermanence. Parenting a child is a noble journey and joyful.

Warm regards,

David R. Dietrich

Father of two | Michigan Psychoanalytic Institute | Birmingham, Michigan, USA

38

∧∧∧∧

Theodore Jacobs

Dear Parent,

As I thought about what I might offer that could be useful to you in raising your children, a memory came to mind. This memory was not directly related to my work as a psychoanalyst, but it referred to an experience that was instrumental in helping guide me as I struggled to find my way as a parent.

The memory concerned a paediatrician, Dr W, who was Chief of the Department of Paediatrics at the medical school I attended. An internationally known researcher and much sought after clinician, Dr W gave no sign of recognising the esteem in which he was held. A man of true modesty, he carried out his role as physician and teacher with impressive skill and quiet confidence. He never drew attention to himself and in morning rounds we students often had to strain to hear the

DOI: 10.4324/9781003385042-40

words of advice he gave to the resident in charge of the case, words that reflected years of study and experience.

I was fortunate in being able to work as a research assistant to Dr W and, in that role, I became acquainted with two of his teenage children, a son and daughter who were volunteers in his laboratory. Rarely have I encountered two such impressive youngsters. Kind, thoughtful, gracious and quite brilliant, they, like their father, were modest and unassuming. Interested as I was in psychiatry and child development, I was curious about how Dr W functioned as a parent; how he had raised two such engaging children. Dr W was not, however, a man who spoke about personal matters and had I not come across his offspring in the way I did, I would not have known that he had any children. Fearful as I was of being out of line by mentioning anything about Dr W's private life, I delayed for several weeks before summoning up the courage to broach the question that had been pressing on my mind. What approach did this great man utilise in raising his children? What was his secret?

One day when I was alone with Dr W in his office, I commented on how much I enjoyed working with his children. Then, tentatively, with much apprehension, I raised the issue of his parenting. Could he tell me something about how he and his wife had raised their children, I asked. Was there any method or philosophy of childrearing that they followed? Dr W looked hard at me and for several long seconds remained silent. I was sure that I had indeed crossed the line and had angered him. Then, quietly, he uttered two words. Benign neglect. I was stunned. What in the world did he mean by that? A feeling of keen disappointment flooded me. I had expected something remarkable from this man, some pearls of wisdom that I could carry with me and make use of when I became a parent.

Just hearing the word, neglect, troubled me. It is well known that neglect is damaging to children. It is, in fact, among the most hurtful experience a child can be subjected to. There is surely nothing positive about neglect. Dr W. read the expression on my face, one of bewilderment and disapproval, and he responded immediately in a tone that was both gentle and caring. "Let me explain", he said. "I see that you are naturally upset by the idea of neglect, and you are right to be so. The last thing children need is to be neglected. On the contrary. They need to thrive in an atmosphere of abundant love and full parental support. But there is such a thing as too much parenting, too much interference with children's needs for autonomy, separateness, individuation.

There is a life force in all humans, a biologically based drive that moves children forward, that propels them to grow and develop according to an innate programme that directs them, as it were, to become the unique individuals they are meant to be. It is important that this force be able to express itself as it fosters essential physical and psychological development. Many well-meaning parents, unaware of the existence of such a natural force and its role in promoting the healthy growth of children, unwittingly suppress it by being too much with their children, offering too much guidance, too much protection, too much planning. They arrange too many activities, lessons and structural programmes. All this planning has a squelching effect on children's needs to follow their own inner dictates. I tell parents that there is a Tom Sawyer and Huck Finn in every child; a need to explore, experiment, discover nature, learn from experience, from trial and error. They need to separate, find their own particular talents and abilities, acquire the capacity to cope and master difficulties."

"Benign neglect is healthy neglect", Dr W continued. "Do children need guidance, teaching, direction from parents? Of course they do, but these should always be given with a light touch, with a readiness to stand aside, and when the child is ready, turn the reins over to him so that he can develop in his own way, guided by an inner force that is his alone."

Benign neglect. Healthy neglect. These were new ideas to me but, as Dr W spoke, I recognised the importance of his words, the wisdom they contained. But what Dr W did not say is how difficult it is for parents to carry out his recommendations, the way of parenting he advised. In many respects, what Dr W suggested goes against our natural impulse, as parents, to protect, guide and influence our children to carry out the ambitions and visions we have for them. At least I found that to be so. It took me many years to develop the necessary trust in my children's judgement, their ability to navigate in the world, for me to be able to let go and stand apart as they found their own voices, their own directions in life. So, although in my case Dr W's advice, his way of parenting, was honoured more in the breach than the observance, when I was able to put his ideas into practice, I learned first-hand how valuable they were, how much they fostered my children's growth, their strengths and their self-reliance.

Benign neglect. An oxymoron if there ever was one. Two words that do not go together, a concept alien to us, to all we have learned about raising children. It took, finally, my being able to make use of Dr W's ideas with my own children, for me to fully appreciate the keen understanding of human development in both its biological and psychological dimensions that they contain. Benign neglect. A puzzling oxymoron, indeed, but one that, if we truly understand the importance of those two words and heed them, serves as a valuable guide in our efforts to navigate the impossible profession of parenting.

Best regards,
Theodore Jacobs
**Father of five and grandfather of three |
The New York and PANY Psychoanalytic
Institutes | New York, USA**

39

∧∧∧∧

Warren Poland

Dear friend, dear fellow Parent,
What to tell a child?

I was scared to death, and with cause. As my wife and I were driving to "Toys 4 Tots" to pick up several surprises for our toddler grandchildren, I felt a shock. Despite the pleasant calm, I suddenly felt a keen gripping pain in my chest, one that radiated to my teeth. I didn't need to be a physician to recognise the symptoms of a heart attack, and, fortunately, we were near a hospital. We entered the emergency room, I began to describe to the clerk my reason for coming, and within a flash I found myself in a bed, surrounded by nurses and attendants, attached to beeping monitors that remined me of the pictures of Command Centre when a spaceship had a crisis.

My own doctor out of town, the hospital assigned me to the young cardiologist just appointed head of their catheterisation

 DOI: 10.4324/9781003385042-41

unit. He wanted to do an immediate catheterisation of my heart. I felt overwhelmed yet clear-headed enough to remember the problems of excessive invasion. I remember saying to him, "Just because you have catheterisation in your blood doesn't mean I have to have it in mine." It is not wise to sound sassy to someone holding your life in his hands. My new young doctor clearly was disdainful of this old psychoanalyst, medical doctor though I be, questioning his expertise. He informed me of his training at the first-rate Peter Bent Brigham Hospital in Boston and wheeled me down the hall to look into the room of a terminal patient attached to even more monitors. Such would be my fate. Already feeling frightened to death, it seemed, I needed to be put into full fear of death.

An hour or so later that afternoon my wife sat by my bedside while I lay forbidden to arise, even to use the toilet. (Using a bedpan was so difficult that I wondered whether his restricting order declaring that limitation was his death wish for me, whether witting or unwitting.) My anxiety was so great that while my wife and I spoke, I kept falling asleep. The doctor did convince me how close I was to death, and I felt horror and grief that I never again would see my children. My mind quickly became fixed, preoccupied by trying to find suitable last words for them, words beyond just love and blessings, final fatherly advice my wife could convey for their future benefit. Even now, speaking of this decades later when they are in their sixties and I am 90 and more certainly facing death, I still feel the pangs of that loving urgency arise.

Through the years my children have turned out to be more different and even more wonderful than realistically I could have hoped. They have taken their lives in directions I could not have imagined, and I take their surpassing me not as a personal threat but as my happiest life achievement. They are improved versions, not second-hand copies. Even in the midst of my crisis facing death, I recognised that they knew the world better than did I. I definitely knew that they had to be and become themselves. Already aware how conscientiously responsible they were, the only final words of advice I could conceive, the ones I told my wife to tell them after I was gone, were, "Protect pleasure!"

That weekend many years ago came to its end. My own doctor returned at about the same time it also became clear that my severe symptoms had been caused by a passing bout of acute esophagitis, a problem that has never recurred. The impact of the weekend, however, has stayed with me, indeed has coloured my life. The result has not been an increase in the fear of death, something deep in my personality already rooted in the background of my anxiety-ridden family for whom it was ever present, stronger than mere reality requires. Such background nervousness remains, but I think it is ever so slightly tamed as a result of the terrified moment when parental love overruled parental fear.

It is a hard thing to be a parent. Children need to learn, and they need to be taught in order to learn. We need to teach our children not to run into the street, not to play with knives. But we also must teach our children how to play hopscotch in the alley behind the house, how to use penknives. Children (and the inner children within ourselves throughout our lives) are always pulled in conflicting urges, on one hand their curiosity reaching for the exploration that makes possible creativity rooted in independence, while on the other hand simultaneously longing for the comfort and security of home. Fear for one's child and wanting to protect that vulnerable precious person is central to being a parent, whether one is a mother or father. Still, supporting and even encouraging a child to choose life also matters. Out of love, we naturally tilt to protectiveness, even naturally to over-protectiveness. We must also protect their growing curiosity.

All of us take better care of those we love than ourselves, more sensitive to dangers for them than for us. At times that is true for doctors too. Doctors are cautious, and so tend to see sickness where something is simply normal for a person. In one famous instance, in his book *The Psychopathology of Everyday Life*, Freud wrote about the meaningfulness that is often behind what was commonly dismissed as "meaningless slips of the tongue". It wasn't pathology or illness that was present, it was normality.

The gifted poet Linda Pastan wrote *To a Daughter Leaving Home*:

When I taught you
at eight to ride
a bicycle, loping along
beside you
as you wobbled away
on two round wheels,
my own mouth rounding
in surprise when you pulled
ahead down the curved
path of the park,
I kept waiting
for the thud
of your crash as I
sprinted to catch up,
while you grew
smaller, more breakable,

with distance,
pumping, pumping
with laughter,
the hair flapping,
behind you like a
handkerchief waving
goodbye.

As has been said, a ship in port is safe, but that's not what ships are for.

My warm regards,
Warren Poland
Father of two, grandfather of three,
great-grandfather of two | Washington, USA

P.S.

Andy Cohen

I think deep down I wanted to be a psychoanalyst because I invented the idea that *analysts know everything*, and I craved that as a mother. But the more I edited these letters, and the more I collaborated with the individual contributors, the more I was reminded that *actually* parenting is a reconciling with *not* knowing. The great surprise of this compilation is that analysts are not experts at parenting, we are just muddling through like everyone else. That said, we are incredibly interested in the muddle and what it all means! And implicit in each letter is that leaning into that – via personal enquiry – then frees us up to support our children in becoming more of themselves. And so, dear Parent, I hope this book was an experiential read and that it has stimulated internal debates that trickle into your home in useful ways. I also hope that if you ever decide to take a deeper dive into any of your own musings that you *now* know where to look. And finally, I hope that that you close this book with a deep sense of respect for yourself, a healthy curiosity, and a few more questions than answers . . .

Take care,
Andy Cohen

Contributors

Kateryna Alpatova is a psychologist, psychoanalytic psychotherapist and candidate of the Ukrainian Psychoanalytic Society (IPA Study Group). She is also the International Psychoanalytical Studies Organisation (IPSO)'s representative for Ukraine and a full member of the Ukrainian Association of Psychoanalytic Psychotherapies (collective member of the European Federation of Psychoanalytic Psychotherapy). She is also a director of Kharkiv Psychoanalysis and Psychotherapy Society. She works in private practice with adults and has a strong interest in Kleinian analysis. Before Russia's large-scale war against Ukraine Katherine lived and worked in Kharkiv.

Deborah Ashdown is a psychoanalytic psychotherapist and candidate psychoanalyst, working in private practice for over 20 years. She typically works with adults, teens, couples and parent/infant dyads. She facilitates Peer Mentorship Programmes in schools as well as community clinical groups for newly qualified psychologists. She has also worked closely with the Ububele Psychotherapy Trust, a community-based mental healthcare initiative aimed at supporting at-risk women and babies, and families in township settings. Deborah is interested in creativity, psychoanalysis, the mind/body relationship, and how the psyche is influenced by neurobiology, evolution, philosophy, history, social anthropology, literature and art. She received a travel award in 2006 to the United States to present her research on Substance Awareness Intervention Programmes for South African youth. She has also been interviewed on prominent local television programs and currently practises in Morningside, Johannesburg.

Ines Bayona is a member of the Colombian Society of Psychoanalysis in Bogota, Colombia. She also has a master's degree in clinical psychology. She is part of scientific groups and editorial groups at her Society, at the International Psychoanalytical Association (IPA) and the Latin American Psychoanalytical Association (FEPAL). She has had a number of papers published in psychoanalytical journals and is also the author and co-author of two books: *Dear Candidate* (2021) and *New Tools for Psychoanalysis* (2023). Currently, her day-to-day work is mostly treating individuals in her private clinical practice, participating in a variety of academic studies, congresses and other activities in various psychoanalytical institutions.

Michael Benn is a psychoanalyst, registered with the IPA, and clinical psychologist. He is primarily a clinician who has worked over the years with adolescents, families, couples and individuals in long-term psychoanalytic/psychodynamic therapy work. He has done psychiatric inpatient therapy with patients in extreme states of crises, also community psychiatric work and trauma work with victims of criminal and political violence through various non-governmental organisations. Michael is the co-founder of Tribe, an organisation that provides therapeutic services for poorer school pupils and teachers. He is co-founder of the Mindful Psychoanalytic Psychology Practice in Johannesburg. He was part of the Life Esidimeni expert witness team to help the families of 144 murdered psychiatric patients. He chairs GRASP (Groups for Reading, and Studying of Psychoanalysis). He is also the founder of "Psychoanalysis and Psychoanalytic Psychotherapy", which is a very large Facebook community with 126,000 members.

Florencia Biotti is a psychologist, child and adolescent psychotherapist and Analyst Member of Buenos Aires Psychoanalytic Association (APdeBA) since 2022. In 2005, she started her career as a teacher at the Universidad de Buenos Aires in the subject of "Psychology of Development: Childhood". She was vice president of IPSO for Latin America between July 2019 and July 2023. Currently she is assistant teacher in the APdeBA Masters in "Psychoanalysis Family and Couples" in the subject "Vinculo fraterno" and member of the Family and Couple Committee (IPA).

Heribert Blass, Dr.med, is a training and supervising psychoanalyst for adults, children and adolescents, a specialist in psychosomatic medicine, psychotherapy and psychiatry, practising in Düsseldorf, Germany. He is also a member of the German Psychoanalytical Association (DPV). Heribert served from 2020 to 2024 as president of the European Psychoanalytic Federation (EPF), and since 2023 as president elect of the IPA. He is also widely published with a strong interest in male sexuality and identity, fatherhood, psychoanalysis in society, psychoanalytic supervision, psychoanalytic institutions, gender dysphoria and transgender identity, child analysis, and others.

Katy Bogliatto, MD, is a child psychiatrist, training analyst of the Belgian Psychoanalytical Society, vice president elect of the IPA (2023–2025). She teaches at the Free University of Brussels, third cycle on the "Certificate in Children & Adolescent Psychotherapeutic Clinic" and on "The Training in Clinical Psychology of Family and Couple Diversity". She also teaches at GECFAPPE (early childhood psychoanalytic family therapy). She is a member of the editorial board of the *Revue Belge de Psychanalyse*. She works in private practice with adults, adolescents, children and young toddlers (parenthood centred psychotherapy) and at the Assisted Reproduction Center of Chirec, Brussels.

Stefano Bolognini is a psychiatrist, training and supervising analyst, former National Scientific Secretary and then president of the Italian Psychoanalytical Society and President of the IPA (2013–2017). For ten years (2002–2012) he was member of the European editorial board of the *International Journal of Psychoanalysis*; he is honorary member of the New York Contemporary Freudian Society (CFS) and of the Los Angeles Institute and Society for Psychoanalytic Studies (LAISPS); honorary member of the Florence Psychoanalytic Center (CPF); member of the advisory board of the International Psychoanalytic University of Berlin (IPU). He is the founder of the IPA Inter-Regional Encyclopedic Dictionary of Psychoanalysis (IRED), where he was chair from 2014 to 2021. He is also the author of several books translated into many languages, his main scientific interests regard psychoanalytic empathy, interpsychic dimension, institutional organisations and issues, educational process and theory of technique. He lives and works in Bologna (Italy), and is a father of three and grandfather of five.

Fred Busch, PhD, is a training and supervising analyst at the Boston Psychoanalytic Society and Institute, and has been invited to teach at many institutes, both in the United States and internationally. He has published eight books, and has published over 80 articles on psychoanalytic technique, along with many book reviews and chapters in books. His work has been translated into numerous languages, and he has been invited to present over 180 papers and clinical workshops nationally and internationally. His latest books from Routledge are: *Creating a Psychoanalytic Mind* (2014); *The Analyst's Reveries: Explorations in Bion's Enigmatic Concept* (2019); *Dear Candidate: Analyst From Around the World Offer Personal Reflections on Psychoanalytic Training, Education, and the Profession* (2020); *A Fresh Look at Psychoanalytic Technique* (2021); *Psychoanalysis at the Crossroads: An International Perspective* (2023); *The Ego and Id: 100 Years Later* (2023); and *How Does Analysis Cure?* (2024). Previously he published *The Ego* at the Center of Clinical Technique (1995) and *Rethinking Clinical Technique* (1999), both now with Rowman & Littlefield.

Cecilia Caruana was trained in APM (Psychoanalytical Association of Madrid) and works as a psychoanalyst on the island of Ibiza, Spain. She is passionate about remembering and thinking about her dreams and those of others. She is deeply interested in the analysis and exploration of the human mind from a dynamic point of view in order to help her patients develop a fuller psychic life.

Liliana Castro is a psychiatrist and psychoanalytic candidate from Oporto, Portugal. She has been actively part of IPSO ExCom from 2021 to 2025, with a special interest in psychoanalytic training, being the IPSO representative in the IPA Psychoanalytic Education Committee from 2023 to 2025. She works both in private practice and in a public psychiatric hospital as clinician and psychotherapist. Liliana works in a university setting, teaching psychiatry to medical students and organising educational programmes for psychiatry residents. Additionally, she has been developing research and clinical work in the field of eating disorders.

Michael J. Diamond, PhD, FIPA, is a training and supervising analyst at the Los Angeles Institute and Society for Psychoanalytic Studies, and is known for his publications in the areas of masculinity, femininity and fathering; psychoanalytic technique; trauma and dissociation; hypnosis, group processes and social action. He has authored five books including *Masculinity and Its Discontents: The Male Psyche and the Inherent Tensions of Maturing Manhood* and *My Father Before Me: How Fathers and Sons Influence Each Other Throughout Their Lives*. He is in private practice in Los Angeles, while teaching, supervising and writing.

David R. Dietrich, PhD, is a psychoanalyst in private practice and a training and supervising analyst at the Michigan Psychoanalytic Institute, where he is also a past president. He is an editor of *The Problem of Loss and Mourning: Psychoanalytic Perspectives* and was a visiting professor of psychoanalysis at the Institute of Medicine, Tribhuvan University, Kathmandu, Nepal in 2010. For years, he was active on the outreach committee of the IPA, helping analysts from around the world, and he taught Discussion Groups on the termination process in analysis at national meetings of the American Psychoanalytic Association. Dr Dietrich has recently taught a seminar to candidates titled "The Zen of Clinical Analysis" and is a two-time winner of the Ira Miller, M.D. Clinical Essay Award for papers he presented to the Michigan Psychoanalytic Society.

CONTRIBUTORS

Giovanni Foresti, MD, PhD, lives in Pavia (Italy). He is training analyst at the Italian Psychoanalytic Society and the IPA. He works in private practice as a psychoanalyst, psychiatrist and organisational consultant and teaches at the Italian Psychoanalytic Society (SPI) National Institute for Training. In the recent years, he served as co-chair for Europe on the Committee "Psychoanalysis and the Mental Health Field", in the IPA board as European representative, in the Executive Committee of the IPA, in the IPA Application Society Committee, and he is now part of the Psychoanalytic Education Committee. His interests are focused on clinical issues, institutional functioning and group dynamics.

Martina Griller–Mushel is a psychoanalytic psychotherapist from Vienna, Austria. As part of her therapy training, she worked with chronic and acute psychiatric patients at the Lower Austrian hospital Maria Gugging, which has since been converted into the *art brut museum gugging*. Martina translated several exhibition catalogues for the Gugging Artists. Her second field of interest is dramatic arts. Martina worked for the Austrian Cultural Institute in London, and the Goethe Institute in Johannesburg as a writer, director and actor. Her master's thesis at the University of the Witwatersrand linked psychology and dramatic arts, addressing the representation of narcissism in two classical plays. Martina worked at a dual diagnostic unit in Johannesburg, where she treated psychiatric patients, who also suffered from addictions or eating disorders. She trained as a group facilitator with Ububele and is currently in private practice in Johannesburg and a senior candidate with SAPA, the South African Psychoanalytic Association.

CONTRIBUTORS

Patricia Harte Bratt, PhD, PsyaD, is a psychoanalyst and psychotherapist in New Jersey and New York City. She is director of Academic Innovation and Communication at the Academy of Clinical and Applied Psychoanalysis (ACAP). She is President of the National Association for the Advancement of Psychoanalysis (NAAP), and of the New Jersey Certified Psychoanalysts Advisory Committee. Dr Bratt developed ACAP's Trauma and Resilience Studies programme and its Critical Incident Support group, providing mental health services to those struggling in war or disaster zones around the world. In 2018 she launched the *iStrive* Center for young adults on the autism spectrum. Her recent book, *Mutual Growth in the Therapeutic Relationship: Reciprocal Resilience*, is published by Routledge. patbratt@comcast.net; www.patriciabratt.com.

Eike Hinze is a psychiatrist/neurologist and training analyst at the Karl-Abraham-Institute in Berlin. He works as an analyst in private practice and is currently chair of the institute's board of training and chair of the IPA committee on "Psychoanalytic Perspectives on Ageing". His main foci of interest, reflected in numerous papers and book contributions, are psychoanalysis of elderly patients, male identity, psychoanalytic training and questions of clinical practice. For many years he has been fostering the development of psychoanalysis in Eastern Europe.

Gohar Homayounpour, PsyD, is a psychoanalyst and award-winning author. She is a member of the IPA, the American Psychoanalytic Association and the Italian Psychoanalytic Society. She is a training and supervising psychoanalyst of the Freudian Group of Tehran, of which she is also founder and past president. She is a member of the scientific board at the Freud museum in Vienna, and of the IPA group Geographies of Psychoanalysis. Her first book, *Doing Psychoanalysis in Tehran* (MIT, 2012) won the Gradiva award and has been translated into many languages. Her latest book is titled *Persian Blues, Psychoanalysis and Mourning* (Routledge, 2022).

Daniel Jacobs is a training and supervising analyst and a past president of the Boston Psychoanalytic Institute and Society. He also served as director of the Hanns Sachs Library and Archives for 24 years. He currently heads the Center for Advanced Psychoanalytic Studies at Princeton. Among his over 40 publications are a co-authored book, *The Supervisory Encounter* (1995), and a novel, *The Distance for Home* (2019). His play, *Enter Hallie*, written with his wife Susan Quinn, will open off Broadway on 6 March 2025.

Theodore Jacobs is a clinical professor of psychiatry (emeritus) at the Albert Einstein College of Medicine. He is a training and supervising analyst in the New York and PANY Psychoanalytic Institutes. He has authored two professional books, *The Use of the Self: Countertransference and Communication in the Analytic Situation* and *The Possible Profession: The Analytic Process of Change*, as well as two novels, *The Year of Durocher* and *The Way it Ends*. Further to this he has published 65 academic papers on a wide variety of analytic topics.

Arthur Leonoff is a supervising and training analyst of the Canadian Psychoanalytic Society and recipient of the Citation of Merit. He is an honorary member of the American Psychoanalytic Association and has served in numerous senior administrative roles in the IPA. He is the current chair of

International New Groups. Dr Leonoff is the author of three books exploring parenting issues in divorce in general as well as in contested and high conflict situations. He is a frequent contributor to the analytic literature and active teacher and clinician.

Maria Lival-Juusela is a clinical psychologist and psychoanalyst at the Finnish Psychoanalytical Society. She is a literary researcher with a PhD from 2009 on the subversive genre of the female Bildungsroman and has subsequently published on cultural memory. She works in private practice in Helsinki and enjoys gardening in her spare time.

Susan Mailer was trained at the Chilean Psychoanalytic Association. She later founded, together with several colleagues, the Psychoanalytic Association of Santiago, known as APSAN. She is a supervising analyst and professor at APSAN's Institute. She has been visiting professor at the Catholic University, the Universidad Diego Portales, Universidad Andrés Bello and Universidad Alberto Hurtado, all in Santiago, Chile. Her articles have been published in Latin American journals and books. In 2019 her memoir, *In Another Place: With and Without My Father, Norman Mailer*, was published in the United States. It was translated by the author and published in 2022 in Chile. She lives in Santiago most of the year, where she has her private practice, supervises and writes.

Corinne Masur is a clinical psychologist, and a child and adult psychoanalyst who lives in the United States in Chester Springs, Pennsylvania. She is also a mother, a friend, a teacher, a photographer, and the author of four books, most recently, *How Children Grieve, What Adults Miss and What They Can Do*

To Help. Corinne has treated children, adolescents and adults for over 40 years and she has led parenting groups for two decades. She currently writes two blogs, one in *Psychology Today* called "Parenting Matters" and one at www.thoughtfulparenting.org.

Kristen Miller Beesley, PhD, is a psychologist and psychoanalyst in metro Detroit, Michigan, United States. She is associate faculty at the Michigan Psychoanalytic Institute, adjunct faculty at University of Detroit Mercy, and she is the Clinic Director for the Mel Bornstein Clinic for Psychotherapy and Psychoanalysis. Dr Miller Beesley became a mother early on in her analytic training and while in her own psychoanalysis. She found that having these simultaneous experiences offered a kind of scaffolding for motherhood that has proven invaluable, while at the same time providing an immersive learning experience, and an opportunity to critically engage with psychoanalytic theory.

Sergio Eduardo Nick is a medical doctor, psychiatrist, psychoanalyst, child and adolescent psychoanalyst (COCAP/IPA). He holds a Post-Grade in Child and Adolescent Psychiatry and Psychotherapy by the Child Orientation Clinic from the Rio de Janeiro Federal University (UFRJ), Post-Grade in Child and Adolescent Law by the Rio de Janeiro University Law School (UERJ). Sergio is also Effective Member of the Brazilian Psychoanalytical Association of Rio de Janeiro/Rio II, Member of the IPA. Former IPA vice president (2017–2021), Latin American board member and the Executive Committee's representative (2023–2025).

Gaetano Pellegrini, PhD, a psychologist-psychotherapist and psychoanalyst, an associate member of the SPI and a member of the IPA. He serves as co-chair of the IPA Scientific Communications Subcommittee. In 2020, he launched the IPA Podcast Talks on Psychoanalysis, which has since published over 160 episodes in seven different languages, creating a significant audio library of psychoanalytic papers. He is a member of the editorial board of the *Rivista di Psicoanalisi*, for which he also curates the Italian podcast, publishing interviews with authors of the featured papers. He is a contributor to the IPA Encyclopedic Dictionary of Psychoanalysis.

Warren Poland has been practising psychoanalysis for over 60 years. He is the author of *Intimacy and Separateness in Psychoanalysis* and *Melting the Darkness: The Dyad and Principles of Clinical Practice*. He received the Sigourney Award for Distinguished Contributions to Psychoanalysis in 2009, the JAPA Journal Prize in 2002 and is former editor of the *JAPA Review of Books*. He is also the past columnist in *American Imago* and has been a member of multiple major psychoanalytic journal editorial boards for over 40 years.

Joan Raphael-Leff is a fellow of the British Psychoanalytical Society, member of the IPA, and founder of COWAP (IPA's international organisation on women and psychoanalysis). Currently retired, she continues to lead the Anna Freud Centre Academic Faculty for Psychoanalytic Research and is Honorary Senior Research Fellow at University College London (UCL). Previously she was professor of psychoanalysis at the University of Essex, UK, and at UCL, and Professor Extraordinary at Stellenbosch, South Africa. Specialising in 1975 in psychoanalytic clinical work and academic research on reproduction and early parenting, she spent many years treating, teaching, supervising and consulting to perinatal projects around the world. Her 14 books and 150+ papers have been translated into many languages.

Carol Richards (née Groener) is married, a mother of two adult children (32 years and 28 years) and lives and works (mainly online) in Clanwilliam, Western Cape. She was born in Port Elizabeth (renamed Gqeberha). When she was seven, the Groener family migrated to Cape Town. After high school Carol completed a nursing career and embarked on a 17-year journey to qualify as a clinical psychologist followed by ten years of training to become a psychoanalyst. Carol was admitted in November 2018 as a member of the South African Psychoanalytic Association and the IPA.

Ashis Roy, PhD, is a psychoanalyst (IPS Kolkata, IPA London). He works with adults, young adults and couples. For more than a decade he was a faculty member at the Centre of Psychotherapy and Clinical Research, Ambedkar University, where he participated in institution building, taught psychoanalysis and trained students to become psychoanalytic psychotherapists. He has an interest in clinical and cultural psychoanalysis and likes to participate in thinking spaces where different schools of psychoanalysis can dialogue with each other. He is a faculty member at CAPA (China–American Psychoanalytic Alliance) and is interested in exploring Asian and South Asian cultures using psychoanalysis. His book, *Intimate Hindu-Muslim Relationships: A Psychoanalytic Exploration of the Self and the Other* (2024) has been published by Yoda Press and is available on amazon.com.

Mariano Ruperthuz Honorato is a psychoanalyst and historian at the Chilean Society of Psychoanalysis (ICHPA) and Psychoanalytic Association of Buenos Aires (APdeBA). He holds a PhD in psychology from the Universidad de Chile, and history from the Universidad de Santiago de Chile. He is research professor at Andrés Bello University in Santiago de Chile, and also works as a researcher at the Freud Museum in London.

Lauren Segal is a South African curator, author and an analyst-in-training, known for her contributions to historical exhibitions and educational media. She holds an honours degree in history from Wits University, Johannesburg and a master's in media studies from London University. Since 2006, Lauren has served as a curator for the Constitution Hill Trust, an institution dedicated to promoting South Africa's Constitution and human rights. She is also a director of Trace, an exhibition and design company specialising in historical sites of conscience. Her work includes curating high-profile exhibitions such as the permanent exhibition at the Johannesburg Holocaust and Genocide Centre and the Mandela Foundation's "A Prisoner in the Garden". Lauren is an accomplished author, with notable works including "Cancer: A Love Story", a memoir of her battle with cancer, and "One Law, One Nation", celebrating South Africa's Constitution. Her publications and conference presentations span topics in political violence, history and reconciliation. In film and television, she has produced educational series such as "Gazlam" and "Takalani Sesame", the latter featuring the first HIV-positive muppet. Lauren Segal continues to work through her multidisciplinary approach, merging history, education and psychoanalysis to foster understanding and empathy.

Claudia Sheftel-Luiz, Ed.M., Harvard University (1982), PsyaD, Boston Graduate School of Psychoanalysis (1997) is the first-place winner of the 2006 Phyllis W. Meadow Award for Excellence in Psychoanalytic Writing (published in *Modern Psychoanalysis*) and first place winner of the 2008 Reader's Digest Best Writer's Website Award, and a 2019 nominee for the NAAP Gradiva Award for her textbook, *The Making of a Psychoanalyst* (Routledge, 2019), reviewed in the *Journal of Modern Psychoanalysis* and described as "arguably the best book written about Modern Psychoanalysis". Dr Luiz treats families and supervises groups virtually. A frequent guest on TV and radio shows, she can be found on Instagram: @drclaudialuiz.

Barbara Stimmel, PhD, was president of the New York Freudian Society, 1998–2003, overlapping with her appointment by Otto Kernberg as North American Secretary of the IPA, 1997–2001. She was the first officer of the IPA from the United States not a member of the American Psychoanalytic Association (APsaA). She was North American Chair of the Berlin IPA Congress, 2007 and is a member of the Culture Committee of the IPA. As a member of APsaA, she was Chair of Supervision Sub-Committee of Board of Professional Standards and is currently on the Supervision Education Committee and the Task Force on Collegiality. She has edited and contributed chapters in several psychoanalytic books, published papers in the major psychoanalytic journals, and presented at many professional conferences. Dr. Stimmel has been on the Psychiatry Chairmen's Committee on Residency Training at Mount Sinai Hospital in New York. She is a member of the Shakespeare Society at the Public Theater in New York.

Alan Sugarman, PhD, practices psychoanalysis with children and adults in Solana Beach, California. He is a training and supervising child, adolescent, and adult psychoanalyst at the

San Diego Psychoanalytic Center. Dr Sugarman is a former and inaugural head of APsaA's Department of Psychoanalytic Education and the inaugural head of its Child and Adolescent Psychoanalytic Department. Currently he is a Director-at-Large on APsaA's board and served as a North American representative to the IPA Board from 2017 to 2019. He has given the Levy-Goldfarb, Marianne Kris and Beata Rank honorary lectures in child psychoanalysis. Aside from publishing widely in psychoanalytic journals, he serves on the editorial boards of the *Psychoanalytic Quarterly, Journal of the American Psychoanalytic Association* and *Psychoanalytic Psychology*.

Ntshediseng Tlooko is a clinical psychologist as well as a senior candidate psychoanalyst with the South African Psychoanalytical Association (SAPA). She completed her Bachelor's degree as well as honour's degree in psychology at the University of Pretoria. She obtained her master's degree in clinical psychology and community counselling at Stellenbosch University. She has presented at the IPCP Ethics Workshop, the Deadly Medicine Conference, the SAPI/SAPA Conference on Fundamentalism and the IPA Congress on the Feminine. Ms. Tlooko has co-authored an article with Coralie Trotter and Bruce Laing, titled "The Mark of the Decanting and the Brick Mother Report", published in *The Psychoanalytic Review* (2023). She was an organising committee member for the SAPI/SAPA Conferences for six years and also worked at the Johannesburg Metro Clinics for seven years.

Johanna Velt is an analyst, a psychiatrist and a child and adolescent psychiatrist. She is member of the Paris Psychoanalytic Society and of the European Society for Child and Adolescent Psychoanalysis (SEPEA). She has her own private practice in

Paris, France. She is interested in many fields, notably research and links with other scientific fields, and child and adolescent analysis. She has written several articles in French and in English, and she is the co-author and co-recipient of the International Journal of Psychoanalysis Award in 2020 for the best article related to coronavirus. She is the Vice-President for Europe of IPSO and she is involved in many committees (IPA podcast team, SPP website, IPA in culture committee, etc.).

Harriet Wolfe, M.D., is president of the IPA, past president of the American Psychoanalytic Association, clinical professor of psychiatry and behavioural sciences at the University of California San Francisco, and training and supervising analyst at the San Francisco Center for Psychoanalysis. Her scholarly interests include clinical applications of psychoanalytic research, organisational processes, female development and therapeutic action. She has co-authored a number of psychoanalytically informed guided activity workbooks for children, parents and teachers to help children cope with natural and manmade disasters. She has a private practice of psychoanalysis, and individual and couple's psychoanalytic psychotherapy in San Francisco.

Acknowledgements

I want to begin by thanking each of the contributors of this book. Even though many of us had to navigate opposing forces to bring these letters into existence, there was an incredible amount of enthusiasm and heart baked into this project. I am incredibly moved by how each of you approached this task, and I am also so grateful for the many word-of-mouth introductions that brought this wonderful group together. I have found working with you all deeply moving and incredibly refreshing – both personally and professionally. I would also like to thank your many private proofreaders (who I never met) but who have had an important hand in helping you each gestate your letters. This definitely had an important metabolising effect on the final book.

A special thank you to Fred Busch and the contributors of *Dear Candidate: Analysts from around the World Offer Personal Reflections on Psychoanalytic Training, Education and the Profession*. Not only did your letters offer valuable advice, but the personal (yet boundaried) nature of your book really touched something in me, in fact, inspiring the initial idea for this book; as you have seen I even borrowed your format! Fred, I also extend a special thank you for those early conversations, words of encouragement and all the critical introductions.

Judith Mitrani, thank you for all the reassurance, your hearty endorsement and for giving me an experience of what it means to really move people with your writing. Elana Afrika-Bredekamp, thank you for your generous endorsement and for bringing some additional home-grown rock star flavour to the project.

Lauren Segal and Deborah Ashdown, my original guinea pigs, thank you for your early "tester" letters. Lauren Segal, Liat Horovitz and Patricia Harte Bratt, thank you for casting an essential eye over early versions of my chapters and for seeing what I couldn't. Thank you also to Gohar Homayounpour, Glynis Ponton, Elda Storck, Gyuri Fodor, Harvey Schwartz and Barnaby B. Barratt for providing much-needed advice at pivotal moments. To Zoë Meyer and your team, thank you for supporting this unusual project, it has been such a pleasure working together. Kim Kur, thank you for assisting with your design flair and for bringing the cover together.

Since this is a parenting book it feels essential to include a respectful nod to my own parents. Perhaps it's only now as a parent myself that I can fully appreciate just how you both rallied to raise me. Thank you for always encouraging me to pursue my creative endeavours, which you instinctively understood as integral to "Andy".

To my patients: who have really taught me so much, I am very grateful. I also want to acknowledge all the seminal people in my life who have nannied, grandparented, mothered, fathered, brothered, sistered and friended me along the way. In important ways each of you have informed how I make my way through the world, this project included. To my analyst: thanks to your insights, this book has become a' pouch to hold vital things. Thank you for gently and lovingly shepherding me and this book into being.

A special acknowledgement must go to my husband, co-pilot and closest ally. You've been the early reader of these letters and a crucial sounding board from start to finish. I can categorically say that this book would not have happened without your fierce support and gentle companionship. To my beautiful growing girls: how lucky I am to mother your grit and your delicacies. I would have to write you each your own book to capture the depth and nuance of who you each are to me. Thank you, a thousand times, for supporting me on all my analytical indulgences, please know dear Family, that you are at the heart of them all.

Bibliography

Aisenstein, M. and Moss, D. (2015) *Desire and It's Discontents*. London: Taylor & Francis.

Arendt, H. (1958) *The Human Condition*. London: The Chicago University Press, 1998.

Biko, S. (1978) *I Write What I Like*. Johannesburg: Heinemann.

Bion, W. (1962) *Learning from Experience*. London: Rowman & Littlefield.

Blass, H. (2017) Väterliche Präsenz in der veränderten westlichen Welt [Paternal Presence in the Changing Western World]. *Zeitschrift für psychoanalytische Theorie und Praxis* [*Journal for Psychoanalytic Theory and Practice*], 32(1).

Bode, S. (2004) *The Forgotten Generation: The War Children Break their Silence*. Stuttgart: Klett-Cora Verlag.

Bolognini, S. (2008) "Ein schwieriges Geschenk": Psychoanalytische Haltung zwischen Anerkennung des Sexuellen und elterlicher Zuwendung ["A Difficult Gift": Psychoanalytic Attitude between Recognition of Sexuality and Parental Care]. In *Gefährdete Begegnungen. Frühjahrstagung der DPV* [*Endangered Encounters. Spring Conference of the DPV*]. Hamburg.

Corpt, E. (2018) The Ethics of Listening in Psychoanalytic Conversations. *Psychoanalysis, Self and Context*, 13(3): 220–228.

Dangarembga, T. (2022) *Black and Female*. London: Faber & Faber.

Freud, S. (1915) Instincts and their Vicissitudes. In *The Standard Edition of the Complete Psychological Works of Sigmund Freud, Vol. 14*. London: Hogarth Press, pp. 109–140.

Freud, S. (1957) On Narcissism. In *The Standard Edition of the Complete Works of Sigmund Freud, Vol. 14 (1914–1916)*. London: Hogarth Press, pp. 67–102.

BIBLIOGRAPHY

Freud, S. (1974) Group Psychology and the Analysis of the Ego. In *The Standard Edition of the Complete Works of Sigmund Freud, Vol. 18 (1920–1922)*. London: Hogarth Press, pp. 67–143.

Hattingh, A. (2023) *"The Journey of a Thousand Miles Begins with One Step" Lao Tzu*. St John's College. Unpublished essay.

Herzog, J.M. (1982) On Father Hunger: The Father's Role in the Modulation of Aggressive Drive and Fantasy. In S.H. Cath, A. Gurwitt and J.M. Ross (Eds), *Father and Child*. Boston: Little, Brown & Co.

Khan, M. (2018) *Hidden Selves: Between Theory and Practice in Psychoanalysis*. London: Routledge.

Lacan, J. (2014) *The Four Fundamental Concepts of Psycho-Analysis*. Abingdon: Routledge.

Larkin, P. (1971) *This Be the Verse*. In *Collected Poems*. London: Faber & Faber and Farrar, Straus and Giroux.

Lear, J. (2014) Mourning and Moral Psychology. *Psychoanalytic Psychology*, 31: 470–481.

Lewis, C.S. (2013/1961) *A Grief Observed*. London: Faber & Faber.

Lorde, A. (1978) *Black Unicorn Poems. A Litany for Survival*. New York: Norton.

McCarthy, C. (2006) *The Road*. Torino: Giulio Einaudi Editore, 2007.

Morrison, T. (1987) *Beloved*. London: Vintage.

Novick, J. and Novick, K. (2010) *Emotional Muscle: Strong Parents, Strong Children*. Bloomington: Xlibris, Corp.

Pastan, L. (1999) *Carnival Evening: New and Selected Poems 1968–1998*. New York: W.W. Norton.

Reik, T. (1983) *Listening with the Third Ear: The Inner Experience of a Psychoanalyst*. New York: Farrar, Straus and Giroux.

Rich, A. (2021) *Of Woman Born: Motherhood as Experience and Institution*. New York: Norton & Company Inc.

Schopenhauer, A. (2000) *Parerga and Paralipomena: Short Philosophical Essays, Vol. 2*. Oxford: Oxford University Press.

Schwartz, H. (2023) *On and Off the Couch, Episode 133: International Commentaries on the State of out Field with Fred Busch, Ph.D.* [Podcast] 30 April 2023. Available at: https://ipaoffthecouch. org/2023/04/30/episode-133-international-commentaries-on-the-state-of-our-field-with-fred-busch-ph-d-chestnut-hill-mass/ (accessed 30 August 2024).

BIBLIOGRAPHY

Stierlin, H. (1974) *Eltern und Kinder* [*Parents and Children*], Erweiterte Ausgabe [Extended Edition] 1980. Frankfurt am Main: Suhrkamp.

Winnicott, D.W. (1949) Hate in the Counter-Transference. *International Journal of Psychoanalysis*, 30: 69–74.

Winnicott, D.W. (1955) *The Collected Works of D.W. Winnicott, Volume 5: 1955–1959*. London: Oxford University Press.

Winnicott, D.W. (1958) *Collected Papers: Through Paediatrics to Psycho-Analysis*. London: Tavistock.

Winnicott, D.W. (1965) Ego Integration in Child Development. In *The Maturational Processes and the Facilitating Environment*. New York: International Universities Press, pp. 56–63.

Winnicott, D.W. (1971) *Playing and Reality*. London: Tavistock.

Winnicott, D.W. (1975) *Through Paediatrics to Psycho-Analysis*. London: Karnac Books.

Index

INDEX

INDEX

INDEX

INDEX

INDEX

INDEX

INDEX

INDEX

For Product Safety Concerns and Information please contact our EU
representative GPSR@taylorandfrancis.com
Taylor & Francis Verlag GmbH, Kaufingerstraße 24, 80331 München, Germany

www.ingramcontent.com/pod-product-compliance
Lightning Source LLC
Chambersburg PA
CBHW051952270326
41929CB00015B/2622

9 781032 471976